Transport Law in Norway

The Authors

The foundation for this description of Norwegian transport law was laid by Bjørn Daehlin and Hans Peter Michelet (*see* below) in the 1990s. The text has been revised several times, but the original structure has been maintained. The revision tasks have gradually been taken over by Hans Jacob Bull and Thor Falkanger – and the last edition in 2013 and the present one have been done solely by them.

Professor Dr juris. Hans Jacob Bull (1941) is Professor of Law at the Scandinavian Institute of Maritime Law (University of Oslo). He is the author of several books and articles on maritime law, insurance and marine insurance law, petroleum law and road transport law.

Professor Dr juris. Thor Falkanger (1934) is Professor of Law at the University of Oslo and works at the Scandinavian Institute of Maritime Law (University of Oslo). He is the author of a number of books and articles on maritime law, real property, mortgages and pledges, bankruptcy and enforcement of claims.

The Authors

Bjørn Daehlin (1959) graduated from the University of Oslo in 1986 and worked as a research assistant at the Scandinavian Institute of Maritime Law from 1984 till 1985. In 1993, he worked as a lawyer with Northern Shipowners Defence Club (Nordisk) in Oslo and is currently Head of Division to the Norwegian Parliamentary Ombudsman for Public Administration. He published (1986) a thesis in contract law on the liability of consulting engineers for designing and engineering work for construction of offshore oil and gas installations.

Hans Peter Michelet† (1925–2003) graduated from the University of Oslo. He worked as a lawyer with Northern Shipowners' Association 1950–1982 and thereafter as managing director of Den Norske Krigsforsikring for Skib 1984–1991. He has written several books and a number of articles on maritime law matters.

Transport Law in Norway

Second Edition

Hans Jacob Bull
Thor Falkanger

This book was originally published as a monograph in the International Encyclopaedia of Laws/Transport Law.

Founding Editor: Roger Blanpain
General Editor: Frank Hendrickx
Volume Editor: Eric Van Hooydonk

Wolters Kluwer

Published by:
Kluwer Law International B.V.
PO Box 316
2400 AH Alphen aan den Rijn
The Netherlands
E-mail: international-sales@wolterskluwer.com
Website: lrus.wolterskluwer.com

Sold and distributed in North, Central and South America by:
Wolters Kluwer Legal & Regulatory U.S.
7201 McKinney Circle
Frederick, MD 21704
United States of America
Email: customer.service@wolterskluwer.com

Sold and distributed in all other countries by:
Air Business Subscriptions
Rockwood House
Haywards Heath
West Sussex
RH16 3DH
United Kingdom
Email: international-customerservice@wolterskluwer.com

Printed on acid-free paper

ISBN 978-94-035-1745-2

e-Book: ISBN 978-94-035-1794-0
web-PDF: ISBN 978-94-035-1842-8

Printed in the United Kingdom.

Table of Contents

List of Abbreviations

AAO	Act on Aviation Operations, 1993
ACL	Act on Conciliation and Litigation, 2005
AEC	Act on Enforcement of Claims, 1992
BIMCO	Baltic and International Maritime Conference (1) I Baltic and International Maritime Council
COTIF	Convention concerning International Carriage by Rail, 1980
CTL	Constructive Total Loss
EEA	European Economic Area
EU	European Union
ICA	Insurance Contract Act, 1989
ICAO	International Civil Aviation Organization
ILO	International Labour Organization
IMO	International Maritime Organization
LNG	Liquefied Natural Gas
LOS	Law of the Sea, 1982
MA	Mortgage Act, 1980
MC	Maritime Code, 1994
MOA	Memorandum of Agreement
MTO	Multimodal Transport Operator
NCA	Norwegian Court of Appeal
NIS	Norwegian International Ship Register
NP	Nordic Marine Insurance Plan 2013, Version 2019
NSB	Norges Statsbaner AS
NSC	Norwegian Supreme Court
PA	Pollution Act, 1981
SAS	Scandinavian Airline Systems
SDR	Special Drawing Rights
SLA	Ship Labour Act, 2013
SSSA	Ship Safety and Security Act, 2007
UNCTAD	United Nations Conference of Trade and Development

List of Abbreviations

UK	United Kingdom
US	United States
YAR	York-Antwerp Rules

General Introduction

§1. Geography

1. Norway is a long, narrow and mountainous country. At its narrowest, it is only 8 km wide. Many peaks go beyond 2,000 m. The country forms a part of the Scandinavian Peninsula and stretches from 57° 58″ to 71° 11″ North. It has a long border to the east with Sweden. In the north-east, it also borders on Finland and Russia, and in the west to the ocean, in particular to the North Sea. The island of Spitsbergen (Svalbard) forms (with surrounding islands) a part of the Norwegian realm. Norway was given limited sovereignty over these islands by the Treaty of Paris of 9 February 1920.

Owing to its long coastline, Norway has also obtained economic sovereignty or specific economic rights over a large area of the North Sea.

The mainland is 324,000 km^2; 386,000 km^2 if Spitsbergen is included. Only about 4.3% of the land is arable.

As from 2020, the country is administratively divided into eleven counties ('fylker'). The capital is Oslo (about 670,000 inhabitants), and the second and third largest cities are Bergen (about 280,000 inhabitants) and Trondheim (about 190,000 inhabitants). The climate may be divided into a coast climate and an inland climate. The former dominates in the western part of the country, with relatively mild winters and a lot of rain, while the east is drier, normally with colder winters and warmer summers.

§2. Demography: Population and Employment

2. Norway has a population (2018) of about 5.3 million people. About one-third live in the cities. In the three northern counties, there are only about 485,000 inhabitants (2018). The fact that the northern part of the country – to a great extent beyond the polar circle – is habitable at all is due to the warm ocean current coming from the United States (US) gulf. This Gulf Stream prevents the Norwegian fjords from freezing during winter and thereby enables the population to obtain a living from the sea.

Traditionally, Norway was a farming, fishing and sea-faring country. There were some exports of forestry, mining and fishing products during the seventeenth and eighteenth century. But from the last half of the nineteenth century, industry gradually emerged, often made possible by foreign capital. Owing to the many rivers and waterfalls, hydro-electric power was cheap to produce. This caused the development of the metallurgical and chemical pulp and paper industry.

Subsequently, when reservoirs of oil and gas were located off the coast in March 1967, the Norwegian oil industry was born.

Today (2018), the working force of about 2,600,000 is divided into 58,000 engaged in farming and fishing; 260,000 engaged in industry and mining, 350,000 in commodity trade, 135,000 in transport, 545,000 in health and social services, and the rest fairly spread over other activities.

The mountainous countryside of Norway, penetrated by deep fjords, steep valleys and often long distances between settlements, did for a long time separate and isolate many parts of the Norwegian population. This brought a great cultural variation which was fortified by the different conditions under which the inhabitants made their living. During the long union with Denmark (1397–1814), the leading classes, particularly within the clergy, civil and military service, were influenced by Danish culture and thereby also by general European culture. The rural populations, to a gradually increasing extent self-owning farmers, continued its slow development, unbroken from medieval times. In some respects, this caused a cultural rift in the population, resulting in giving Norway two official languages, one allegedly being closer to Danish. These two languages stem from the same root and therefore are not very different. They are, e.g., much more similar than French and Flemish. Efforts have been made to merge the two languages into one, but so far this has proved to be a slow process.

Apart from this, the Norwegian population is quite homogenous, with the exception of a small contingency (about 40,000 of Sami people.). Since the Second World War, Norway has also received a great number of inhabitants, coming from all parts of the world, gradually transforming Norway into a more multicultural society than before.

§3. Political and Legal System

3. Norway is an ancient kingdom, reckoning its history as one state from the year 872. After union with Denmark for about 400 years (1397–1814) and with Sweden for about 100 years (1814–1905), Norway again became a completely separate and independent state in 1905. The same year the Norwegians also elected their own king. Today Norway is a constitutional monarchy with parliamentary government. The 169 members of the Parliament ('Stortinget') are elected every fourth year. The government will normally be chosen from the largest party in the Parliament.

4. Norway has a written Constitution. The Constitution was adopted in 1814, before the union with Sweden, and was inspired by the ideas of the American Constitution and the French Revolution – adapted to the special circumstances of Norway. There have been few substantial changes in this Constitution over the years, but from later years inclusion of clauses regarding human rights should be noted. The most important change is the development of the parliamentary system, which has been adopted more or less in spite of the Constitution. The Constitution was rewritten in 2014; this was first and foremost an update of the language, but at the same time former non-written principles were included.

Norway is not a member of the European Union (EU), but Norway is part of the EU economic co-operation through the *European Economic Area Agreement* (the EEA Agreement). The EEA Agreement was made part of Norwegian law by the enactment of Parliament of 27 November 1992, No. 109.

There is a general feeling in Norway that Norwegian society offers freedom of speech, welfare and social security for the individual beyond the standard of many nations. Norway has ratified and now incorporated to a binding extent for Norway the central treaties on human rights.

Norway has also ratified a number of significant conventions prepared by the International Labour Organization (ILO).

5. The Norwegian judicial system consists of the Reconciliation Board ('Forliksrådet'), which has the power to pass judgments in smaller matters, sixty-three Courts of First Instance, which are normally presided over by one judge, six Courts of Appeal, normally with three judges sitting in each case, and the Supreme Court seated in Oslo, normally sitting with five judges. The courts, and in particular the Supreme Court, are also empowered to handle questions regarding constitutional rights, e.g., whether a particular enactment by the Parliament is against the Constitution. For constitutional responsibility, there is a special Court of Impeachment, the composition of which is laid down in the Constitution.

The Norwegian legal system lies somewhere between the English and the Continental approach. There is no comprehensive legal code, neither for civil, nor for criminal matters, but many of the major sections of law have been codified into separate statues, e.g., on sale and purchase of goods, on tort, on maritime matters, on general criminal law, and on mortgages and pledges.

In Norwegian law, there is also a strong element of common law (unwritten law). Decisions and reasoning of the Supreme Court are normally followed. Since Norway has agreed and implemented the EEA Agreement, Norway has also accepted the decisions of the European Court in Luxembourg prior to the conclusion of the EEA Agreement as relevant sources of law. Additionally, Norway is inclined to accept later EU Court decisions although no express commitment under international law has been made in that respect. Norway is, however, not subject to the jurisdiction of the European Court.

§4. General Introduction Relating to Transportation

6. Owing to the country's geographic particularity, transportation has traditionally mainly relied on ships sailing along the coast. Indeed, the very name Norway meant 'the way to the North', signifying that this was a natural way to sail. The mountains made the building of roads and transportation over land very difficult, therefore the inland traffic was kept to a minimum. Before roads and rail developed after the middle of the nineteenth century, travelling between the south and north of Norway went more by sailing vessels on the sea than by foot or horse inland.

The close contact with the sea has made the Norwegians a sea-faring nation for a long time. When the English repealed the Navigation Act in 1849, enabling foreigners to compete in transporting goods to and from England, they gave the Norwegians a chance to build a greater merchant fleet. Since then, Norway has played a significant role – in peace and war – with its large and modern merchant fleet, which at times ranked as number four in the world.

I. Inland Waterways and Ports

7. Commercial carriage of passengers or goods on inland waterways is in Norway – unlike parts of the European continent – no longer a practical way of transportation. The few canals that originally were constructed for commercial transport are today only an attraction to leisure time boat traffic.

II. Railroads

8. The commencement of railway transport in Norway may be dated to the inauguration in 1854 of the railway tracks between the capital Oslo and Eidsvoll (Eidsvoll being the place where the Norwegian Constitution was agreed in 1814). The distance was approximately 68 km and the transport was performed by steam locomotives.

The railway network today is generally operated by electrified locomotives, but diesel locomotives are needed on certain routes.

The topography of Norway – with mountains and valleys – makes construction of railway tracks costly. Furthermore, parts of Norway are thinly populated, meaning that the infrastructure needed for railway operations can hardly be funded solely through the price asked for railway transport.

For years, members of Parliament have debated whether or not to have railway transport also to the very north of Norway. So far, no firm steps have been taken. The railway tracks going north now stop in Bodø in the county of Nordland. A separate railway track runs from Narvik to he prosperous iron ore fields in Northern Sweden (Kiruna) and connects tot he rest of the Swedish railroad network. The two most northern counties – Troms and Finnmark – do not provide railway transport within their territory.

Looking at the rest of the Norwegian territory as a whole, the railroad network serves most major cities, but the network as such can hardly be described as dense if compared to the railroad network in most countries on the European continent.

Railway tracks with mountain passages as part of the travel distance may, during wintertime, encounter tough weather (snow). Despite heavy snow handling equipment, the carriage may be prevented. Delay or prevented transport due to the weather is nevertheless not a frequent experience.

The main track between the two major cities – Oslo in the east and Bergen on the west coast in the county of Hordaland – is a scenic route with a mountain passage. The distance is about 471 km, and the track was completed as early as 1909. Another important track is the south line from Oslo via Kristiansand in the south to

Stavanger on the west coast in the county of Rogaland (about 586 km and completed in 1944). The south line does not require any mountain passage. There is a main track from Oslo via the Dovre mountains to Trondheim (about 553 km, completed in 1921). Finally, the main track north runs from Trondheim to Bodø (729 km, completed 1962) and includes a mountain passage which crosses the polar circle.

In Norway, carriage of cars with passengers on railway wagons is not part of any regular railway route as on the European continent.

The railway offers a number of efficient inter-city connections to serve passengers living outside but working in Oslo.

The performance of railway services in Norway has, for many years, been the responsibility of the Norwegian State Railways (NSB). Today the infrastructure is owned by a state company (Bane NOR SF), and most of the passenger service is provided by the state-owned company NSB AS and most of the cargo carriage by CargoNet AS, which also is state-owned.

The operation of railway services experience competition in transport of both passengers and goods from other means of transport, in particular transport by air and by road, but to some extent also from waterborne transport with bulk/product carrier vessels and Hurtigruten. Hurtigruten is primarily a passenger line whose vessels sail regular schedules from Bergen in the south of the west coast via, *inter alia*, Trondheim, Tromsø and North Cape, to Kirkenes close to the Russian-Norwegian border.

III. Road Systems

9. Just as for railroad tracks, the topography in Norway makes the construction of efficient road systems very costly compared to many other European countries. In addition, the often hard winter climate requires many resources, not only to keep the roads open for traffic during the winter but also in terms of maintenance of the road surfaces following the winter season. Nearly every year, even main road connections between major cities, e.g., Oslo–Bergen, may, during wintertime, be blocked for short periods by severe weather on mountain passages.

The road system in Norway is dense only in and to some extent surrounding the major cities, in particular, Oslo, Bergen, Trondheim, Stavanger and Kristiansand. Still, the road system is, of course, the most important and closely-knit transportation system and reaches all over the populated areas of Norway, from Lindesnes in the south to the North Cape. In the western and northern parts of Norway, the many fjordsrequire buses, cars and trailers often to be taken on ferries performing a sea passage as a part of the regular road network.

The speed limits in Norway are the same for cars, buses and trailers. The regular limit outside densely populated areas is 80 km/h. Highways permit 90/110 km/h. There are a few highways with two lanes in each direction, mainly located around Oslo and some of the other major cities. For a bus or trailer driver from the European continent with a destination in Norway, it may be useful to take into consideration that the travel distances (km) in Norway often will require substantially more time behind the wheel than the same distance on the European continent.

The main roads between the major cities in Norway are basically parallel to the corresponding railway routes and with similar mileage (*see* section II. above). There are the main routes to Sweden – between Oslo and Stockholm (about 520 km) and Oslo and Gotenborg (about 295 km).

IV. Airports

10. Norway is, on the world map, hardly in the centre of any international flight connections. A large number of busy international destinations nevertheless are served by direct flights from the main airports in Norway. However, many international destinations from Norway will require a connection through, e.g., Heathrow in London, Kastrup in Copenhagen or Schiphol in the Netherlands.

The main airport in Norway, Gardermoen Airport, opened in October 1998 and is located to the north of Oslo. Most of its passengers are taken there by high-speed trains running from the outskirts of Oslo and through the city. The travelling time is nineteen minutes from the city.

The great travelling distance between the south and the north of Norway makes air carriage a frequent and necessary way of transporting passengers and mail to many destinations within the country. All major cities have access to airports in the immediate vicinity or at least within reasonable travelling time by bus.

The major airlines with Norwegian roots are Scandinavian Airline Systems (SAS) and Norwegian Air Shuttle ASA. SAS is partly owned by the states of Sweden, Denmark and Norway.

V. Pipelines

A. *Facts*

11. In Norway, the oil and gas resources are located on the Norwegian continental shelf. Of the eighty-five fields that are currently in production, sixty-six are located in the North Sea, seventeen in the Norwegian Sea and two in the Barents Sea (2018). Pipeline transport of petroleum takes place through lines on the seabed.

In 1965, the Ministry of Industry (at that time) granted the first licences to explore and develop petroleum (production licence) for specific areas on and under the seabed (blocks). The production licence is a permit to fully explore (drill) and, with certain reservations, to develop and produce from a commercially exploitable field. The reservations relate to the requirements for further permits or approvals from the ministry in order for the ministry to maintain a certain control on exactly how the licensees intend to develop, produce and land the petroleum.

Following the first licence round, the Balder field was discovered in March 1967, although the field was not commercially applied for and approved to be exploited until 1996 (floating production facility). The Ekofisk field, presently operated by ConocoPhillips was located in December 1969 and proven to be a major discovery early in 1970.

Since then, a number of discoveries have been made – some mainly gas and some mainly oil. The last major oil reservoir, Johan Sverdrup, operated by Equinor (former Statoil), was discovered in 2010. Some well-known fields still producing are Sleipner (Equinor), Statfjord (Equinor), Gullfaks (Equinor), Heidrun (Equinor), Snorre (Equinor), Oseberg (Equinor), Troll (Equinor) and Valhall (Aker BP). Other major producing fields today are Gina Krogh, Grane, Kvitebjørn, Njord, Snøhvit, Tyrihans, Visund and Åsgard (all Equinor), Ivar Aasen and Skarv (both Aker BP), Maria and Vega (both Wintershall), Goliat (ENI), Edvard Grieg (Lundin) and Ormen Lange (Shell), whereas Aasta Hansteen, Johan Sverdrup, Martin Linge (all Equinor) and others are expected to start production in the near future.

A discovery that has been declared commercial and to be exploited by the licensees, and approved for development by the Ministry of Petroleum and Energy, will bring with it a decision on how to land the petroleum. On many oil fields, oil is landed directly on to tankers (buoy-landing). In other cases, oil and gas are transported by pipeline to onshore facilities. Oil, wet gas and liquefied natural gas (LNG) are transferred to ships at onshore facilities, while dry gas is moved by pipeline to the United Kingdom (UK) and continental Europe.

As for gas pipelines, Norway's first large pipelines were laid early in the 1970s. From dedicated gas transport solutions for individual fields, the gas transport system has been transformed into an integrated system serving most of the Norwegian continental shelf. The transport capacity of the Norwegian pipeline network is currently (2018) about 120 billion cubic metre dry gas per year. Three onshore gas processing plants – Kårstø, Kollsnes and Nyhamna – are integrated with the pipeline network, and receive rich gas from the fields. Dry gas is separated from the rich gas for onward pipeline transport to receiving terminals abroad. There are four receiving terminals for Norwegian gas in continental Europe (two in Germany (Emden and Dornum), one in Belgium (Zeebrügge) and one in France (Dunkerque)) and two in the UK (Easington and St. Fergus). The total length of the Norwegian gas pipeline network is about 8,800 km. Most of the gas transport infrastructure is jointly owned through the joint venture Gassled, while the 100% state-owned company Gassco is the neutral and independent operator.

As for oil and condensate pipelines, it was considered most appropriate to build onshore oil terminals for some of the larger field developments in Norway. Other fields were subsequently connected to this infrastructure. The oil transport system is not as closely regulated as the gas transport infrastructure. Today, oil transport infrastructure on the Norwegian shelf is divided into four different systems. Oil pipelines from fields in the North Sea run to the Norwegian terminals Sture, Mongstad and Kårstø and to Teeside in the UK. At the Norwegian terminals, oil is stored in rock caverns before most of it is loaded on to tankers for export.

The complexity of the pipeline systems makes a detailed description of the pipeline network excessive in this context. The following will concentrate on some major projects.

Norpipe is a 36-inch gas pipeline running roughly 440 km from Ekofisk to Emden (Germany), on stream from September 1977, and a 34-inch oil pipeline running roughly 354 km from Ekofisk to Teesside (England).

Statpipe handles wet and dry gas from several fields (*inter alia*, Statfjord) and is a system of some 880 km pipelines landing at a terminal in Kårstø (Norway) and interconnecting, *inter alia*, Heimdal and Norpipe to Emden – on stream from October 1985.

Zeepipe includes gas pipelines from the field Sleipner to Zeebrugge (Belgium) and from Kollsnes processing plant to Sleipner and Draupner, which in turn are interconnected. The section that connects Sleipner and Draupner links Zeepipe with Statpipe. The pipeline also transports dry gas which the Kollsnes terminal receives from the Troll field.

The Troll field gas is partly processed offshore and further treated to be shipped to the European continent from Kollsnes. The Troll gas may supply under more gas sales contracts, but will usually be transported via Sleipner and the Draupner riser platform. Draupner is linked, *inter alia*, to the Norpipe, the Europipe I and the Franpipe systems. Europipe I (1995) runs from the Draupner riser platform and ties in gas from other sources to be landed in Emden. Franpipe (1998) runs from Draupner to Dunkerque (France). Europipe II (1999) runs from Kårstø to Dornum (Germany).

Frigg pipelines previously served the Frigg field in the British and Norwegian sector. The gas was landed in St. Fergus (UK). Today, the Frigg pipelines are tied up with a new pipeline from Heimdal (Vesterled, 2001), serving fields in the Oseberg area. The Åsgard Transport pipeline (2000) runs from the Åsgard field to Kårstø, and serves several fields in the Haltenbanken area. The Haltenpipe (2001) transports gas from the Heidrun field to the industrial facility at Tjeldbergodden, which is located in Møre og Romsdal county.

B. Law

12. The legal framework for the petroleum industry – including the pipeline transports – has been developed over more than fifty years. The basis was an act of 1963 mainly declaring the ownership in, *inter alia*, any petroleum resources to belong to the state of Norway. At the same time, the 1963 Act granted the ministry the powers to promulgate all necessary regulations. This was initially effected in 1965 and revised in 1972.

The decree of 1972 contained an express provision to the effect that the licensees would need a separate permit to land the petroleum outside Norway (section 34). The provision formed the basis for ministry practice, also to review in more detail and approve plans for the specific development of the field facilities.

Later, extensive regulations and administrative practice were absorbed and legislated in the *Petroleum Act* of 1985. The presently prevailing legislation on the public interests of petroleum law is the *Petroleum Act* of 29 November 1996 No. 72.

The licensees of the various production licences do not always own an interest in the transportation systems (pipelines). This is particularly true when it comes to gas pipelines, where most of the transportation systems are owned by Gassled, with Gassco as the operator, *see* above. Generally, the use of pipeline infrastructure will be subject to terms to be agreed on between the pipeline owner and the shipper of oil or gas (freedom of contract). To ensure prudent resource management and efficient operation of the transportation system, and to secure the owner of the system a reasonable profit, the Ministry of Petroleum and Energy will survey and approve the agreements. For gas transport through pipelines, relevant tariff rules have been provided for in Regulation 20 December 2002 No. 1724.

VI. Important Data Relating to Transport Activity

13. Below, some data relating to domestic transport activity is set out. The source of the information is the Official Statistics of Norway issued by the Statistics Bureau of Norway (2016 figures):

- Railway: 4,500 mill. passenger km, 2,000 mill. ton km.
- Air: 4,300 mill. passenger km, 15 mill. ton km.
- Road: 71,000 mill. passenger km, 20,000 mill. ton km.
- Sea: 870 mill. passenger km, 20,000 mill. ton km.

Transport from the Norwegian continental shelf to the main land: 30,500 mill. ton km.

VII. Ministries Responsible for Transport Policy

14. The overall legal framework on transport law and transport policy is set out by Parliament mainly by enactments (legislation) and, somewhat indirectly, through the allocation of budget funds available for the transport sectors each year.

Within the frame of the legislation by Parliament, general regulations based on applicable statutory law are usually promulgated by the relevant ministry, or to some extent by the relevant directorate. Additionally, individual decisions are made by the relevant ministry, e.g., by the Ministry of Transport and Communications granting licences to commercial operations of air transport against a remuneration.

The Government – consisting of the Prime Minister and the other ministers – has of course an important influence on transport policy. According to the Constitution, a number of resolutions have to be passed by the Government sitting with the King in council. In daily work, most assignments are handled by the Ministry of Transport and Communications. This is particularly true for aspects of public transport law. Regarding private transport law (contract law in particular), the Ministry of Justice and Public Security plays an important role. In the following, a brief outline on the allocation of responsibility for transport law policy and adoption of regulations, including implementation of international conventions binding on Norway, will be made.

The handling of maritime private law is divided between the Ministry of Justice and Public Security and the Ministry of Trade, Industry and Fisheries, while requirements on safety for the vessel and its manning, etc., are the responsibility of the latter and the Maritime Directorate.

The law on *international road carriage of goods* (the CMR) and domestic road carriage of goods are handled by the Ministry of Justice and Public Security. The law on transport of passengers is divided between the Ministry of Justice and Public Security and the Ministry of Transport and Communications. The latter grants permit to commercial passenger transport operations and also deals with aspects of public law relating to carriage by road, such as safety, together with the Directorate of Public Roads.

As to *railway transport, international carriage of passengers and goods* according to the Convention concerning International Carriage by Rail (COTIF) (with appendixes relating to the CIV and to the CIM with annexes), are handled by the Ministry of Transport and Communications, which also carries the overall political responsibility for the NSB. The law on domestic carriage of passengers is, however, the responsibility of the Ministry of Justice and Public Security.

The Ministry of Transport and Communications holds the overall responsibility on air transport public law, e.g., according to the Chicago Convention, and the Ministry is assisted by the Civil Aviation Administration. The *air transport private law* (in particular contract law based on the Montreal Convention and relevant EU-legislation is handled by the Ministry of Justice.

Pipeline *transport of oil and gas* is a fragment of the petroleum law, which is handled by the Ministry of Oil and Energy.

Part I. Introduction

Chapter 1. Definitions and Notions

§1. Maritime Law and Transport Law

15. It may be said that 'maritime law' comprises the legal rules connected with vessels, the latter word taken broadly. Thus, matters concerning sale and purchase of vessels, liens and mortgages attaching to them, contracts regarding construction and repair of ships, not to mention all the chartering contracts related to vessels, might be considered parts of maritime law. But not all questions regarding maritime activity can be addressed in the present context. For instance, the important field of marine insurance will only come in as a background, and the almost classic law on charter parties is only mentioned briefly.

The term 'transport law' obviously is a wider concept than maritime law. It comprises also the law connected with transportation by road trailers, railway vehicles and aircraft. The rules are similar in many respects. Sometimes they differ for good reasons – due first of all to factual circumstances; sometimes they differ with no apparent rational explanation.

The law on road, railway, air and multimodal (combined) transport will be presented in a more limited context compared to the outline of maritime law. For these modes, the presentation will focus on the contract law applicable to transport of passengers or goods.

§2. The Law of the Sea

16. By the law of the sea (LOS), one normally has in mind the international and intergovernmental agreements regarding the rights and obligations of states to use and/or protect international waters. Although the treaties entered into regarding such matters may indeed affect traffic at sea, they will not be dealt with here. But it should be noted that Norway has agreed to/ratified the following treaties:

- *The Convention on the Continental Shelf*, Geneva 1958.
- *The United Nations Convention on the Law of the Sea*, Montego Bay 1982 (UNCLOS).
- *The United Nations Agreement Relating to the Implementation of Part XI of the United Nations Convention on the Law of the Sea of 10 December 1982*, New York 1994.

- *The United Nations Agreement for the Implementation of the Provisions of the United Nations Convention on the Law of the Sea of 10 December 1982 relating to the Conservation and Management of Straddling Fish Stocks and Highly Migratory Fish Stocks*, New York 1995.
- *The Agreement on the Privileges and Immunities of the International Tribunal for the Law of the Sea*, New York 1997.
- *The Protocol on the Privileges and Immunities of the International Seabed Authority*, Kingston 1998.

The Convention on the Continental Shelf has in particular been of importance to Norway as it formed the international legal basis for the exploration and exploitation of oil and gas in the Norwegian part of the North Sea, which again gave rise to the development of the Norwegian petroleum industry (*see also* General Introduction, V.A. above).

Chapter 2. Main Sources of Transport Law

§1. Maritime Law

I. Treaties

17. Norway has always tried to play an active part in the creation of international treaties in the maritime field. Among the most significant treaties ratified by Norway and transformed into or incorporated in Norwegian legislation are (spring 2019):

- *The International Convention for the Unification of Certain Rules of Law Relating to Collision Between Vessels*, Brussels 1910.
- *The International Convention for the Unification of Certain Rules of Law Relating to Bills of Lading*, Brussels 1924 as modified by the amending Protocols of 1968 (Hague-Visby Rules) and 1979.
- *The International Convention for the Unification of Certain Rules Concerning the Immunity of State-Owned Ships*, Brussels 1926 and the additional protocol of 1934.
- *The International Convention for the Unification of Certain Rules Relating to the Arrest of SeaGoing Ships*, Brussels 1952.
- *The International Convention Relating to the Registration of Rights in Respect of Vessels under Construction*, Brussels 1967 (not yet in force).
- *The International Convention for the Unification of Certain Rules Relating to Maritime Liens and Mortgages*, Brussels 1967 (not yet in force).
- *The International Convention Relating to Intervention on the High Seas in Cases of Oil Pollution Casualties*, Brussels 1969 and the additional protocol of 1973 (Intervention Convention).
- *The International Convention on Civil Liability for Oil Pollution Damage*, Brussels 1969 as modified by the amending Protocol of 1992 (CLC 1992).
- *The Special Trade Passenger Ships Agreement*, London 1971 and the additional Protocol of 1973.
- *The International Convention on the Establishment of an International Fund for Compensation for Oil Pollution Damage*, Brussels 1971 as modified by the amending Protocol of 1992 (Fund Convention 1992) and the additional Protocol of 2003.
- *The Convention Relating to Civil Liability in the Field of Maritime Carriage of Nuclear Material*, Brussels 1971.
- *The Convention on the International Regulations for Preventing Collisions at Sea*, London 1972 as amended (COLREG 1972).
- *The International Convention for the Prevention of Pollution from Ships*, London 1973 as modified by the amending Protocols of 1978 and 1997 (MARPOL 1978/1997).
- *The Athens Convention Relating to the Carriage of Passengers and Their Luggage by Sea, 1974*, as amended by the Protocol of 2002.
- *The International Convention for the Safety of Life at Sea*, London 1974 as amended (SOLAS 1974) and the additional Protocols of 1978 and 1988.

- *The International Convention on Salvage*, London 1989.
- *The Convention on Limitation of Liability for Maritime Claims*, London 1976 as amended by the Protocol of 1996.
- *The International Convention on Liability and Compensation for Damage in Connection with the Carriage of Hazardous and Noxious Substances by Sea*, London 1996 (HNS 1996) as amended by the Protocol of 2010 (HNS Convention 2010).
- *The International Convention on Arrest of Ships*, Geneva 1999.
- *The International Convention on Civil Liability for Bunker Oil Pollution Damage*, London 2001.
- *The International Convention for the Control and Management of Ships' Ballast Water and Sediments, 2004.*
- *The Hong Kong International Convention for the Safe and Environmentally Sound Recycling of Ships, 2009.*
- *The Nairobli International Convention on Removal of Wrecks, 2007.*

18. In addition, Norway has signed the following treaties:

- *The United Nations Convention on the Carriage of Goods by Sea*, Hamburg 1978 (Hamburg Rules).
- *The International Convention on Maritime Liens and Mortgages*, Geneva 1993.
- *The United Nations Convention on Contracts for the International Carriage of Goods Wholly or Partly by Sea*, New York 2008 (Rotterdam Rules, not yet in force).

As for the Rotterdam Rules – signed by Norway and other countries in Rotterdam 23 September 2009 – a committee appointed by the Ministry of Justice gave in 2012 a report on implementation of the Rotterdam Rules in the Maritime Code (MC) (NOU 2012: 10). Implementation is recommended and the necessary amendments in the legislation are described. However, no legislative action has yet been taken.

II. EU/EEA Law

19. As a result of Norway's accession to the EEA Agreement, important EU legislation concerning maritime law has been implemented in national legislation.

III. National Legislation

20. The *Norwegian Maritime Code* of 24 June 1994 No. 39 comprises provisions on all the main topics concerning legal maritime matters and is practically identical to 'sister-statutes' in Denmark, Sweden and Finland. The current MC replaces a previous one dated 20 July 1893. Although the 1893 version had retained its date, its provisions had been revised, modernized and enlarged. Also, the 1994 MC has been amended several times, in particular, to satisfy the requirements of international conventions on salvage, pollution liability and limitation of liability. In the following, the Norwegian MC will be referred to as 'MC', or '1994 MC'. When referring to the previous code the abbreviation '1893 MC' is used.

The *Ship Safety and Security Act* (SSSA) of 16 February 2007 No. 9 was enacted to ensure the safe management and operation of ships. To a great extent the Act relies on international legislation, most importantly the rules and standards established by the International Maritime Organization (IMO), the ILO and the EU.

The *Ship Labour Act* (SLA) of 21 June 2013 No. 102 regulates the labour conditions of seafarers and replaced the *Seamen's Act* of 30 May 1975 No. 18, was in 2013 superceded by.

In 1987, the Norwegian International Ship Register (NIS) was established. The relevant provisions for registration are laid down in Act of 12 June 1987 No. 48 *Relating to the NIS Act.*

§2. Rail Transport

I. Treaties

21. Norway has ratified the *Convention concerning International Carriage by Rail*, Bern 1980 as modified by the 1999 Protocol (COTIF).

II. EU/EEA Law

22. In 2007, the EU enacted Regulation (EC) 1371/2007 on Rail Passengers' Rights and Obligations regarding Rail Journeys and Services throughout the Community. This was implemented by Regulation of 3 September 2010 No. 1241.

III. National Legislation

23. National legislation on railway transportation includes the following acts:

- The *Act on the Convention concerning International Carriage by Rail* of 10 December 2004 No. 82 (COTIF Act), makes COTIF, together with its appendices, applicable as enacted law.
- The *Act on the Liability of the Railroad Service towards Passengers* of 10 June 1977 No. 73 regulates the railways liability for damage to passengers and their luggage.
- Lastly, there is the *Act on the Building and Operation of Railways, including Tramways, Underground Railways and Suburban Railways, etc.* of 11 June 1993 No. 100 (Railways Act).

24. Supplementary to the legislation on railroad transport, the standard conditions of carriers and freight forwarders are generally applied, namely: the *Standard Conditions of Carriage* of the NSB (NSB CC, valid from 4 December 2013), the

General Carriage Terms and Conditions of the freight train operator CargoNet AS of 31 December 2016 (valid from 1 January 2017) and the *General Conditions of the Nordic Association of Freight Forwarders* (NSAB 2015, valid from 1 January 2016).

§3. Road Transport

I. Treaties

25. Norway has ratified the *International Convention on the Contract for the International Carriage of Goods by Road*, done in Geneva in 1956, including the additional Protocol of 1978 (CMR). In addition, Norway has signed the *Additional Protocol to the CMR concerning the Electric Consignment* of 2008.

II. National Legislation

26. The CMR was made part of Norwegian internal law first by the *Act on International Carriage of Goods by Road* of 31 January 1969 No. 3. Later, a revision took place that resulted in the *Act on Carriage of Goods by Road* of 20 December 1974 No. 68 (the CGR Act). The Act comprises both international and domestic carriage of goods by road.

The *Act on Liability for Vehicles* of 3 February 1961 applies, *inter alia*, when personal injury is suffered by passengers in connection with transport by road in a vehicle.

§4. Air Transport

I. Treaties

27. Air transport and airlines are to a great extent subject to public administrative law. Norway has implemented the *Chicago Convention on International Aviation* of 1944, as well as the *International Air Service Transit Agreement* and the *International Air Transport Agreement* of the same date.

As for air transport private law, the following conventions have been ratified by Norway:

- *The Convention for the Unification of Certain Rules Relating to International Carriage by Air, Warsaw* 1929 (Warsaw Convention) and the amending Protocols of 1955 (Hague Protocol) and 1975 No. 1-4 (Montreal Protocols).
- *The Convention on the International Recognition of Rights in Aircraft*, Geneva 1948.

- *The Convention, Supplementary to the Warsaw Convention, for the Unification of Certain Rules Relating to International Carriage by Air Performed by a Person Other than the Contracting Carrier*, Guadalajara 1961 (Guadalajara Convention).
- *The Convention for the Unification of Certain Rules for International Carriage by Air*, Montreal 1999 (Montreal Convention).
- *Convention on International Interests in Mobile Equipment* of 2001 (Cape Town-Convention) with *Protocol to the Convention on International Interests in Mobile Equipment on Matters specific to Aircraft Equipment* of 2001.

II. EU/EEA Law

28. Norway has implemented Regulation (EC) 2027/97 on Air Carrier Liability in Respect of the Carriage of Passengers and their Baggage by Air of 9 October 1997, as amended by Regulation (EC) 889/2002, as well as Regulation (EC) 785/2004 on Insurance Requirements for Air Carriers and Aircraft Operators of 21 April 2004.

III. National Legislation

29. The prevailing national legislation on both air transport public law and air transport private law is the *Act on Aviation Operations* of 11 June 1993 No. 101 (the AAO Act).

§5. Multimodal Transport

30. There are no binding international conventions specifically governing multimodal transports. Norway participated, however, in the United Nations Conference of Trade and Development (UNCTAD) work that resulted in the *United Nations Convention on International Multimodal Transport of Goods*, signed in Geneva 1980 (the UNCTAD Convention 1980). The convention has not been ratified by Norway and has not otherwise become effective according to its terms.

Chapter 3. Jurisdiction and Courts

31. There is no specific admiralty jurisdiction in Norway, nor are there special admiralty courts.

The Act on Conciliation and Litigation in Civil Matters of 17 June 2005 No. 90 (ACL) Chapter 4 has rules on venue. The main rule in section 44 is that litigation can be commenced in the court district where the defendant is domiciled or, if the defendant is a company (a legal entity), where the company according to registration in the Register of Business Enterprises has its head office.

Section 4-5 offers a number of optional venues. Actions regarding contractual questions may be brought 'where the obligation upon which the action is based has been performed or is to be performed'. Actions for damages based upon tort may be brought 'in the place where the damage originated or where its effects occurred or may occur'. In employment questions, the suit may be brought 'at the place of work or at the place where the employee performs his work. If there is no such place, the action may be brought at the place of business from where the employee was employed'. Section 4-5 has also particular rules for maritime relations. Actions in such matters may be brought 'in the judicial district where the vessel's port of registry is situated, and if the vessel has been arrested, an action relating to the claim for the money secured by such arrest may be brought at the place where such arrest took place'. Putting up security to avoid arrest has the same effect.

The code provides for venue in international matters. Section 4-3 says that a dispute in such matter may only be brought before the Norwegian courts if the facts of the case have a sufficiently strong connection to Norway.

Furthermore, it should be mentioned that section 4-6 has rules on agreed venue: an action may be 'filed with the court agreed upon by the parties' – thus excluding or supplementing the venues provided by sections 4-3 to 4-5. Such agreement may have been reached after the dispute was a fact, but also beforehand, the typical example is jurisdiction clauses in charter parties.

In addition, there may be special rules on jurisdiction in other acts than ACL. One example is MC section 203 on the jurisdiction of Norwegian courts regarding oil pollution damage; another is section 6-5 of the SLA of 21 June 2013 No. 102 directing suits relating to employment to Norwegian courts.

Of particular importance is the *Lugano Convention* of 30 October 2007 between the EEA and EU countries. The rules regulate, *inter alia*, which countries' courts shall be deemed competent to adjudicate private law cross-border disputes.

Chapter 4. State Immunity

32. The jurisdiction of Norwegian courts is 'subject to such limitations as are recognized in international law or that derive from any agreement with a foreign State' (ACL section 1-2). A similar provision is in the Act on Enforcement of Claims of 26 June 1992 No. 86 (AEC) section 1-4. The latter act has also some specific provisions regarding foreign vessels in section 1-5, and – which is of particular interest – on foreign state vessels in section 1-6. The rules on foreign state vessels reflect the international conventions ratified by Norway. The essence is that a foreign state vessel (owned or chartered) is not subject to the enforcement rules when the vessel is 'exclusively used for state purposes of a public law nature'.

Chapter 5. Transport Intermediaries

33. In complex transportation arrangements, one needs intermediaries to obtain smooth implementation of the various demands. Of particular importance are the freight forwarders. Originally, they were true intermediaries: giving information and advice on transportation possibilities – with one mode of transportation or combinations, and, furthermore, participating in the contract negotiations and the writing of the contract between the cargo owner and the carrier. Today a freight forwarder is very often the *contractual* carrier – sometimes using transport vehicles owned by him (in particular: trucks), very often on the basis of an underlying contract he has with the actual (performing) carrier (the shipowner, the railway operator etc.). In Scandinavia, there has been a standard set of rules regarding the services of a freight forwarder. The present version is '*General conditions of the Nordic association of freight forwarders*' of 2015 (abbreviated: NSAB 2015) and is a result of negotiations between the freight forwarders' association and a number of organizations on the cargo side. It is indicative that section 3 after having listed the services a freight forwarder may provide describes the freight forwarder 'as a contracting party', before a description of his role 'as intermediary'.

When the freight forwarder gives a promise of transportation, i.e., assumes the responsibility of a carrier, his obligations and rights are described in NSAB 2015 sections 15–21. His period of liability is 'between the moment when the goods have been taken over until the moment the goods have been delivered' (section 15). The basic rule is that liability for damage or delay depends upon fault or neglect, see section 16 stating that there is no liability if loss, depreciation or delay is caused by 'circumstances which the freight forwarder could not avoid and the consequences of which he was unable to prevent' (letter h). When there is liability, the freight forwarder is entitled to limit his liability to 8.33 SDR per kg 'of the part of the goods which has been lost, depreciated or damaged' (section 22). However, there is an important special rule in section 2 – the 'network clause':

> 'If a certain mode of transport has been expressly agreed upon, or if it is proved that loss, depreciation, damage or delay has ocurred whilst the goods were carried by a particular means of transport, the freight forwarder shall be liable in accordance with the law applicable to such mode of transport and commonly used conditions of carriage, to the extent that these deviate from what is laid down in § 6, section 2 and 3 or §§ 15 - 21.'

In the maritime sector the shipbrokers and the agents are very important.

The shipbroker will normally represent one of the parties to the contract – the charterer or the owner, or the yard or the purchaser of a new building. His task will be to bring the parties together, e.g., resulting in a charter party between the shipowner and the charterer. Only by conclusion of a binding charter party can the broker normally earn his remuneration (the commission).

In Norway, there are several large ship brokering firms also working in the international shipping market. Often a Norwegian shipbroker will conclude a contract between non-Norwegian parties.

There is no separate statute governing shipbrokers, but statutes for brokers dealing with real estate and dealing with securities may by way of analogy be relevant, and so may general principles of contract law. There are a great number of Norwegian court decisions and arbitration awards dealing with questions as to when a shipbroker is entitled to commission.

Regarding agents, one should distinguish between port, liner and forwarding agents.

The duties of the port agent are to assist the party appointing him, owner or charterer, in expediting the stay of the vessel in port. A central part of his work is to help the master, *inter alia* by ensuring that all relevant documents are obtained and signed as quickly as possible.

The liner agent is usually contractually tied to one or more liner carriers. His task is to provide cargo to the liner service, advertise sailings, collect freights and arrange documentation.

In Norway, there is no statute spelling out the rights and obligations of these categories of intermediaries. There are, however, statutory laws from 1916 and 1992 on certain sales agents, but these statutes will not be directly applicable. The legal position of the agent – both towards his principal and towards third parties – will, therefore, depend upon general principles of contract law, the basic idea being that an agent (if he describes himself as such) will not be bound as against third parties, while the principal on whose behalf the agent acts, normally will be bound.

Part II. Maritime Law

Thor Falkanger & Hans Jacob Bull

34. Since the 1890s, Norway, Denmark and Sweden have had MCs, regulating first of all commercial shipping. These codes have been drafted – and updated – in close co-operation between the Nordic countries, and have been and still are practically speaking identical. The codes are not built on foreign law. They reflect, of course, a number of international conventions, and the drafters have been well-acquainted with non-Scandinavian maritime law, in particular, English jurisprudence. The present Norwegian one is from 24 June 1994 No. 39 – in the following abbreviated MC.

This Nordic basis has been strengthened by the law report Nordiske Domme i Sjøfartsanliggender (*Nordic Court Decisions concerning Maritime Matters*), abbreviated ND, published each year since 1899, lately also comprising judgments on road transport.

A private translation of the Norwegian Code to English is found in MarIus No. 435 (2014), and the quotes in the following are from this translation.

Chapter 1. The Vessel

§1. Registration and Nationality of Vessels

35. In Norway, there are two ship registers – the ordinary (NOR) and the international (NIS). The rules on the ordinary register, which are discussed first, are found in MC, in particular in Chapter 2.

The MC does not give a general definition of 'ship' or 'vessel'. The concept is more or less taken for granted. But some indications are given in as much as MC section 11 states that the obligation to register concerns vessels of more than 15 m of length. If the vessel is shorter, it may be registered on certain conditions.

The question of nationality is, however, defined in particular in MC section 1. A vessel is considered Norwegian where it is owned:

(1) by a Norwegian citizen;
(2) by a partnership where the owners are fully liable if at least 6/10 is owned by Norwegian citizens (including Norwegian companies);
(3) by a limited partnership where Norwegian citizens hold at least 6/10 of the capital of the limited partnership; or
(4) by a company with limited liability where at least 6/10 of the capital and voting power are on the hands of Norwegian citizens, and in addition, certain requirements as to the composition of the board of directors and the principal place of business for the limited company are met.

Most important is No. 4. The nationality requirement (which is applicable in Nos 2 and 3 as well) is satisfied, e.g., if say 60% of the stock capital is owned by a company which in itself fulfils the national requirements. Furthermore, equal with Norwegian nationality (of a person or a company) is an EEC-state nationality.

The formal rule is that vessels fulfilling the above requirements have to be registered in NOR, but there are two important exceptions.

The first one is connected with the Norwegian International Register. By the Act of 12 June 1987 No. 48, Norway established the Norwegian International Register (NIS). The purpose was mainly to prevent Norwegian owners flagging out their vessels to flags of 'convenience' ('open registers') whereby they might obtain considerably reduced running costs, first and foremost in their crew expenses. However, registration is open also for non-Norwegian vessels. The requirements for registration in NIS are:

(1) the owner of the vessel fulfils the requirements for entry into NOR; or
(2) the owner is a limited joint-stock company or a limited partnership with its main office in Norway, or a partnership ('partrederi') with a managing owner satisfying the requirements in MC Chapter 5;
(3) even if the owner does not fulfil the conditions of 1 and 2 above, if he has a representative in Norway authorized to accept writ of summons and fulfilling the MC Chapter 5 requirements for a managing owner.

The owner of a Norwegian vessel is free to choose registration in NIS instead of NOR, but registration in NIS has certain disadvantages: vessels registered in NIS are not permitted to carry cargo or passengers between Norwegian ports or operate in regular passenger traffic between Norway and other countries. However, vessels mainly employed in foreign waters are permitted to carry cargo (i) between Norwegian ports as part of regular service between Norwegian and foreign ports, or (ii) as petroleum cargo in bulk from the Norwegian shelf, or (ii) occasionaly for periods not exceeding 3 months.

The second exception to registration in NOR is a very wide one: the owner is free to register in any other register, which means that not much remains of the old obligation for the Norwegian owner to register in NOR. His obligation is today that the vessel has to be registered – where depends upon the owner's own considerations.

MC Chapter 2 contains detailed rules, supplemented by Regulations, as to how one should proceed when entering a vessel into the NOR register. The procedure for NIS registration is basically the same as for NOR.

The purpose of registration is twofold: It gives the authorities an instrument to supervise that vessels flying the Norwegian flag comply with safety requirements as well as other aspects of public law. The other effect is that registration of ownership and rights – section 20 prescribes which private rights pertaining to it may be entered and noted – gives protection as against third parties and bankruptcy. For example, when the vessel has been mortgaged the mortgage first registered will normally have priority, and if the sale of the vessel is registered the sale will normally be respected by the bankruptcy estate when the owner goes bankrupt after the sale has been registered.

§2. Registration of New Buildings and Constructions Not Considered as Vessels

36. Not only sailing vessels, but also vessels under construction, and even the new building contract, may be registered in a special section of the ship register. This possibility is mainly due to facilitating financing of the vessel. For instance; if the new building is owned by the yard up to delivery to the buyer, the yard may use the vessel under construction as security for bank credit during the building period; if ownership is with the buyer, he may use the new building as security for loans used for paying instalments to the yard.

For similar reasons, constructions not qualifying as vessels may to some extent be registered, e.g., floating cranes and docks, barges and hovercraft, *see* MC section 33. Floating installations used on the continental shelf can also be registered, *see* MC section 507; when they are permanently on-site, registration depends upon the rules in Chapter 6 in the Act on Petroleum Activities of 29 November 1996.

§3. Acquisition and Ownership

37. Norwegian citizens and companies may today buy and sell vessels without public law restrictions. Normally, the sale of a vessel is also exempted from value-added tax claims.

The normal way to acquire a vessel is either to enter into or take over a new building contract, or to buy a sailing vessel (second-hand sale). You may also inherit a ship, but this is, of course, a rare event for commercial ships. Normally, a person would inherit shares in a company owning ships, rather than the vessel itself. The vessels are movables, and if Norwegian law is to be applied, it would be the *Sales of Goods Act* of 13 May 1988 No. 27 which would offer the supplemental legislation to the agreed terms. This act is supplemental also regarding new building contracts.

It should be noted that the contract for sale and purchase of sailing vessels mostly used in international transactions stems from the 'Norwegian Sale Form' under the name of *Memorandum of Agreement* ('MOA'), originally prepared by the Norwegian Shipbrokers' Association and issued in 1956. In 1993, this contract was amended, and adopted by the shipping community via the Baltic and International Maritime Council (BIMCO) –'Saleform 1993'. The present version is Sale form 2012. The contract leaves it open for the parties to agree upon where possible disputes shall be arbitrated.

38. The *shipowner* may be an individual. In this case, the form of ownership will then be described as a *sole or individual proprietorship*. If a ship is owned by several partners, all with unlimited liability for the debts of the company, this is referred to as a *shipowning partnership or part owners* (part owners is a direct translation of the Norwegian term '*part-redere*'). If only one or more of the partners have unlimited liability, while the others are only liable up to the amount they have invested, there is a *limited partnership* ('*kommandittselskap*'). If the liability of all the participants in the venture is limited to the amount they have invested, there is a *corporation* or *limited company*. In the case of shipowning partnerships, it is correct to say that the partners themselves own the ship. However, in the corporation, in legal terms the corporation is the shipowner rather than the individual shareholders. Financially speaking, it may be relevant to describe a major shareholder as owning the ship, but legally this is incorrect.

The owner may delegate the performance of some, or all, of the operational functions typically associated with ownership of ships to others. The participants in a limited partnership will usually delegate the day-to-day management of the ship to a commercial manager. Often also manning and technical management is taken care of by a management company. In some cases, there is a specific requirement for a managing owner to be appointed, i.e., in the case of shipowning partnerships (MC sections 3 and 103). Where a Norwegian corporation owns a ship, a particular person or entity must represent the corporation, namely the board of directors.

Generally speaking, there has in Norwegian shipping been a tendency to have several vessels in one company, rather than to have one company for each vessel.

Chapter 2. Maritime Liens and Mortgages

§1. Maritime Liens

I. Introduction

39. A maritime lien is an encumbrance on a ship prescribed by law; it takes effect without an agreement or a judicial or administrative decision. The underlying idea is that a person or company having a claim of a certain nature against the owner deserves a preferred security for his claim. The Norwegian word for maritime lien is '*sjoepant*' (the Norwegian word '*pant*' covers also enforcement liens (execution liens) and mortgages).

Maritime liens have three important characteristics:

(1) they give security, protected against third parties without registration;
(2) they have priority ahead of all other encumbrances; and
(3) they are subject to a short limitation period.

Obviously there is a conflict of interest between typically the banks financing the acquisition and operation of a vessel and the creditors having their claims secured by maritime liens. The bank may experience that the value of the mortgage diminishes when the number of maritime liens increases. Clearly, this will influence the willingness to supply such credit which the shipowner in most cases is dependent upon. This conflict has led to a reduction of the number of claims which are secured by a maritime lien, reflected in the Brussels Conventions of 1926 and 1967. The Norwegian rules are based upon the 1967 Convention. Norway has not adhered to the new convention of 1993, but the stipulations contained therein do not differ very much from existing Norwegian law.

A maritime lien attaches to the ship and her appurtenances (*see* MC section 45 on appurtenances). Ships under construction cannot be subject to a maritime lien prior to the launching.

II. Categories of Maritime Liens

40. MC section 51 first subsection provides:

> Claims against an owner are secured by maritime liens against the ship, in so far as they relate to:
>
> 1. wages and other sums due to the master and other persons employed on board in respect of their employment on the vessel;
> 2. port, canal and other waterway dues and pilotage dues;
> 3. damages in respect of loss of life or personal injury occurring in direct connection with the operation of the ship;

4. damages in respect of loss of or damage to property, occurring in direct connection with the operation of the ship, provided the claim is not capable of being based on contract;
5. salvage reward, compensation for wreck removal, and general average contribution.

When a claim falls within the list in MC section 51 first subsection (1)-(5), it is in principle irrelevant whether the claim is based on contract, tort, statute or case law.

A maritime lien shall arise also if the claim is against the owner, charterer, manager or any person to whom the shipowner has delegated his or her functions, *see* second subsection. The effect of this stipulation is as follows.

The shipowner ordinarily puts the ship to commercial use and finances its activities. When this function is transferred to another party through a lease or a bare boat charter, the charterer becomes the '*owner pro hac vice*' – manning, maintaining and utilizing the vessel. The charterer is then normally liable if, for example, the ship collides through negligence with another ship. However, the damaged ship will have a tort claim which is secured by a maritime lien in the vessel. The shipowner therefore becomes indirectly liable; he may have to cover the claim in order to avoid a forced sale of the ship. The rationale is that liability for collisions is an operational risk, and the shipowner should not be able to side-step the security the maritime lien gives to the claimant, simply by delegating ownership functions to, e.g., a bareboat charterer. The same applies where one of the other parties listed in MC section 51 second subsection becomes personally liable for a claim. For example, where A runs the catering services on board a cruise ship as an independent contractor, then waiter B will be employed by A, not the shipowner. If A does not pay the wages, B's claim will be secured by a maritime lien in the ship. If a person unlawfully takes control of the ship, no maritime liens arise, because the shipowner has not transferred his functions to this person. When a government requisitions a ship, this is not considered 'unlawful' in this sense, but the rules on sovereign immunity make the rules on maritime liens ineffective.

Some remarks will be made as to the various categories of claims as mentioned below.

MC section 51 first subsection (1) applies to 'wages and other sums due to the master and other persons employed on board.' There is no requirement for a claimant to have been hired by the shipowner, nor is it necessary for the claimant to belong to the 'actual' crew (cf. the example of the waiter above). It is irrelevant whether the person has been employed on a permanent basis or merely been hired for a short time. It is not necessary for the claimant to be contractually bound for service on a specific ship. For example, a seaman with a 'company contract' (i.e., a contract to serve on several of the company's vessels) is entitled to a maritime lien for non-payment of wages. A's claim resulting from service onboard ship A will be secured by a maritime lien in ship A, but not ship B.

'Wages and other sums' is interpreted quite broadly. It is irrelevant whether payment is made in the form of wages or other compensation. The gross claim is secured. Where the shipowner deducts tax from wages, the tax authority's claim against the shipowner will be secured by a maritime lien in that the authority subrogates the seaman's maritime lien right. In addition, a claim arising instead of, or in addition to, an ordinary wage claim, is secured by a maritime lien (e.g., a claim arising from unjustified termination, a claim for maintenance, for free trips home, etc.).

41. MC section 51 first subsection (2) covers various fees. An examination of the legislative history reveals that only public fees are secured, i.e., fees based on statute or public regulations with a public body as the creditor.

42. MC section 51 first subsubsection (3) and (4) apply to personal injury and property damage sustained in 'direct connection with the operation of the ship'. Whether the deceased or injured person, or the destroyed or damaged property, was on board the ship, on another ship, floating on the water or located on land, is irrelevant. The decisive factor is whether the damage is sufficiently proximate to the operation of the ship. Legislative history shows that this formulation was chosen to ensure correspondence between maritime liens and P&I insurance cover. The rationale is that claims covered by the P&I policy will normally be so closely connected with the ship that it is appropriate for them to be secured by maritime liens.

Pollution from a vessel may cause substantial damage to a wide range of persons. The owner of the vessel (and others) has wide-ranging liability for such damage (*see* Chapter 13 below). Claims of this type are secured by a maritime lien insofar as there is damage to property or personal injury. If, for example, a beach is damaged by a vessel discharging oil, a claim by owners of the beach will be secured by a maritime lien. In the case of liability in accordance with MC section 191 (convention-based liability), maritime liens are of less practical importance because the shipowner is obliged to carry liability insurance (MC section 197).

There is one significant exception relating to property damage claims. A maritime lien does not arise if the claim can be based on contract. This primarily means that maritime liens cannot arise in connection with damage to or loss of cargo, or damage to or loss of passengers' luggage.

An additional exclusion (involving both personal injury and property damage) is found in MC section 51 subsection 3 for cases where the damage is caused by nuclear materials; regulation of this type of liability is left to special legislation.

43. Finally, MC section 51 first subsection (5) provides a maritime lien for salvage claims, i.e., for efforts qualifying as salvage under the rules in MC section 441. The same applies to tort claims for wreck removal, i.e., there is a maritime lien in the wreck, or in the ship which is to blame (also stated in the *Harbour Act* of 17 April 2009 No. 19 section 35). Finally, claims for general average contributions qualify for a maritime lien under MC section 51 first subsubsection (5).

44. Claims secured by a maritime lien may carry interest, typically in accordance with the *Act on Interest on Late Payment* of 17 December 1976 No. 100. There is a long case law tradition that maritime liens cover the interest component of the claim as well as the litigation costs. This is also the situation under today's rules.

III. Enforcement of Maritime Liens

45. Maritime liens are subject to a limitation period of one year (MC section 55). The one year period is calculated from the date the claim arose, e.g., the day the damage occurred, compare MC section 51.

Commencement of an ordinary court case does not affect limitation. MC section 55 states that limitation can only be prevented in one way: by arresting the vessel. To obtain an arrest in these circumstances it is, as per the ACL in Civil Matters of 17 June 2005 No. 90 section 33-2 subsection 3, sufficient to have a claim which is due and secured by a maritime lien. The petition for an arrest prior to the expiry of the limitation period will not breach the limitation; the arrest must be granted and formally served on board (i.e., served upon the master) or implemented (*see* MC section 55 second sentence). The arrest must be followed up and a forced sale must take place, otherwise the effect of the arrest is lost, compare the one year limit in ACL section 33-10 subsection 1 letter c.

The courts have, however, accepted that an arrest by A is sufficient to stop time running, even if it does not lead to a forced sale, provided that another creditor demands a forced sale before A's one year period expires and the forced sale takes place. According to the *travaux preparatoires* to the enforcement rules, a forced auction also prevents extinction of a maritime lien, meaning that a maritime lien which arose during the one year period prior to the date of the forced sale is protected.

When a creditor is legally prevented from arresting the vessel, the limitation period does not run (MC section 55 subsection 2).

Ordinarily, the threat of arrest or implementing the arrest will force the shipowner to put up security, allowing the parties to resolve the dispute without the ship being detained. If security is not provided amicably, a difficult situation may arise. For example, where the crew invokes a maritime lien in respect of wage claims, they must – within one year of the time the claim arose – arrest the vessel and demand a forced sale of the vessel. An arrest is not, however, sufficient ground for a sale; in most instances, a judgment for the claim is required. Altogether, this is a serious matter for the claimant, especially when the general rule in MC section 95 subsection 2 is that an arrested ship must remain where it is until a forced sale has taken place or forced use has been implemented. At the request of a maritime lien holder, the court may, however, decide that the shipowner is entitled to operate the vessel. Moreover, security can be demanded from the claimant in connection with an arrest (ACL section 33-4 subsection 1), and the party arresting the ship may become liable for the loss caused by the arrest (ACL section 32-11).

IV. Ranking

46. A maritime lien in the vessel is effective without registration. In fact, registration is not allowed (MC section 20 subsection 1(1); the registrar is not able to decide for instance whether a lien has arisen in an alleged collision, and this type of liens has a short lifetime). A maritime lien has priority ahead of all other claims (MC section 52 subsection 1). In other words, mortgages and enforcement liens are pushed aside, as are possessory liens (MC section 54 second subsection). Among maritime liens, priority is generally decided by the category number in MC section 51 subsection 1. Thus a wage claim secured by a maritime lien (No. 1) must be paid in full before any payment can be made on a claim for damage to property (No. 4). Claims in the same category have equal status.

Salvage claims under No. 5, however, have special status; they have better priority than older maritime lien claims, and among the No. 5 claims a more recent claim will have priority. For example, a maritime lien for salvage in February ranks prior to a maritime lien for wages from January, but after a maritime lien for wages from March and likewise after a maritime lien for salvage in April. The special rules for salvage claims can be explained by the fact that a salvage operation 'salves' the security for holders of older maritime liens: without the salvage effort, the security would have been lost.

Generally, possessory liens have lower priority than maritime liens and mortgages. However, there is one exception: a shipbuilder's or a repair yard's possessory lien has a lower priority than a maritime lien, but a higher priority than mortgages and enforcement liens (MC section 54 second subsection).

V. Choice of Law

47. Mortgagees benefit from the reduced threat from maritime liens in Norway, but a threat is still posed by liens arising in foreign countries under foreign law.

A typical case would be a supplier's lien arising under American law during a Norwegian ship's call at an American port. MC section 75 deals with this problem, providing that a Norwegian court will only recognize a claim as being secured by a maritime lien if it is so entitled under Norwegian law. This means that the American supplier's liens will not be recognized by the Norwegian court, but as soon as the ship calls an American port, the maritime lien may be invoked there. The fact that the ship is Norwegian and that the law of the flag state does not allow a maritime lien to arise in relation to a supplier's claim, is considered irrelevant by the American courts.

In case of foreign-registered ships, the Norwegian court may apply foreign rules on maritime liens, but only to the extent that foreign maritime liens not based on Norwegian law are given priority behind maritime liens, possessory liens and recorded claims (MC section 75 subsection 2).

VI. Liens on Cargo

48. Liens on cargo are not regulated in the 1967 Convention. However, MC section 61 provides for lien on cargo. Such a lien shall attach to cargo for:

(1) a claim in respect of a salvage reward and a general average contribution;
(2) a claim arising in consequence of the fact that the carrier or the master in accordance with his statutory authority, has entered into a contract, taken

action or incurred expenditure on the account of the cargo-owner, and a cargo-owner's claim for compensation for goods sold for the benefit of other cargo-owners;

(3) a claim by the carrier arising out of a chartering agreement, in so far as the claim can properly be brought against the person claiming delivery.

The lien on cargo is extinguished when the cargo is delivered by the carrier (section 63), and it is subject to limitation unless suit is commenced within one year from the day the claim arose (section 64).

§2. Ship Mortgages

I. General Concepts

49. In our times, it is rare that a ship is paid for with money belonging to the purchaser or contractor. He will usually need to borrow at least part of the purchase price. Lending money to a potential shipowner may be a risky business. The financial institution providing the money will therefore wish some security in addition to the personal claim it may have against the borrower. This security is obtained by a mortgage (Norway: '*pant*').

Theoretically speaking, the establishment of a mortgage falls into three stages:

(1) Establishment of a loan agreement.
(2) Agreement to the effect that the loan shall be secured by (*inter alia*) a mortgage.
(3) The creation of the mortgage deed itself.

In Norway, there is a separate statute regarding granting of preferred security in assets, including mortgages: the *Mortgage Act* of 8 February 1980 No. 2 (MA). Section 1-1 defines the rights of the mortgagee as follows:

> By a right under a mortgage is meant a special right to seek satisfaction of a claim in specific property (the attached property).

This means that the lender (the creditor) normally has both a *personal* claim against the debtor and a claim in rem against the asset, namely the ship. Today the mortgage is a short formal document. The rights of the mortgagee will depend upon terms of the loan agreement, and these terms will be decisive if the question of forfeiture of the mortgage arises.

A mortgagee may, even with a duly registered ship mortgage, feel that he is uncomfortably exposed. The ship – the object of the mortgage – may be wholly or partly destroyed, and the security thereby accordingly threatened. The mortgagee, therefore, normally will insist that the vessel shall be insured against, in particular, hull and machinery risks and war risks (hull insurance). Additionally, it will also be in the interest of the mortgagee that the vessel be insured against potential liability towards third parties (P&I insurance). One reason for the lender to insist on adequate P&I cover is, of course, the exposure to maritime liens that may rank better than any registered mortgage. Occasionally, there are separate assignments of insurance proceeds in favour of the mortgagee. However, normally the mortgagee is secured by a clause in the mortgage together with being duly noted as co-insured with the owner by the hull and machinery and war risk insurers. Some lenders also require a separate mortgagee interest cover. The common concept of insurance is that the rights of the mortgagee are derived from the legal position of the owner (mortgagor). Accordingly, if the owner should be denied, e.g., hull insurance cover for having caused the incident wilfully, the position of the mortgagee also is seriously jeopardized unless a separate mortgagee interest insurance has been taken out.

II. Creation of Ship Mortgages

50. The MA section 1-2 subsection 2 establishes the principle that a mortgage can only be valid if its basis is in statute. Such a basis as regards ship mortgages is found in MC section 41.

If the provision is strictly construed, it only covers mortgages of the whole ship, but it is generally accepted that mortgages of a part of the ship can be arranged (a part owner may wish to mortgage his share in the vessel, *see* paragraph No. 51 below).

The scope of a mortgage is determined by interpreting the mortgage agreement. On this point, MC section 45 has important rules which are partly mandatory and partly supplementary. Subsection 1 states that the mortgage, or, for that matter, other charges on a ship, also attach to the ship's separate parts and appurtenances. An item temporarily brought ashore may still be considered an appurtenance and thus covered by the mortgage. An example would be electronic equipment brought ashore for adjustment or repair.

The rule in subsection 1 implies that if, for instance, new electronic equipment was acquired, it would be covered by an existing registered mortgage, and certainly by a subsequently registered mortgage. In addition, the establishment of separate charges in appurtenances (or parts of a ship) is not allowed. Thus an attempt to reserve property rights in electronic equipment would not be upheld, nor would it be valid between the parties. The rationale is primarily that electronic equipment is so important that it is practically in the same category as, e.g., propulsion machinery, and therefore the financing plan should be structured to allow the acquisition of equipment through equity capital and ordinary credit secured by a mortgage. It would be unsatisfactory if, in connection with a forced sale, a ship could be stripped of equipment if suppliers exercised liens in the equipment for the outstanding balance of the purchase price.

There are some exceptions, however. First of all, under MC section 45 subsection 2 leases of appurtenances will be upheld. This exception is applicable to leases of, for example, Decca equipment. A pre-condition, however, is that the shipowner can terminate the lease with less than six months' notice. If a longer termination period is agreed upon, the item is within the scope of the mortgage, regardless of whether it is a genuine lease agreement ('operating leasing') or a so-called financial leasing, which implies that the lessee has paid for the object at the expiry of the lease period.

A further exception (MC section 45 subsection 3) is available for registered small vessels with a length not exceeding 10 m (*see* MC section 11 subsection 3 allowing registration of fishing vessels required to be registered under the Act 26 March 1999 No. 15 relating to the right to participate in fishing and catching (Participants Act), and vessels used exclusively or mainly in trade). For machinery and electronic equipment on such vessels, the reservation of property rights will be valid because of the special financing needs of such small vessels.

51. It has been an issue whether a part-owner should be entitled to mortgage his share in the vessel, for example, his 20% interest in the partnership and consequently his ideal 20% interest in the vessel. MC section 113 presents a compromise: this can be done, but only with the approval of the other owners. A consequence of such approval is that the creditors of the part-owner can obtain enforcement lien on the relevant part, *see* MC section 119. Legal protection against the creditors or bankruptcy estate of the part-owner mortgagor is obtained by registration in the ship registry. The register will list the part-owners, and the mortgaging of one of the part owner's property rights will appear in theship's sheet in the register.

The problems that can arise when part of a ship is mortgaged can be illustrated by a simple example. Take a ship owned with equal parts by A, B and C. First, the ship is mortgaged to X for NOK 5 million. Subsequently A mortgages his part for NOK 1 million, and finally, the whole ship is mortgaged to Y for NOK 3 million. If Y demands a forced sale of the ship, the Enforcement of Claims Act section 11-20 requires that the lowest acceptable purchase sum shall give full satisfaction to those with higher-ranking security in the ship. This means at least NOK 5 million to X, but how much should be allotted to A's separate creditor? And if A's separate creditor attempts to realize his security, what is then the lowest acceptable price? The answer to these problems is uncertain.

52. Rights under a new building contract or rights to the actual new building can be mortgaged, *see* MC section 41 subsection 2. Rules on the scope of mortgages are given in section 43 in respect of new buildings in Norway. The main engine and hull sections built by the yard or brought from a subcontractor to the yard are subject to the mortgage unless otherwise provided in the loan agreement. Furthermore, unless there is an agreement to the contrary, materials (e.g., steel plates) brought to the building yard form part of the mortgage. A pre-condition is that the materials are distinctly marked or otherwise identified for incorporation into the ship. The painting of a building number on the plates will be considered sufficient. The charge on materials and equipment is extinguished when they are sold and taken away from the yard, provided the acquiring party neither knew nor ought to have known that the sale was against the interests of the mortgagee. If the plate supplier has reserved property rights in the plates (a seller's lien), the reservation will rank above a mortgage in the ship under construction – *see* MA section 3-15 subsection 2. However, the supplier's lien will lapse when the plates are incorporated into the construction (*see* the MA section 3-19) or once the plates are cut (*see* the MA section 3-20); the rights of the mortgagee of the new building are then correspondingly expanded.

Sections being built at another yard in Norway may also be included, i.e., the mortgagee has security in such sections even before they arrive at the main yard. Also, sections built at a foreign yard may be included but only from the time that delivery from that yard has taken place.

53. The mortgage may attach to several objects, typically several vessels or even the shipowner's whole fleet of specified ships. The MA section 1-12 answers some of the questions that such an arrangement may give rise to.

54. An important question is whether the rights of the mortgagee can pass to another object. MC section 72 provides that a creditor with a maritime lien will not benefit from insurance or tort sums that become due when the vessel is damaged or lost. The mortgagee is treated differently and may have an independent claim against the tortfeasor and the insurance company, *see* Nordic Marine Insurance Plan (NP) clause 7-1.

III. Formalities Relating to the Creation of a Mortgage

A. Mortgage Deed and Loan Agreement

55. Apart from authentication of the signatures of the person(s) signing the mortgage on behalf of the mortgagor, there are no formal requirements that have to be observed in order to create a valid mortgage deed. The person(s) signing the contract must obviously have the necessary authority to bind the mortgagor. This is of particular importance where the vessel is owned by a corporation or partnership. The NOR and NIS registry will demand verification that the corporate requirements for binding the company (mortgagor) have been adhered to in order to allow the mortgage registered.

The Norwegian merchant banks use a standardized ship mortgage deed. This is a fairly simple document with a few clauses. The tendency is clearly that the mortgage deed contains only the data relevant for registration, including, of course, other encumbrances on the ship (e.g., clause on no further mortgaging). The important document is the loan agreement, today often a lengthy document with a detailed regulation of the rights and obligations of both parties on (*inter alia*):

- regular payment of interest and instalments;
- use and maintenance of the ship;
- insurances to be taken out;
- sale and further mortgaging of the ship;
- accelerated payment and forced sale.

B. Registration

56. The principle of legal protection being available solely through registration applies not only to ships subject to mandatory registration but also to ships and new buildings which are eligible for registration (MC section 11 subsection 3 and section 33). In order to get full protection of a mortgage on a new building or, for example, a pleasure craft with a length of 12 m, it is necessary to register the mortgage, and this has as a pre-condition that the owner has seen to it that the new building/the craft is registered.

Mortgages on ships registered in NIS are subject to the same rules; registration is necessary in order to get full protection.

IV. Ranking

57. The MA stipulates in section 1-13:

> When two or more have security rights [a term including mortgages, execution liens and maritime liens] in the same asset, that right takes priority which was first incurred, if nothing else has been specifically agreed, or follows from the rules of legal protection.

The rules on legal protection do make important modifications so that the practical rules are those stated in MC section 23:

> Registered acquisitions of rights rank in priority before those not registered.
> In the event of a conflict between registered acquisitions of rights, priority is given to the acquisition of rights first entered in the journal.
> Acquisitions of rights entered in the journal at the same time have equal rank. Executions and arrests have nevertheless rank prior to other acquisitions of rights. When several attachments are registered at the same time, the oldest attachment has priority.

However, it should be noted that maritime liens have priority before mortgages and execution liens, even if the maritime lien arose after registration of the mortgage or the execution lien (MC section 62), and furthermore that a registered contractual right ranks after an earlier non-registered right, if the acquirer of the contractual right at the time of registration 'knew or ought to have known about the earlier right' (MC section 24).

The Enforcement of Claims Act stipulates in section 11-20 that at a forced sale, no offer can be accepted if it does not cover the claims of those who have better priority than the mortgagee demanding the forced sale.

V. Validity Period of Mortgage

58. As stated above, a mortgage transaction consists of two components: the loan for which the borrower is personally liable, and the security given in the vessel (the mortgage). These two components will almost always be present when a ship is mortgaged (while a personal claim against the owner may not exist if a maritime lien is incurred, e.g., while the vessel is on a bareboat charter). The loan and the mortgage would thus normally exist for the same period of time: the mortgage ceases (is deleted as an encumbrance on the vessel) when the debt has been repaid. The owner can make it a condition for his payment that he gets a receipt to the effect that he has repaid the mortgage-loan in part or in full, and upon full repayment he can demand the return of the mortgage deed, enabling him to have the encumbrance deleted from the ship register. There is not, however, an absolute link between the contractual claim for repayment of the loan and the mortgage encumbrance. If the contractual claim becomes time-barred, the mortgage encumbrance will survive, and the creditor can use the mortgage as a basis for a forced sale of the vessel – hopefully thereby getting full satisfaction. Should he not get full satisfaction, the time-bar means that he is precluded from seizing other assets belonging to the shipowner.

It should also be noted that it is fully possible to 're-use' a mortgage. When a loan, secured by a mortgage, has been partly or fully repaid, the mortgagor and the mortgagee may agree that the mortgage shall secure a new loan. Such 're-use' may, however, cause priority problems in relation to encumbrances with lower priority than the original mortgage.

When the mortgage object, in our case a ship, is destroyed, the security has disappeared (but if the vessel is insured there is a right of subrogation to the insurance compensation, *see* MC section 72 where this rule is implied). However, the liability for the personal loan continues. Indeed, this loan is normally deemed to have fallen due by default if the mortgaged ship is lost, or severely damaged.

VI. Assignment of Mortgage

59. The MA stipulates in section 1-10 that assignment of the mortgage may validly take place (e.g., when the owner changes bank connection). The mortgagee may also use the mortgage as security for his own debt (re-pledge). The assignment or re-pledge does not need to comply with any particular form. It is done by signing an assignment on the mortgage deed by the mortgage holder, together with delivery of the document to the assignee. A ship mortgage deed containing an unconditional debt undertaking is, under Norwegian law, a negotiable document unless expressly stated to the contrary on the deed ('non-negotiable').

An assignment of the personal claim will normally be considered to imply a transfer of the mortgage as well and vice versa. The subsequent mortgagee will, as a main rule, be in the same legal position as the previous mortgagee was in.

VII. Ship Mortgage and International Law

60. Under international law, a state can only enforce claims against assets which are within its own territory. From this follows that a Norwegian ship can only be subject to a forced sale in the country/state where the ship is at any given time, in Norway or abroad. Similarly, a foreign vessel which happens to be in Norway may under certain conditions be sold here. When the court gives its final approval of a forced sale, one of the conditions is that the vessel at that time is in Norwegian waters. However, *preparations* for a forced sale may be initiated even when the vessel is abroad.

61. Rights in the vessel created abroad may be transferred to the Norwegian register when the vessel is entered there. Such rights are relevant when the vessel is subject to a forced sale (or forced use) in Norway. Special rules apply to maritime liens. A claim may be secured by a maritime lien based on the law of the country where the claim arose, but the lien is recognized only if the claim would have been secured under Norwegian law.

A Norwegian mortgage duly registered in the NOR or NIS register will normally be respected abroad. This means that the mortgagee will be paid what is due to him when costs, etc., and possibly maritime liens and other mortgages with a better priority, have been covered. The effects in Norway of such a sale are stated in MC section 76:

> If a ship is sold by forced sale abroad, all maritime liens, registered mortgages and other encumbrances on the ship cease to attach provided that, at the time of the sale, the ship was in the territory of the State in question and that the sale was performed in accordance with the laws of that State and the provisions of the 1967 International Convention on Maritime Liens and Mortgages.

To what extent the Norwegian authorities will respect a forced sale abroad if the conditions stipulated in section 76 are not observed is not spelled out, neither in the MC nor elsewhere.

§3. Sale of the Vessel

62. The fact that the vessel is mortgaged does not prevent the owner from selling it. This is explicitly stated in the MA section 1-11 subsection 1. However, it is also said that sale may not take place 'if the opposite follows from agreement'. The banks will almost invariably deny the owner the right to sell the vessel without the consent of the mortgagee. Such restriction will, as long as it appears from the register, preclude registration of change of ownership.

The sale of a vessel – in particular when the intention is to transfer to a register in another country – may involve a lot of paperwork. The climax is on the so-called closing day: There is a meeting with seller and buyer, together with their lawyers, as well as representatives of the seller's and buyer's banks. The purpose of the meeting is to ascertain whether the necessary documents are present, duly signed and authorized. During the meeting, one obtains confirmation, typically by telephone, that delivery of the vessel has taken place in conformity with the sales contract. Thereafter, the last documents can be signed and instructions be given regarding deregistration and new registration in the register selected by the buyer. The necessary groundwork in the registers is usually done in good time before the closing day, leaving only the finishing touches for the closing day.

A sale – with transfer of title in the same Norwegian register or to a foreign register – does not in principle affect the mortgage. Obviously, there may be difficulties when a vessel is transferred from the Norwegian register to a foreign register; *see* in this respect MC section 28 subsection 2:

> If an encumbrance has been registered on a ship, the ship shall not be deleted without the written consent of the beneficiary of the encumbrance, but a note of the facts which would otherwise have resulted in deletion shall be made on the ship's sheet in the Register. In such event the encumbrance retains its priority, but no new establishments of rights can be registered.

§4. Extinction of Ship Mortgages and Liens

I. Extinction: General

63. The normal cause for extinction will, of course, be paid by the debtor of the claim secured by the mortgage. The same result is achieved when payment of the claim is made in connection with a forced sale when the purchase price is sufficient to cover the mortgage debt. If payment of the claim is made by a third party the mortgage will, however, continue to exist, and the intervening payer will subrogate to both the contractual claim and the rights flowing from the mortgage.

On forced sale and bankruptcy proceedings not giving full payment, *see* III. and IV. below.

MC section 29 contains rules regarding deletion of encumbrances, i.e., the encumbrances are removed from the register; they will not appear on subsequent printouts from the ship register. Deletion will follow on presentation of evidence that the encumbrance or charge no longer attaches to the ship; in most instances, the required evidence is a receipt or a statement from the mortgagee. Another example is an auction bill of sale which shows that the mortgage has lapsed (*see* III. below).

MC section 30 contains various rules concerning time limitation of the legal protection obtained by registration. When the time has expired, the registrar should delete the encumbrance on his own initiative.

II. Waiver by the Creditor

64. The mortgage may be extinguished wholly or partly by consent of the creditor, i.e., consent to delete or discharge the mortgage.

III. Forced Public Sale

A. General

65. Enforcement of the rights flowing from the mortgage (foreclosure) is regulated in detail in the 1992 AEC, supplemented to some extent by the rules in the 2005 ACL in Civil Cases. The demand for a forced sale of the vessel is submitted to the ordinary Court of First Instance. The application must be addressed to the court in whose district the vessel is or is expected to be in the near future (section 11-3). This should be seen in connection with section 11-10, which contains rules on where the vessel has to be during the actual sale. The court's confirmation of a sale can ordinarily be given only if the vessel is in Norway at the time. However, a request for forced use can be put forward at the registered owner's domicile even if the vessel is not in Norway. In this way, the vessel can be brought to Norway where a sale can take place.

A condition for allowing a forced sale is that the claimant can show 'an enforcement ground'. Such grounds are listed in AEC section 11-2. The most important one is 'a registered mortgage'. A 'registered execution lien' is also an enforcement ground, while a maritime lien in most cases is not – which means that, generally, the holder of a maritime lien has to obtain an ordinary judgment for his claim before he can demand a forced sale. It follows from section 11-1, compare section 4-4, that the claim secured by the mortgage must be due either according to ordinary rules on repayment or due to declaration of premature repayment.

The application must be presented to the debtor (the defendant) (AEC section 11-7). After he has had the possibility to give his views, the court decides whether to grant the application (section 11-9). If the application is granted, the court has to choose between a forced (compulsory) auction and an assisted sale (section 11-12). The court's decision will primarily be based on which alternative is likely to result in the highest net proceeds. In most cases, this means an assisted sale is preferred.

B. Sale by an Assistant of the Court

66. When the court chooses this alternative, it appoints an assistant. In most cases, this will be a professional ship broker who is familiar with the market for the type of vessel in question. The broker will circulate the vessel's particulars and as far as possible follow the procedures applying to ordinary sales. When the broker has obtained one or more offers, which he considers to be reasonable, these will be put before the creditor (i.e., the party who demanded the forced sale). The creditor then has to decide whether he wants the court to confirm a sale on the basis of the bid which he finds acceptable (section 11-28). If the creditor decides to proceed with the sale, the assistant must notify the owner, other parties with rights in the vessel and the court (section 11-29). The court must then verify that the conditions for confirmation are met. If this is the case, the court makes a formal declaration (decree) that the vessel is sold (section 11-30).

67. There are two important rules setting the lowest limit for an acceptable offer. First, a sale must give full satisfaction for all parties with rights ranking higher in priority than that of the creditor demanding the forced sale (section 11-20). A simple illustration: there are mortgages in a vessel ranking in this order: A 100, B 90 and C 80. If C demands foreclosure, the lowest acceptable bid must cover A and B (190). It is not necessary for C to get any satisfaction. If A is the claimant there is no limit in respect of the principle in section 11-20.

The second rule is that the court shall not confirm a sale if it considers that further sales efforts may result in higher net proceeds (section 11-30 subsection 2 letter a).

The confirmation decree may be appealed within one month (section 11-34).

The so-called settlement day occurs three months after the assistant's presentation of the offers to the court and the holders of rights in the vessel. The purchase price must be paid by this time. However, the buyer is entitled to wait fourteen days from the date when the confirmation decree is final (section 11-27); if this right is exercised he must in addition pay interest at 6% *pro anno*.

At the same time as delivering the confirmation decree or at a later stage, the court also delivers a distribution decree, i.e., decides how the purchase price shall be distributed (section 11-36). First, the expenses are covered, including the assistant's fee. Thereafter, secured creditors are paid according to their priority. This is because a forced sale is in principle a general settlement of all monetary claims on the vessel, i.e., the buyer gets the vessel free of monetary encumbrances and the mortgages are deleted in the ship register. There is a right of appeal also against this decree. Payment takes place when the confirmation and the distribution decrees are final (section 11-38). The secured claims normally accrue interest and such interest is secured under the mortgage. The system in AEC is that all claims are calculated forward to the settlement date, i.e., what each claim amounts to on that day when interest and costs secured are added. These sums are relevant when applying the principle in section 11-20 as well as when distributing the proceeds in accordance with section 11-36.

As stated above: after the sale, the vessel is free of all monetary encumbrances. The mortgagee not having got full satisfaction will usually have a non-secured claim against the owner for the non-paid part.

For non-monetary encumbrances the system is different. For example, the fate of a registered right of pre-emption will depend upon its priority. If it has priority before the claimant, there will be no sale unless the buyer accepts the vessel with this encumbrance (section 11-20). With priority after the claimant the vessel shall first be offered on the condition that the right attaches; if no bid is obtained the right will be 'set aside' (section 11-21), meaning that it will cease as an encumbrance, but a right to monetary compensation remains, if the purchase price so allows. In this context, it should be noted that charterparties are outside the category 'non-monetary encumbrances'; they cannot be registered (MC section 20).

C. Forced Auction

68. The rules on forced auction in AEC are relatively few and brief (sections 11-43 to 11-54) as there are a number of references to the rules on assisted sales. The following points should be noted.

When the court decides on a forced auction, the actual auction may be held by the court or by an enforcement officer. After the auction has been sufficiently advertised in the press etc. and decisions have been made on the auction conditions (sales conditions), the actual auction will take place. Bidding continues until the director declares the public meeting closed. Then it is up to the claimant to decide whether any of the bids are acceptable (section 11-50). The claimant is usually obliged to elect the highest bid. As with an assisted sale, the bid must be at least sufficient to cover all encumbrances with higher priority than the claim which is the basis for the sale. Also as in the case of an assisted sale, the court must check that the price is within the law requirements, and that the procedural rules have been followed, before issuing a decree of confirmation (section 11-51). The court also distributes the sale proceeds through a distribution decree. The same principles apply as under an assisted sale (section 11-52). The effects of a confirmed auction sale – for the claimant as well as other parties with a right in the vessel – are the same as in an assisted sale.

IV. Bankruptcy

69. If the shipowner is declared bankrupt (*see* Act on Bankruptcy of 8 June 1984 No. 58), the bankruptcy estate will sell the assets and distribute the money among the creditors. The bankruptcy does not preclude the mortgagee from having the ship sold in the manner mentioned above, in other words, the mortgage remains intact. However, the estate may decide to dispose of the ship. Very often the vessel is mortgaged for sums exceeding the value of the vessel, and the estate may then decide to abandon the ship, i.e., transferring it to one of the mortgagees. The estate has also the possibility of selling the ship in such a way that mortgages exceeding the value of the vessel are (wholly or partly) extinguished (Bankruptcy Act sections 117a–117c). Furthermore, the bankruptcy estate has the possibility to sell the vessel in accordance with the rules applying to forced sale (Act on Creditors Right to Seize the Assets of the Debtor of 8 June 1984 No. 59 section 8-15); here the bankruptcy estate is treated as if it had first priority, which means that the principle in AEC section 11-20 is not applicable.

Chapter 3. Master and Crew

70. The central piece of legislation in Norway relating to the employment status of a ship's master and crew is the SLA (Act of 21 June 2013 No. 102 concerning employment protection for employees on board ships, etc.). The act must be viewed in tandem with the SSSA (Act of 16 February 2007 No. 9 relating to ship safety and security), in particular, Chapter 4 concerning working environment and personal safety. Although the general Working Environment Act of 17 June 2005 No. 62 does not apply to employment on ships, it has long been an important aim that employees onboard Norwegian ships should have the same legal protection in their work as those employed on land. Consequently, the provisions in the Working Environment Act were taken as a starting point in the drafting of the SLA. When interpreting the SLA, support and inspiration may be found in the general act and legal practice relating to it.

Norway is a party to the Maritime Labour Convention 2006 (MLC), which came into effect in 2013. The incorporation of MLC into Norwegian law made for certain challenges. In many ways, the Convention is 'old fashioned' by comparison with what is regarded in Norway today as efficient practical legislation. It is built up on the basis that employees onboard ships do not have permanent employment, a state of affairs which Norway departed from in 1985, and consequently, it contains hardly any provisions concerning employment protection. Nor has the Convention taken much note of the practice, usual in international shipping today, whereby the owner of the ship, the manager of the ship and the employer of those who work onboard the ship are not necessarily one and the same company. When Norway and numerous other nations found it expedient, nonetheless, to ratify the Convention and incorporate its provisions into their domestic law, it was prompted by the wish to participate in achieving an international 'minimum' standard for those who work at sea.

The master stands in a unique position amongst those who work on board ships. He has the highest level of authority on board the ship, but will at the same time be an employee in the legal sense (SLA section 1-2 subsection 1). The provisions in the SLA and the SSSA, which is presented below (paragraph Nos. 76 to 83), will consequently apply to him as well as to the rest of the crew. In addition Chapter 6 of the MC contains a number of particular provisions with reference to the master. These provisions compare with similar provisions in the other Nordic MCs. Some of the situations dealt with corresponding to those dealt with in the SLA and SSSA, but the regulation in the MC is not altogether harmonized with them.

§1. Master

I. Appointment of the Master

71. In order to be eligible as master on board a Norwegian vessel, it is necessary to hold a master's license, *see* Regulation 22 December 2011 No. 1523 section 28, with references to sections 23–27, which has its basis in the SSSA of 16 February 2007 No. 9 section 16.

The appointment of a master is, in principle, not different from the procedure followed when hiring other members of the crew. Reference is therefore made to the presentation in paragraph No. 78 below.

II. The Public Functions of the Master

72. The master is the highest authority on board the ship. The SSSA and, on individual points, the SLA also makes him a figure with central responsibility for compliance with the provisions of the acts, see so far as the SSSA is concerned sections 8, 19, 29 and 37 with supplementing regulations.

In addition, MC Chapter 6 deals exclusively with the position and duties of the master. Both his public and private functions are regulated. This applies for example to MC section 131 concerning the ship's seaworthiness, MC section 132 concerning navigation, MC section 133 concerning the ship's books, MC section 134 concerning loading and discharging and MC section 135 concerning the master's duties if the ship – or another ship – run into difficulties.

A primary duty for the master is to keep law and order on board. To achieve and maintain this, the master may use force. If the vessel is in danger, or there is mutiny among the crew, it is allowed to use the means which are necessary to establish order and obedience (SSSA section 40). If a serious crime has been committed on board, and the vessel is not in a Norwegian port, the master shall investigate, secure proofs and obtain statements. He may also take steps and use necessary force to take control of the suspect (SLA section 9-3).

III. The Private Law Functions of the Master

73. Some of the master's public duties, e.g., maintaining the safety of a vessel, are at the same time private law functions inasmuch as it is the master's obligation towards his employer (the shipowner) as well as the crew and the cargo owner to exercise due diligence in this respect. One may, therefore, say that it is not always possible to distinguish between the master's public and private law functions.

MC section 137 empowers the master to enter into contracts on behalf of the shipowner. The authority of the master in this respect is stated as follows in subsections 1 and 3:

> The master, in his capacity as such, has authority to enter into contracts on behalf of the owner relating to the conservation of the ship or the performance of the voyage and to make agreements for the carriage of goods on the voyage, or of passengers if the ship is intended for that purpose. He or she can also act as plaintiff in lawsuits relating to the ship. In lawsuits relating to the ship the master may receive proclamations and communications on behalf of the owner of the ship, provided that this is not contrary to the obligations of Norway under international law.

If money is required for any of the purposes mentioned, and the instructions of the owner cannot be awaited, the master shall seek to raise the money in the most convenient way. He or she may then, according to the circumstances, raise loans or pledge or sell goods belonging to the shipowner and even, if necessary, pledge or sell cargo. Even if the transaction was unnecessary, the contract shall nevertheless be binding if the third party acted in good faith.

The master may also enter into contracts on behalf of the cargo owners without any special authority (MC section 138).

The contracts entered into on the basis of such authority is binding on the shipowner or the cargo owner respectively, while the master himself is not bound (MC section 139). In practice, such authority is less used than previously owing to improved communications.

Otherwise, the master will be under the instructions of the owner as to where to go and what to transport. However, the owner may by contract, e.g., a time charter party, cede those rights to a charterer. In such a case, the master will have duties to both the owner and the charterer. This may at times put the master in awkward situations, in particular, if the instructions which the master receives are in conflict with stipulations in the charter party. The same type of conflict may arise in relation to the cargo. The master may have an obligation to sign bills of lading 'as presented', while at the same time he is bound to ascertain that the contents of the bill of lading are correct. Considerable pressure is then sometimes put on the master to co-operate on terms which may go beyond what is legally prudent for him to follow.

IV. Special Duties of the Master

74. The above explanations have outlined the unique and important position of the master. His main duties may be summed up: to take care of the ship and the persons on board as well as the interests of the cargo. Modern communication systems make it possible for the master to give extensive reports to the shipowner, and for the shipowner to give frequent and detailed instructions to the master, almost from minute to minute when difficulties arise. The everyday decisions are, of course, a matter for the master. However, even in difficult situations the master may have to act on his own – immediate action is required, or the decision depends upon facts which cannot adequately be conveyed to or assessed by the owner. In such situations, the responsibility and authority to make decisions will rest with the master, for example on whether to accept assistance from a salvage vessel, to jettison cargo, seek a port of refuge, etc.

V. The Liability of the Master

75. The master is not personally liable for the contracts entered into on behalf of the owner or the cargo-owner (MC section 139). As for loss caused by his negligence, MC section 140 prescribes:

> The master is liable to compensate any loss caused through fault or neglect in his or her service pursuant to the general law of torts, cf. Section 2-3 of Act relating to Compensation in Certain Circumstances.

Section 2-3 in the mentioned act of 13 June 1969 No. 26 provides that the liability of an employee may be reduced when this is considered reasonable taking into account his behaviour, economic status, his position and the circumstances in general.

§2. CREW

I. The Contract of Employment of Crew Members

76. Traditionally, a contract of employment was for service on a named vessel. The tying of the employment contract to a specific ship had several implications. For example, the contract came to an end if the ship was lost or subject to long-term repairs.

Gradually, so-called shipping company contracts became more widespread. These are agreements whereby the seaman is employed to serve on board a vessel belonging to the owner. If the ship he is working on is sold, he can continue service on another of the shipping company's ships. This right and duty to serve on any of the shipping company's ships applies unless otherwise is agreed in writing or laid down in a collective wage agreement. For a shipping company with only a few ships, the provision has little practical importance. It should be noted that requirements with respect to certificates and special qualifications may prevent a transfer to another vessel. Moreover, the seaman is not obliged to accept a transfer to a different or less senior position.

The above principles are now refined and embodied in the SLA. The SLA proceeds from the starting point that it is the employer who has primary responsibility to an employee in the working relationship. In order to emphasise this, the Act uses the designation 'employer' for him, cf SLA section 2-1, thereby adopting the concept to be found in the Working Environment Act. At the same time, the Act also imposes duties on 'the shipowner'. The concept of 'the shipowner' is reserved for those who manage the ship, *see* SLA section 2-3, which makes reference to SSSA section 4 for a more precise definition: The shipowner is the entity which is identified in the Ship's Safety Management Certificate as the managing company, *see* subsection 1, and will often, but not always, be the actual owner of the ship. In a 'traditional' shipping company the owning function, management function and employer function will be collected together under one roof; it is the entity which owns the ship, who also manages it and engages the master and crew. This model, however, does not give a full picture of today's reality in the Norwegian shipping industry. Even if 'traditional' shipowners can still be found, ships today are more often than not manned by a company other than the one which manages them (and equally it may be yet another company which actually owns the ship.) In such cases, it is the crewing company which is the employer of the employee according to the SLA.

SLA section 2-2 subsections 1 and 2 state that it is the employer who has primary responsibility towards the employee. The employer shall *ensure* that the provisions laid down in and pursuant to the Act and the employment agreement are complied with and is accordingly *responsible* to the employee for the fulfilment of the financial requirements and rights which are accorded to him by the Act.

Obligations towards the employee are, however, imposed also upon the shipowner, *see* SLA section 2-4. These obligations are of a slightly different kind. If the shipowner is someone other than the employer, the shipowner has a duty in accordance with subsection 1 to *see to it* that the provisions laid down in and pursuant to the Act or in the employment agreements are complied with. This *see to it* duty involves the shipowner in following up and checking that the employer satisfies the employee's rights. The shipowner must therefore have a system in operation which makes it possible to keep a necessary check on the employer. In addition to the *see to it* duty pursuant to subsection 1, the shipowner has also an independent *ensure that*-duty pursuant to subsection 2 in those cases where the Act expressly requires it, namely with reference to the rules contained in Chapters 8, 9 and 10.

The shipowner also has *financial* responsibility towards the employee. It follows from SLA section 2-4 subsection 3 that the shipowner is jointly and severally liable with the employer for the payment of salary, holiday pay and 'any financial claims that employees working onboard the ship are entitled to pursuant to the provisions set out in Chapter 4 of this Act'. The intention of the provision is to ensure that the employee can make good his valid rights under the MLC directly against the shipowner. Other financial obligations which the employer might have towards employees, such as responsibility for unfair dismissal and other claims connected with employment protection are on the other hand not subject to joint and several liability.

In maritime employment relationships, as in most other employment relationships, collective wage agreements play an important role. These agreements are entered into between the employer and employee organizations and set various restrictions on the contents of individual contracts. For example, the seamen can demand to be paid at the rate set by the collective agreement, even if their employment contracts set a lower rate of remuneration. The collective wage agreements clarify and extend the rights granted by the SLA.

The SLA section 1-2 define the scope of the act. The main rule is that the act applies to an employee working onboard Norwegian vessels under a contract of employment with an employer. The nature of the employment is irrelevant, whether it be navigation, galley duty or running a hairdressing salon onboard a cruise vessel. The act, except for Chapters 8–10, will not apply to persons who work on Norwegian ships without being in the position of an employee towards an employer, *see* SLA section 1-2 subsection 1 second sentence. Neither will the act apply to employees who are only working on board when the vessel is in port (longshoremen, watchmen, etc.), *see* SLA section 1-2 subsection 2 letter a).

The SLA section 1-2 subsection 1 states in express terms that the provisions of the act may not be departed from by an agreement which is to the detriment of the employee, unless the act or relevant regulations expressly provide otherwise.

77. As mentioned above, NIS-registered ships are also subject to Norwegian law unless explicitly otherwise provided in or pursuant to a statute, *see* NIS Act section 3 subsection 1. Such exceptions are particularly relevant to the position of the crew. The NIS Act section 6 contains the main principles. Terms relating to pay and working conditions must be fixed in a collective wage agreement (in writing), with a Norwegian or foreign trade union as the negotiating party on the employee's side. Subsection 3 first sentence establishes that a collective wage agreement must specify that it is subject to Norwegian law and the competence of Norwegian courts. The second sentence nonetheless contains an opportunity to agree that disputes shall be determined in other countries pursuant to their procedural rules. A pre-condition is, however, that Norwegian substantive rules will be applied. Should this not be so, the Norwegian court will, in extreme cases, have a basis for rejecting the jurisdiction clause.

The individual employment contract must specify that it is subject to Norwegian law and that disputes shall be determined by the Norwegian courts, subject to the employee's right to bring claims in his country of residence (section 6 subsection 4). The extent to which such claims can be brought in the country of residence will depend on the rules of that country.

The NIS Act section 7 has an important reference to the rules in the Ship Safety Act regarding working and resting time, and section 8 provides that essential parts of the SLA are applicable.

II. Recruiting

78. The employment contract must be in writing and include information on factors of major significance for the employment relationship, *see* SLA section 3-1 subsection 1. The employee is appointed on a permanent basis, *see* section 3-4 subsection 1 first sentence, but the parties may agree on a probationary period not exceeding six months, *see* section 3-2 subsection 1. In case the employer have a need for a short-term engagement, section 3-4 provides the possibility of entering into contracts for temporary appointments, but the conditions for this are restricted, *see* subsection 1.

III. The Duties of the Employer and Employee

79. The employee's duties will be specified in the employment contract, or follow from custom or regulations that are applicable to his position. Collective wage agreements also contain important provisions describing employment duties. The work must be performed on the ship specified, but as we have seen, an employee may be transferred to another ship belonging to or operated by the employer.

In recent years, the traditional working pattern has been modified by the development of so-called alternating service. If an employee has a duty to alternate, he can be asked to take on a different position in his own department (as it is referred to in the collective wage agreement) or to work in another department. The work, however, must be of a type that the employee is or can become qualified to carry out. The collective wage agreements contain other specific rules.

The SLA does not stipulate any requirements as to the qualifications of individual employees. This subject is dealt with in the requirements set out in SSSA section 16 and accompanying regulations, see in particular the regulation of 22 December 2011 No. 1523 concerning seamen's qualifications and certificates. In addition SSSA section 17 establishes requirements as to health and SSSA section 18 a minimum age of 16 for any person working onboard ships, both provisions having supplementary regulations.

A person working onboard a ship, whether as employee or independent contractor, is entitled to require that his workplace and leisure time living space satisfy his reasonable demands for safety, hygiene and well-being. The provisions concerning this are to be found in SSSA Chapter 4 'Working environment and personal safety', which cover both safety and welfare. Section 21 sets out a main principle: 'necessary safety measures and precautions shall be taken in order to avoid or reduce any hazard to life and health and to ensure a fully satisfactory working environment for persons who are working on board.' Further, pursuant to section 22 the work on board 'shall be arranged and carried out so as to safeguard life, health and working environment in a good and suitable way.' The chapter also contains provisions about working hours and hours of rest (sections 23 and 24), living and recreational environment (section 25), catering (section 26) and medicaments and right to treatment of sick persons (section 27). The responsibility for ensuring that all this is taken care of is shared between the shipowner, the master, the employer and others who work onboard.

The SLA contains no provisions dealing with how much salary an employee is entitled to. The rate of pay, including basic wages, extras and overtime, depends on the collective wage agreements and the specific contract. SLA Chapter 4, however, has detailed rules as to calculation and payment of salary and right for the employer to make deductions. Salary accrues from the date specified in the employment contract or at the latest from the day the employee enters into service', *see* section 4-1 first paragraph. The chapter also has rules regarding the frequency of wage payments, the sending home of wages, and limitation on the right to make deductions. In the case of illness or injury, the employee is entitled to demand salary for as long as the employment lasts, but the entitlement lapses if the employee is entitled to sickness payments pursuant to the relevant national social security scheme and in any event twelve months from the date the disability arose, *see* section 4-4.

80. In addition to salary, an employee is entitled to free accommodation and board. When commencing and terminating services the employee will normally be entitled to free passage from or to his home, including free accommodation and board. There are other instances where an employee is entitled to free passage home, *see* SLA section 4-6 subsection 1 letter a) with regard to free passage home after six months' continuous service in foreign trade on the same ship or on ships belonging to the same employer. Finally, in the event of illness or injury, the seaman, whether an employee or an independent contractor, is entitled to nursing care from the shipowner, *see* section 8-1. Reference is also made to the rules in section 8-2 regarding the shipowner's obligation regarding death and burial.

81. As mentioned in Chapter 2, §1.II. above, a seaman's claims are secured by a maritime lien.

IV. Termination

82. In principle, employment is for an unspecified period of time with a mutual right of termination. The initial notice period is one month, but three months for masters. The period increases with the length of service (two months after five years, three months after ten years), *see* SLA section 5-2 subsections 1 and 2. If the employee is engaged for a probationary period (*see* paragraph No. 78 above), the period of notice on either side is fourteen days, *see* section 5-2 third paragraph. Notice of termination must be in writing, *see* section 5-3 subsection 1.

Before making a decision regarding termination, to the extent that it is practically possible the employer is to discuss the matter with the employee and the employee's elected representatives, *see* SLA section 5-1 subsection 1 first sentence. The subject matter for discussion will be the basis for a possible dismissal and how a choice is to be made between several employees as to who should be dismissed, *see* second sentence. Insufficient consultation may be significant in an evaluation as to whether dismissal is unfair.

83. The SLA contains two sets of regulation regarding termination of the employment of an employee: ordinary dismissal (dismissal with notice) and summary dismissal (dismissal without notice). Summary dismissal is an option for the employer if the employee has committed a gross breach of duty or other serious breach of the contract of employment, *see* SLA section 5-14 subsection 1. Summary dismissal involves the employee withdrawing from work with immediate effect and his entitlement to salary ceasing. Since summary dismissal is a drastic measure, it must appear necessary that the employee withdraws immediately. The decision must be made on the basis of a quite broad evaluation of the whole situation where, having regard to the employee and to the employer's undertaking, it does not appear unreasonable or inappropriate to dismiss the employee summarily. The summary dismissal may be tried by the courts. If the summary dismissal is regarded as unfair, the dismissal will be set aside if the employee so demands, *see* section 5-14 subsection 3 first sentence. However, even if the summary dismissal must be regarded as unfair, in special cases and if so claimed by the employer, the court may decide that the employment should be terminated if, after weighing the interests of the parties, the court finds it 'clearly unreasonable' that employment should continue, *see* second sentence. In practice, this approach will only rarely be applied. A more practical solution is that an unfair summary dismissal is upheld as a dismissal with notice if that is objectively justified and the employer asks for it, *see* third sentence.

If there is reason to believe that an employee has done something that may involve summary dismissal and the needs of the undertaking justify it, the employer may suspend the employee while the matter is being investigated in accordance with section 5-13 subsection 1. Suspension is accordingly an immediate but temporary withdrawal during the time it takes to investigate whether the conditions for summary dismissal are met. The employee retains his right to be paid salary during the period of suspension, *see* subsection 3. Suspension shall be revoked as soon as the conditions laid down in the subsection 1 are no longer fulfilled, *see* subsection 2 first sentence.

As regards ordinary dismissal (dismissal with notice), section 5-6 subsection 1 prescribes that the employee may not be dismissed 'unless it is objectively justified on the basis of circumstances relating tot he undertaking, the employer or the employee'. Dismissal without reasonable cause is to be considered invalid, *see* section 5-11 subsection 1. Consequently, the employee is entitled to retain his job, and, if he wishes, to return to the position he was dismissed from. In 'special cases' the court may nevertheless decide that the employment should be terminated if, after weighing the interests of the parties, anything else would be 'clearly unreasonable,' *see* second sentence. Generally it will be very difficult for an employer to make good an assertion of this kind. The employee is also entitled to claim compensation if he has been unfairly dismissed, whether he continues in the job or leaves, *see* section 5-11 subsection 2 first sentence. The compensation will be assessed at the amount the court deems 'reasonable' having regard to the financial loss, circumstances relating to the employer and employee and other facts of the case, *see* second sentence. It is assumed that the compensation will at the least cover financial loss and may in addition incorporate an element of compensation for non-economic loss.

In determining whether a dismissal is justified, the situation at the time of dismissal is the underlying basis of the enquiry. The onus is on the employer to show that the dismissal is fair, but the employee must establish that what he is being blamed for, such as absence without permission or refusal to comply with orders, is excusable.

When deciding whether the dismissal is justified section 5-6 subsection 1 indicates at the outset that regard must be had to the 'circumstances relating to the undertaking.' What is meant by the concept of 'undertaking' is the business which the employer carries on. Subsections 2–4 contain special provisions linked to the circumstances relating to the undertaking. Subsection 2 states that a dismissal based on curtailed operations or rationalization measures will not be fair if the employer has other suitable work which he can offer to the employee, *see* first sentence. The need to reduce the crew is therefore not sufficient in itself. But there has to be an available position or need for work which is not covered by existing availability, which the employee has to be regarded as qualified to do. The second sentence goes one step further; in determining whether a dismissal is justified by curtailed operations or rationalization measures, the needs of the undertaking are to be weighed against the disadvantages caused to the employee by the dismissal.

Subsection 3 establishes that registration of a ship in the NIS register constitutes due grounds for dismissal if the employer has no other suitable work to offer to the employee. Subsection 4 prescribes that transfer of ownership of the total undertaking cannot in itself be used as a reason for dismissal. The provision presupposes that rights and obligations in relation to employment matters are taken over by the new owners upon the transfer. If the new employer opts to go through with dismissal, the evaluation should lay weight on whether the dismissal would have been considered reasonable if the transfer had not taken place, *see* second sentence.

Section 5-6 subsection 1 also makes reference to 'circumstances relating to the employee' when deciding whether a dismissal is objectively justified. If the employee does not satisfy the demands which viewed objectively can reasonably be made upon him, then the condition may be fulfilled. More often than not the grounds for dismissal will rest on repeated acts of misconduct where the employee has received one or more warnings. Experience indicates that neglect of duty is a significant group which covers everything from failure to comply with orders to work done badly. Smuggling is an area of misconduct which is frequently encountered in practice as is alcohol or drug abuse in or in connection with the service.

The employee has special protection against dismissal in the event of illness or injury, *see* section 5-7, pregnancy and following the birth or adoption of a child, *see* section 5-8, and military service, *see* section 5-9. These provisions do not prohibit dismissal as such, but the employee cannot be given notice on the basis of these factors. Pursuant to section 5-12 subsection 1 first sentence an employment contract can always be terminated when the employee reaches the age of 70. Even a lower age limit may apply if the limit is objectively justified and is not seen as a disproportionate intervention, *see* second sentence.

An employee finding that dismissal with or without notice is unlawful, may demand negotiations with the employer, *see* section 6-1. If the dispute is not resolved in this way the case may be brought before a Norwegian court within specific time limits, *see* section 6-2:

> person working on board a ship, whether as an employee or as an independent contractor, is entitled to leave service on board in certain defined situations, see section 9-5. It is important to emphasise that leaving service on board pursuant tot o this section will not have any bearing on the employment contract with the employer, which will continue to remain in force.

SLA Chapter 7 contains rules which regulate the employee's entitlement to leave of absence. The rules do not give the employee a general right to payments during such leave of absence; this is generally dependent on other statutory provisions in the National Insurance Act (in the event of pregnancy, birth and adoption) or on collective bargaining agreements.

Chapter 4. Liability and Limitation of Liability in Maritime Law

§1. The General Principles

84. The traditional approach under Norwegian law is that liability for damages is triggered by negligence. That means that anyone acting in a negligent or culpable manner (fault), whether through an act or an omission, causing damage to a third party, is liable for the damage. A further condition for liability is normally that the damage is sufficiently proximate – the connection between the fault of the tortfeasor and the damage should not be too remote.

In addition to the person thus being held liable, some other person or a legal entity may become liable for the same damage. This is true if the person causing the damage is acting as employee ('servant') or in the service of such person or entity, according to the principles of vicarious liability.

There is also a third form of liability, *strict liability* i.e., liability is imposed without the presence of any culpable conduct.

Independently of the above, a person or a legal entity may, of course, enter into contracts whereby rights and obligations arise. Whether and to what extent there is *contractual liability*, will normally be decided by the terms of the contract, unless there are relevant statutory stipulations regulating the question of liability, supplementing or modifying what follows from the contract.

§2. Liability of a Shipowner and the Crew

85. A *shipowner* may incur liability on any of the aforementioned bases, depending on the claim and the individual circumstances.

The *crew*, including the master and officers, will normally incur liability only through negligent behaviour. Although liability for the crew exists in principle, it should be noted that a claim against a crew member may be reduced or rejected with reference to the stipulations in section 2-3 of the Tort Act of 1969. Moreover, in practice, it is not very important whether the injured party can sue the master or the crew because they will not have sufficient assets to meet the claim. Should, however, a member of the crew be held liable, he will have some protection in MC 282 subsection 2 if the claim is related to the cargo: Anyone for whom the carrier is responsible has the right to plead the same exceptions and limitations as the carrier.

Thus, the question of whether the shipowner is liable is the really important question. Such liability may arise directly from the owner's own fault – for example: the shipowner has been negligent in hiring a master whom he should have known to be incompetent, or: the shipowner has given insufficient instructions regarding the handling of cargo or the navigation of the ship. Where the shipowner is a limited company, decisions/actions made by the corporate bodies, i.e., the general assembly and in particular the board of directors, are considered as acts of the company as such. In addition, it follows from the general rules in the Tort Act section 2-1 that the company may be vicariously liable for the acts and omissions of the management, including the president and the managing director of the company. The vicarious liability regulated in this section is of a general nature; an employer is liable for the consequences of an employed's negligence 'during the execution of work or service for the employer'. We have, however, a specific regulation of the vicarious liability of the shipowner in MC section 151, which we now will consider. MC section 151 subsection 1 reads:

> The shipowner shall be liable to compensate damage caused in the service by the fault or negligence of the master, crew, pilot, tug or others performing work in the service of the ship.

Two main questions arise in this context:

(1) For whom is the shipowner liable? For what categories of employees and people/companies rendering service to the ship can he be held responsible?
(2) What is the meaning of 'performing work in the service of the ship'?

To the first question. The *master* and *crew* are expressly mentioned in MC section 151. The crew includes employees on deck and in the engine room, as well as in the galley. Fishermen are included in the case of a fishing vessel, while on a passenger vessel all persons working onboard serving the passengers are included (e.g., barbers, musicians). The existence of an employment contract between the shipowner and the crew member is not a condition for liability under section 151. Independent contractors and their employees may also cause liability for the shipowner, for example, the waiter hired by A, where A is an independent contractor in charge of the restaurant onboard the passenger ship.

86. *Pilots and tugs* are also expressly mentioned in MC section 151. Pilots are included to make it clear that the shipowner is liable for the actions also of a compulsory pilot (a pilot which it is obligatory to have on board, for instance in narrow waters). Tugs were added when the code was revised in 1972 because of a need to clarify whether the shipowner of a towed vessel is liable for errors committed by a tug. It is now clear that the shipowner *is* liable.

87. The shipowner is, generally, liable for damage caused by *longshoremen and other assistants* working while the ship is in port. Loading and discharging operations are work in the service of the ship, and the same is true of the weighing/counting of cargo. Mooring, watch and maintenance (cleaning) is also work in the service of the ship. Errors committed by various agents may also result in liability for the shipowner, regardless of whether the person is permanently employed by the shipowning company or is an independent contractor (but there is a limit to what can be considered as falling within section 151, *see* paragraph No. 90 below).

88. When the *ship agent* commits an error, the shipowner may be held liable, regardless of whether the agent is permanently employed by the shipowner or is an independent contractor. The decisive factor is whether the error which caused damages occurred in the performance of his service to the vessel. The shipbroker is normally considered to be an independent intermediary for whom the shipowner is not responsible under section 151.

89. Generally, the shipowner is not liable for faults on board *icebreakers* and *salving vessels*. The owner is liable, however, if the ship is taken in tow at its own request. Shipyards, repairers, classification societies, technical consultants, etc., may all commit errors during assignments for the shipowner. Whether liability arises under section 151 depends on the nature of the work. If the work can be categorized as typical of the shipowner's activities, the owner will be liable even if he has delegated the work to a technical consultant. Major works carried out at a shipyard are good examples of work which does not result in liability for the shipowner under section 151 (although the shipowner may be liable for negligence in the choice of shipyard or for insufficient supervision/control of the work). Neither is the shipowner liable for errors by charting and lighthouse services. Another example: It is commonly accepted that if electronic navigation equipment is taken ashore for repairs, the shipowner will not be liable according to section 151 in case of sloppy work, eventually leading to a collision (but also here the owner may be held liable if he has been negligent in his choice of repairman).

90. To the second question. Even if the person in question is one for whom the shipowner normally is liable, it does not follow that all the (negligent) acts of this person lead to liability for the shipowner. The employer/employee relationship must have commenced. A shipowner is not liable under section 151 for the actions of a seaman who is *en route* to the ship, is travelling home for vacation or has finished his term of employment. In this respect, it is immaterial e.g., whether the trip home is paid by the shipowner or whether the hire runs on the seaman's voyage to the ship. He is not 'performing work in the service of the ship'.

The shipowner may be liable for the acts of a person employed on an ad hoc basis. A typical example is liability for longshoremen. Their work is on the ship or at least in close physical contact with the ship, and so is the inspection of the ship by the technical expert engaged by the owner. Even work performed far away from the ship may result in liability for the shipowner. He would be liable for damage arising from negligent instructions regarding maintenance problems on the vessel, given by a technical expert who has not visited the ship.

An area that has proved problematic in relation to the shipowner's liability is that of voyage and time charters. Is the shipowner liable for the negligence of longshoremen engaged by the voyage or time charterer? Case law from recent years shows that the shipowning company is liable for independent contractors and people who perform work which has such a connection to the operation of the ship that it must be considered 'work in the service of the ship'. This would include liability for longshoremen hired by the charterer.

There may also be doubt in the case of public servants. From a broad perspective, their work is in the interests of the ship, but this is not necessarily sufficient to impose vicarious liability under section 151 (e.g., acts of the medical authorities). There must be a closer connection. An example is a compulsory pilot, for whom the shipowner is liable according to the text of section 151.

When deciding the scope of the vicarious liability the order aspect is important. If the shipowner is entitled to give orders as to how the work shall be carried out and to supervise the performance as well as check the quality of the work afterwards, he will ordinarily be liable for the errors of those providing the service. This is typically the position towards the crew. However, the shipowner is not exempted from vicarious liability where he has not these rights or the possibility of exercising them in respect of persons working in connection with the ship. Where pilots or tugs are concerned, the shipowner will, in practice, be unable to give instructions. This may also be the case when a stevedore company is engaged to perform loading and discharging operations. He is nevertheless liable. In these instances, legal doctrine has suggested that the borderline should be drawn with a view to what are typical shipowning functions: The shipowner should not be able to avoid liability by delegating typical tasks to independent contractors.

91. As mentioned, the shipowner may become liable, even if no fault has been committed: he is held *strictly liable*.

Statutory provisions on strict liability in maritime law are found in MC Chapter 10, which deals with oil pollution. Under these rules, the registered owner of a ship (and not a bareboat charterer) is strictly liable for damage or loss resulting from pollution caused by oil which has escaped or been released from the ship. This liability also encompasses expenses associated with efforts to prevent or minimize contamination.

Another example of liability being imposed regardless of fault is found in the rules applying to emergency situations – the Tort Act section 1-4. Under certain circumstances, the law allows another person's property to be damaged in an emergency. Even though criminal liability does not arise in such a case, compensation for the damage must be paid on a strict basis.

92. Also, the Norwegian courts have decided that there is strict liability in certain circumstances. This is based on the premise that persons who engage in particular dangerous activities must expect that damage occasionally will occur. It seems more appropriate that the person running this particular business should carry the loss than a third party, who often are damaged incidentally. An important consideration in many of such cases is: Who ought to take out an insurance against the damage which has now occurred? This type of liability has often been referred to as '*liability for dangerous enterprises*'. To some extent this label is appropriate, but it is also somewhat misleading, as strict liability can be applied also against an enterprise that one cannot really describe as 'dangerous'.

There has been some uncertainty about the role of strict liability in the context of maritime law, i.e., whether a shipowner should be held strictly liable for damage caused by a ship. The rules on collision between ships are based on liability in negligence only. However, in two decisions, the Supreme Court has imposed strict liability where ships have collided with and damaged land-based installations after a breakdown had made reversing impossible (ND 1921 401 and ND 1952 320). Another important step towards strict liability in the field of maritime law was taken in a case where strict liability was imposed for personal injury caused by a loading boom falling down (ND 1969 389 NSC). However, on the other side, compensation on the basis of strict liability was denied by the Supreme Court where a submarine surfaced and damaged a trawl (ND 1973 348).

93. The above discussion has been confined to liability in tort, i.e., liability arising outside contractual relations. Contractual liability results when a contract is not properly performed (e.g., the terms of a shipbuilding contract, a mortgage, a bill of lading or a charterparty are not complied with). In principle, only a party to a contract can become liable under its provisions. Other parties who in one way or another, interfere and prevent proper performance, may be liable in tort. There are, however, a number of areas where there is no clear dividing line between the two types of liability. For example, the carrier may be sued on the basis of contract or tort when the cargo is damaged, but MC section 282 subsection 1 has given the carrier the right to be adjudged on the basis of contract even if the claim is framed as a claim in tort. The crew member who actually caused the damage can, in principle, be held liable by the cargo owner in tort only. However, the law has given him (as mentioned in No. 86) protection: He is entitled to be judged in accordance with the same contractual rules as the carrier, *see* MC section 282 subsection 2.

Unless there are express provisions to the contrary, liability for breach of chartering contracts is only imposed in cases of negligence (fault). For example, for the carrier to be liable for the charterer's losses if the ship arrives too late at the loading port, the carrier or the persons for whom he is responsible must normally have been negligent (culpable). Mandatory statutory provisions apply in many situations, restricting the complete freedom when drafting contract terms. A clear example of such provision is MC section 275, which sets out the shipowner's (actually the carrier's) minimum obligations with respect to the cargo (MC section 254).

94. Where there is, in principle, freedom of contract, the question may nevertheless arise to what extent a contractual stipulation deserves recognition by the courts. Are there some limits? If an exemption clause in an individual contract has unreasonable consequences, it can be set aside by the court under the provisions of section 36 of the Agreements Act of 31 May 1918 No. 4. But are there general legal principles which prevent a party from reducing or totally disclaiming liability?

The traditional view has been that a distinction should be made between the acts of the contracting party and the acts of those who assist in performing the contract ('the servants'). This distinction is reflected in some statutes (e.g., MC section 276 on the exclusion of the right to plead exceptions in respect of damage due to navigational error or fire). It has been a common understanding that exceptions for significant degrees of negligence are valid in respect of acts of the servants, but that there is considerably less scope for limitation regarding the conduct of the party himself. Generally, a party may exclude liability for the consequences of his own ordinary negligence (*culpa levis*), but hardly for gross negligence (*culpa lata*). This restriction is also considered to apply to his closest collaborators, or in a company: those with the leading positions (ND 1994 136). This means that errors by, for example, the president, the finance director or the technical director will be treated as the party's own fault; if one of them has caused damage by gross negligence an exclusion or limitation clause will not be valid.

§3. Limitation of Liability

95. Shipowners have a long-established right according to special legislation to limit their liability for damage caused by a ship. This does not mean, however, that the rules (which have no counterpart in non-transport law) are justifiable in the light of modern legal thinking. The idea behind this type of limitation is that shipping shall be protected against the enormous claims (the catastrophic liability); today this is, first of all, an insurance question: is limitation necessary for obtaining adequate insurance cover?

The various systems for limiting liability, differing from one country to another, were undesirable from an international point of view. Efforts were therefore made to harmonize the legislation by way of conventions. The first convention, made in Brussels in 1924, was replaced in 1957 by the new Brussels Convention, which in turn was replaced by the London Convention of 1976, all of which have subsequently been incorporated into Norwegian legislation. The rules of the 1976 Convention are now contained in MC Chapter 9 – with amendments in 2002 implementing the 1996 Protocol to the 1976 Convention, whereby the limitation amounts were increased. A further increase came by Act of 12 June 2009.

A characteristic feature of these rules is that limitation applies to *all* claims (so long as they are within the itemized list) arising in connection with one particular incident (e.g., a collision). As a result, the term 'global limitation' is frequently used. The present rules differ from the older ones in the sense that fewer types of claim are subject to limitation, and that the limitation amounts have been increased considerably.

Damage from oil may be of catastrophic dimensions – in particular when there is oil spill from a tanker, but also bunker oil may cause enormous problems. The liability connected with oil spills and the possibility of limiting liability have led to special conventions and national legislation. This legislation is discussed below in Chapter 13. In the present chapter, there are only some short remarks in paragraph No. 117 on the relationship between the two limitation regimes: the general one in MC Chapter 9 and the special ones for oil pollution.

§4. Ships for Which the Limitations of Liability Can Be Invoked

96. In general, the rules in MC Chapter 9 apply to all constructions that can be considered vessels. In the case of pleasure craft, it has been argued that the maximum liability is unreasonably low because the limitation fund depends on the vessel's tonnage. Today, however, this argument has little force because of the imposition of a minimum liability (MC section 175 Nos 2 and 3). Warships and other state-owned or operated vessels may be immune from arrest and enforcement proceedings (under both international and domestic rules), but claims for damages can, of course, be brought before the court. This raises the question of whether the state is entitled to invoke the limitation rules. An argument against is that the state generally will be able to cover the liability in full, making the limitation rules unnecessary. Nevertheless, it has been clear for some time that liability for damage caused by warships, etc., can be limited (ND 1949 532 NSC). However, warships should not be considered on the same footing as merchant vessels in all respects (MC section 181 first paragraph). The minimum liability applicable in the case of certain state-owned ships is higher than for other vessels. Moreover, the limitation rules do not apply at all if damage results from a type of action that is particular to a warship. For example, it is not considered reasonable for the state to be able to limit liability if a ship is torpedoed by accident (which was established under the previous rules, *see* the Swedish Supreme Court decision in ND 1978 353).

§5. Claims Subject to Limitation

97. The categories of claims for which liability can be limited are specified in MC section 172 and 172a, and these should be seen in conjunction with section 173 excepting some claims from limitation. Claims listed in section 172 and 172a fall within the 1996 Protocol, but regarding the claims in section 172a Norway made reservation when accepting the Protocol, and this has made it possible to have special limitation rules for the claims.

The legal basis for liability is irrelevant (e.g., whether the claim is based on negligence or strict liability). It is also generally irrelevant whether the claim is in tort or contract.

The right to limit liability must be seen as a privilege and consequently, there is reason to interpret the rules strictly (as opposed to allowing limitation in situations which are similar to those expressly listed). This does not mean, however, that only liability for the immediate and direct claims listed in section 172 can be limited. Both recourse actions and claims for consequential damages may be subject to limitation.

If a claim is outside the listed categories in section 172 and 172a, other rules may lead to some kind of limitation of liability. An example is the special relief offered to the tortfeasor by the Tort Act section 5-2; another is the package or kilo limitation which the carrier can plead when cargo is damaged, *see* MC section 280. It should be noted that the possibility of pleading the rules of MC Chapter 9 does not preclude the application, e.g., of the package limitation: When a cargo has been lost, the damage has to be calculated with a view to MC section 280, and it is the total of the amounts thus arrived at which may be subject to limitation under section 172 No. 1.

98. MC section 172 No. 1 applies to claims for personal injury and property damage, insofar as the damage has occurred on board or in direct connection with the operation of the ship or a salvage operation. An example of damage occurring on board would be personal injury suffered by a passenger (in the case of crew, there is an exception in section 173 No. 5). Damage to cargo on board is the most important category in this provision. For example, an error by the pilot may lead to a collision and – if certain exceptions offered by MC are not applicable – liability for the owner for damage to cargo.

Liability for personal injury and property damage on board the ship that has been run into will be subject to limitation because the damage has occurred 'in direct connection with the operation of the ship'. The situation is the same if the master of a tug causes a collision between the towed vessel and another ship or a pier. In the case in ND 1984 129, the Supreme Court concluded that damage which a trawl caused to fishing nets was also subject to limitation.

99. Under No. 2, losses arising from delay can be limited insofar as they arise in connection with a contract for the transport of goods or passengers. For example, if a passenger has to go ashore before reaching his intended destination because the vessel has grounded, his claim for lodging, meals, etc., will fall within No. 2.

100. No. 3 provides a right to limit liability for damages other than those for personal injury, property damage and delay, insofar as the claim does not arise out of contract. For example, liability for loss of profits by a factory which loses its electricity supply following the negligent anchoring of the ship near a sub-sea cable is subject to limitation under this provision. According to the preparatory works to this section also liability for blocking a waterway falls within No. 3. If there were no specific reference in the legislative history, it would probably be doubtful whether liability for blockage would be considered as arising 'in direct connection with the operation of the ship'.

101. No. 4 gives the right to limitation of claims in respect of 'measures taken to avert or minimize losses for which liability would be limited, including losses caused by such measures'. When for example chemicals threaten to escape from the stranded vessel the authorities may take measures to prevent or minimize damage. The claim eventually presented to the owner is subject to limitation. If such measures are taken by the owner himself, his expenditures cannot be covered by the limitation fund (which is in contrast to what applies in case of oil pollution, *see* Chapter 13 §3. below).

102. Claims relating to cleaning efforts after maritime accidents, etc., are also to some extent subject to limitation, but as mentioned above, the possibility to make reservations to the limitation convention has led to a special regime for vessels with tonnage exceeding 300 tonnes. MC section 172a describes the claims and section 175a the limitation amount for such claims. Regardless of the basis for the claim, a right of limitation arises for:

- Claims on the occasion of 'raising, removal, destruction or rendering harmless a ship which is sunk, stranded, abandoned or wrecked, as well as everything that is or has been on board the vessel' (section 172a No. 1). As an illustration, *see* Supreme Court decision in ND 1954 267: The harbour authorities engaged a private firm to remove the vessel, and the bill was presented to the owner, who was entitled to limit his liability. Today the owner's obligation of removal is stated in the Harbour and Fairway Act of 17 April 2009 Chapter 5.
- Claims for 'removal, destruction or rendering harmless the ship's cargo' (No. 2). Bunker oil is not cargo, but in case of removal where the vessel is stranded and bunker oil is streaming out, the claim may fall within No. 1.

– Claims arising from 'measures taken to avert or minimize losses for which liability would be limited under this Section' (No. 3), similarly as according to MC section 172 No. 4 above.

§6. Claims Excluded from Limitation

103. MC section 173 contains a series of exceptions to the right to limit liability, grouped in six numbers. According to No. 1, claims for salvage (including so-called special compensation, *see* Chapter 9 §3. below) and general average contributions cannot be limited, nor can claims which arise out of contract and involve measures falling within section 172 No. 4 (measures to avert loss, etc.) or section 172a subsection 1 (all claims mentioned in paragraph No. 102 above). According to No. 2, oil pollution claims as described in sections 191 and 207 (*see* Chapter 13 below) cannot be limited. According to Nos 3 and 4, the same applies to nuclear damage. No. 5 states that personal injury claims are not subject to limitation if the injured person is an employee for whom the person claiming limitation is responsible and the injured has 'duties connected with the operation of the ship or with salvage'. For example: A claim brought by the seaman's widow and/or children for loss of their provider is not subject to limitation. Finally No. 6 prescribes that claims for interest and legal costs cannot be limited.

§7. Counterclaims

104. A shipowner who faces a claim for which he can limit liability may have a counterclaim arising out of the same incident. The question then is whether the liability should be limited to the gross or net claim against the shipowner (i.e., before or after set-off). The latter method is known as the single liability principle. To illustrate: Ships A and B collide, the damage to A is 500, while the damage to B is 700. Both ships are equally to blame. The limitation fund for A is 70, while B's is 100. Under the single liability method, A is liable for 1/2 x 700 –1/2 x 500 = 100, and this liability is limited to 70. Under the cross liability method, A is liable for 1/2 x 700 = 350, which is limited to 70. B is liable for 1/1 x 500 = 250, which is limited to 100. In the end, the cross liability method means that B pays A: 100 – 70 = 30, while the single liability method leads to payment of 70 from A to B.

MC section 172 subsection 2 declares that the single liability method (in accordance with the convention rules) shall be applied, i.e., limitation can only be 'demanded for that part of the claim which exceeds the counterclaim'.

§8. Conduct Excluding Limitation

105. Where the owner (or another party entitled to limit liability, *see* §9. below) has himself committed the error which triggered liability (rather than the error being committed by someone for whom he is responsible), it seems unreasonable that he should be entitled to limit the liability. Nonetheless, the statute allows this, provided that there is not a very significant degree of culpability or fault (owner's privity). Pursuant to MC section 174, liability cannot be limited when the liable person has 'caused the loss deliberately or through gross negligence and with knowledge that such loss would probably result' (*see* paragraph No. 107).

The liable party is first and foremost the owner. In the case of a sole proprietorship, the owner is not difficult to identify. In a partnership, it will be one or more of the part owners. Where a corporation is involved, difficulties arise in determining which errors are to be considered as those of 'the liable person'. An error committed by one of the company's corporate bodies (the general assembly or board of directors) will clearly be considered as conduct barring limitation. It is probably necessary to go even further in equating actions of employees with those of the shipowner himself ('identification'). This applies generally to shipowning entities, not just to limited companies or corporations. The London Convention of 1976 does not provide a solution to this problem, leaving it to domestic law. The position under Norwegian law is unclear, partly because there are few court decisions in this area. However, it is probably safe to say that a Norwegian court would be cautious in establishing grounds for identification. The prevailing view is that identification would result if the error were committed by management personnel within the shipowning company with a fairly significant level of responsibility. Thus, if a technical director of the shipowning company were to be at fault, this might be considered as excluding the right to limit.

The most common situation is that an employee (a crew member) makes the error which triggers liability. Even the most indefensible conduct will not threaten the owner's right of limitation unless he can be grossly blamed regarding instructions to and supervision of the crew.

106. There has been much debate about the position of the master/owner. A typical question is whether the shipowning company – established as a corporation – can limit liability when the error is committed by the master who is also the main shareholder and/or sole board member. The answer is that the right to limit liability is not lost if the error is committed by the master/owner in his capacity as master (*see* Supreme Court decision in ND 1958 122).

107. The conduct barring the right of limitation is described in section 174. If the damage is caused by an intentional act (deliberately or by wilful misconduct) the answer is clear – the liability is unlimited. In cases of negligence, liability will usually be unlimited if there is gross negligence. In objective terms, gross negligence occurs when the relevant action carries a substantial risk of causing harm. Subjectively, the person who did the action must have or should have known that there was great risk involved. If there is a high degree of subjective culpability, the level of objective risk may be reduced.

In addition, section 174 establishes a requirement that the person who caused the damage must have understood that damage would probably result. In objective terms, there must be quite a significant probability of loss or damage before the right to limit liability is lost. It is not enough that the person who caused the damage ought to have understood that loss or damage would probably result. He must in fact have understood that the act would probably cause damage ('conscious gross negligence').

MC section 174 employs the terminology of ordinary tort law and must, therefore, be interpreted in accordance with ordinary principles. The level of care that must be exercised should be stricter in relation to persons exercising management functions than employees or assistants. One would expect the owner himself to exercise greater care than the crew.

§9. Persons Entitled to Limit

108. MC section 171 names the persons protected by these rules. Most important in practice is the shipowner's right to limit liability. A bareboat charterer will be entitled to limitation as a consequence of his status as '*owner pro tempore*', but also the time and voyage charterers are given the right to limit liability. This would apply, for example, if an entire cargo is lost in an accident and the bills of lading impose liability on the time charter carrier. The charterer's right to limitation is also important in relation to claims arising between owner and charterer. Thus a charterer is entitled to limit his liability in connection with damage inflicted on a time chartered vessel. The final person mentioned in section 171 first sentence is the manager or operator (e.g., the managing owner in a shipowning partnership or an independent management company).

109. The second sentence grants a right of limitation to 'anyone performing services directly connected with salvage, including measures as mentioned in section 172 subsection 1 No. 4 and section 172a subsection 1' (*see* above in paragraph No. 101 regarding measures to avoid or mitigate damages, removal of wrecks, etc.). That the liability of the salving vessel itself can be limited follows from the first sentence of the provision. More problematic is liability which arises as a result of actions not occurring on board the salving vessel. The English courts found that the earlier Convention did not allow a right of limitation when a diver from the salving vessel – after he had left the vessel – shot a bolt into the hull of the salved vessel. The present Convention (and statute) is drafted so that there is a right of limitation in such cases.

110. Under subsection 2, limitation of liability shall also be available to persons for whom the owner or others mentioned in subsection 1 are vicariously liable. All persons who can be said to be members of the crew are entitled to limit their liability. Such persons do not have to be employed by the owner. Even a waiter employed by an independent contractor running the ship's restaurant can limit his liability (it is, of course, very unlikely that a waiter's liability would be sufficient to trigger the global limitation rules). A pilot can limit liability whether he is employed by the owner or by the state. It is assumed that the right to limit liability applies internally as well, e.g., between owner and crew.

Finally, subsection 3 provides protection for the insurer. If the claimant pursues the insurer directly, he cannot obtain larger damages than he would have if he had sued the assured (who in turn would have been indemnified by the insurer).

§10. Generally on Limitation Funds

111. As mentioned above, the purpose of global limitation is to protect shipowners from excessive liability. The rules are therefore structured so that limitation takes effect when the total liability arising from a particular incident – with one or more creditors – has reached a pre-determined ceiling. If the claims exceed the ceiling, the amount available – the limitation fund – has to be distributed between the creditors, like in a bankruptcy settlement.

The limitation fund is traditionally tied to the vessel's tonnage. This system is still employed, although there is now a mandatory minimum amount. Once a certain size of tonnage is reached (this is now measured in tonnage units) an amount is added for each further tonnage unit based on a regressive scale, i.e., the greater the tonnage, the lesser the addition per tonne. Special rules apply to passenger vessels regarding the calculation of maximum liability.

To ensure that limitation funds do not vary too much from country to country, the amounts are fixed in Special Drawing Rights (SDR).

For one incident there may be a number of claims, and if they are of substance limitation may be demanded and the creditors will get partial compensation. There is one limitation amount for the claims listed in section 172a, *see* section 175a. For the claims listed in section 172 it is more complicated, *see* section 175. Claims from passengers on the liable vessel have a special limitation amount, and claims for personal injury to others are also subject to a special regulation. If these two groups do not get full compensation they compete with the non-paid part of their claims in the general limitation amount, together with all other claims subject to limitation.

§11. Limitation Fund

112. MC section 175 No. 1 sets a ceiling for liability towards passengers. The limitation fund is calculated according to the number of passengers stated in the ship's certificate. It is irrelevant how many passengers actually are on board the ship at the time of the incident which triggers the liability. The limitation amount is now 175,000 SDR multiplied by the number of passengers that the ship is registered to carry. An owner cannot limit liability for claims from the crew on his own ship, *see* MC section 173 No. 5.

MC section 175 No. 2 contains rules applying to all other personal injury claims which are subject to limitation. An example would be claims from passengers or crew on a ship that has been run into. The minimum amount is 2,000,000 SDR, but with additional amounts per tonne for vessels with tonnage exceeding 2000. Tonne is defined in No. 6 as 'gross tonnage' measured in accordance with the Convention on Tonnage Measurement of Ships of 1969.

MC section 175 No. 3 applies to all other claims subject to limitation, e.g., claims for property damage. In addition, all personal injury claims not covered by the amount under No. 2 are entitled to compensation from the No. 3 fund; they compete on an equal basis with the other claims (section 176 subsection 2). The limitation under No. 3 is based on a similar system as under No. 2, but the minimum amount is 1,000,000 SDR and the additional amounts, depending upon the size of the vessel, are lower.

In a few cases, the limitation fund is calculated in accordance with special rules. The most important cases are mentioned below.

The salvor's limitation fund will normally be calculated based on the salvage vessel's tonnage. But if salvage takes place without the use of the vessel (e.g., by using a diver), or the salvor works from the salved vessel (e.g., after having been set aboard by helicopter), a nominal tonnage of 1,500 tons applies (MC section 175 No. 5 and section 175a subsection 2).

For warships and other ships engaged in non-commercial State activity the minimum liability for claims under section 175 Nos 2 and 3 and section 175a is calculated on the basis of 5,000 tons (section 181 subsection 1) – however, with the exclusion of the right of limitation where the damage or loss is due to 'the particular characteristics or use of warships.'

For ships built or equipped to drill for subsea natural resources the limits for claims under section 175 No. 2 is 36 million SDR, and for claims under section 175 No. 3 and section 175a the limit is 60 million SDR (section 181 subsection 2).

113. In the instances enumerated in section 172a on limitation in connection with clean-up efforts relating to maritime accidents, etc., the liability limits are defined in section 175a. There is a minimum of 2,000,000 SDR, and for vessels exceeding 1,000 tonnes additional amounts per tonne are added on a regressive scale.

114. The limitation fund applies to claims arising from *one incident*- MC section 175 No. 4, compare section 175a subsection 2. If *two* accidents occur on the same voyage, we may have two limitation funds. Whether there in this sense are one or two accidents may be difficult to decide. From court practice, see the Supreme Court decision in ND 1984 129: Within seventy minutes the vessel caused damage to seven chains of nets; this was considered to be one incident. Even if there is considerably more time between the occurrences of damage, there may be one incident: In ND 1987 160, the Supreme Court decided that delivery of contaminated bunker oil to two vessels was one incident since the cause of damage to the vessels was faulty cleaning of the tank from which both vessels got their bunker oil.

§12. PROCEDURE

115. When a claim is made against a party entitled to limit liability, it would seem natural to set aside a fund equivalent to the amount to which liability can be limited. The creditors could then divide the fund between themselves, and the liable party (defendant) would no longer have anything to do with the matter. However, limitation of liability under MC Chapter 9 (in contrast to limitation under Chapter 10) does not depend on whether the party entitled to limitation establishes such a fund (MC section 180). If the number of creditors is small it may not be necessary or expedient to establish a fund. A settlement can then be arranged amicably, or the limitation rules can be invoked if the debtor is sued for claims for which he is entitled to limit liability. But if creditors subsequently file claims which have not been given consideration during such an informal allocation of the limitation fund, the debtor remains liable. In addition to the amount already paid informally, he is obliged to pay the new creditor as if the claim had been filed before the initial payment had been made. The primary advantage of establishing a limitation is that this risk is avoided.

A limitation fund can only be established when a petition has been filed for an arrest or other enforcement proceedings, or if a suit has been filed in relation to a claim that can be limited, and then only with the court where the arrest or other relief has been requested (section 177 subsection 1). A creditor may seek to arrest one of the owner's vessels in a jurisdiction where the legal rules are favourable ('forum shopping'). The owner is not allowed to forestall the creditors by establishing a fund in a jurisdiction favourable to him. He has to wait until arrest or other conservatory proceedings have been commenced.

116. Once the limitation fund has been established, there is no longer any point in creditors pursuing individual claims for which liability can be limited. The creditors are secured through the fund. Individual enforcement of claims after the establishment of a fund could, therefore, be prohibited. MC sections 178–179 do not go so far. The court has considerable discretion to evaluate whether the creditor will suffer unreasonably if he is forced to pursue his claim in the foreign jurisdiction where the limitation fund is established. The Norwegian rules prohibit individual pursuit of claims in Norway to a much greater extent than is required under the London Convention.

117. MC Chapter 10 (sections 191 et seq.) contains rules relating to limitation of liability for oil pollution (*see* Chapter 13 below). If liability is limited pursuant to these rules there will be no concurrent limitation under MC Chapter 9. It is, therefore, necessary to distinguish the situations to which each chapter applies:

> Chapter 10. is primarily an incorporation of the Bunker Oil Pollution Damage Convention of 1992. *See* section 183 on strict liability and section 190 on geographical application. The liability is subject to limitation under Chapter 9, *see* section 185.
>
> Chapter 10.II is primarily an incorporation of the 1992 Liability Convention and the 1992 Fund Convention. The owner is strictly liable for damage or loss caused outside the ship by contamination resulting from the escape or discharge of oil from the vessel (section 191), but he has a right to limit his liability (section 194). In this case, a special fund is established (which is not discussed here). Should one incident cause both pollution damage and

other types of damage, funds can be established both under Chapters 9 and 10. Claims must then be submitted according to their nature, either to the global limitation fund or to the oil pollution fund. In addition, section 207 has some special rules on oil spill liability not covered by the convention.

Chapter 5. Charterparties

§1. Definitions and Varieties of Charterparties

118. A charter party is a contract between two parties – the owner/carrier and the charterer – relating to the performance of transportation services by a ship, or to make a ship's transportation capacity available. Traditionally, one distinguishes between voyage charter parties, charter parties for consecutive voyages and quantity contracts, and time and bareboat charter parties.

The background for concluding a charter party is often a sale of goods, necessitating transportation – sometimes concerning a quantity that cannot easily be transported by a liner vessel – requiring the full cargo capacity of a ship or even more than one ship. The availability of liner service, the quantities involved and the flexibility in accommodating the wishes of seller and buyer will determine the type of transport agreement preferred.

However, a contract of affreightment is not always based on an actual or prospective sale of goods. A shipping line may, e.g., need further tonnage because one of their own vessels has had an accident or someone wishes to test whether there are possibilities of creating a regular shipping service in a particular trade or area, without investing too much capital either by purchasing or building the vessel needed. It may also be that someone has a more or less well-founded belief that the shipping market, in general, or in a special segment, will rise in the near future and therefore wishes to secure tonnage, either to cover foreseeable needs or for purely speculative purposes. In such cases, a party may wish to enter into a time charterparty. By this type of charterparty the owner keeps control of the ship, its crew and its equipment, i.e., the owner retains the nautical management of the vessel, while the time charterer takes over its commercial management.

The characteristics of these contracts may be summarized in this way: Under a voyage charter the owner of the vessel will normally be responsible for the vessel's arrival at the agreed port at an agreed time, there picking up a specified cargo and bringing it to the agreed port of discharge – against remuneration (voyage freight calculated on the basis of units carried or fixed as a lump sum). A special form is the charter for consecutive voyages, e.g., five voyages performed without interruption between A and B.

In time chartering, the owner places a fully manned and equipped vessel at the disposal of the time charterer who is then entitled to the carrying services of the vessel: The time charterer decides what cargo the vessel shall carry and the ports of loading and discharge (within the limits stated in the contract). The remuneration to the owner, for keeping the vessel in an operative state and performing the voyages requested by the charterer, is a fixed amount per time unit, e.g., USD X per day.

The bareboat charter parties vary from the above types of charters inasmuch as this contract – as the name indicates – only relates to hiring of the hull itself. In other words, the owner of the vessel does not undertake any transportation, nor does he man or operate the vessel. The owner places the naked hull ('*coque nue*') at the disposal of the charterer. Thereafter, it is up to the latter to man, navigate and operate the vessel. The best known standard forms of bareboat charter parties are probably Barecon A and Barecon 89 (and Barecon B for new buildings financed by mortgage).

The quantity contract is used where there is a reasonably constant and predictable transport requirement. The shipowner may then undertake to have cargo transported at more or less prefixed intervals from A to B. The shipowner is usually relatively free to choose the ships necessary. The typical pattern is that there is a head agreement covering the main items; for each voyage the terms of an agreed voyage charter are applicable.

119. The position that the charterer has acquired by a charter party may to a great extent be used as a basis for further contracts. Thus, it may happen that on the same voyage, there may be more than one charter party. In the extreme, shipowner A may have bareboat chartered his vessel to B, and B may have time chartered the vessel to C. C as time chartered owner may have time chartered the vessel to D. D as sub-charterer may again have sub-chartered the vessel for a specific voyage to E. Thus, when a question arises it is important to refer it to the relevant contract.

120. It is a difficult and time-consuming process to draft a charter party from scratch. There are therefore a number of standard forms of charter parties upon which the parties may base their negotiations and contract, and to which they may add further clauses to meet their particular needs. These standard charter parties either have been drafted to be usable in as many trades as possible (e.g., Gencon), or to meet the special circumstances of a particular trade (e.g., Norgrain for grain, Baltcon for coal, C (Ore) 7 for ore, Shell time for oil). Many charterers may insist on basing a possible contract on one of the forms. They may even have their own '*pro forma*' charter party, with terms which they may be unwilling to deviate too much from.

121. Many of the charter parties stipulate that possible disputes shall be decided in London or New York, according to the law governing in the country of litigation, *lex fori*. Nevertheless, many disputes have over the years been decided by Norwegian courts or by arbitration in Norway. Many of them are printed in ND (*see* paragraph No. 34).

Owing to the fact that the 1994 MC as well as the 1893 MC are quite similar for the Scandinavian countries, the court decisions in these countries will also be relevant for Norwegian judges, although not binding on them. Many of these decisions concern charter parties. There is also a fairly rich legal literature, to which it is referred to in pleadings and paid regard to in the judgments.

§2. STATUTORY PROVISIONS

I. General

122. Since the 1890s, Norway, Denmark and Sweden have had MCs regulating *inter alia* many of the legal issues frequently arising under charter parties. The present rules are found in MC 1994 Chapter 14, entitled 'chartering of ships', comprising sections 321–394. The chapter is divided into four major subdivisions: I. General provisions, II. Voyage chartering, III. Quantity contracts and IV. Time charter parties. There are no provisions relating to bareboat charter parties.

The main rule is that for these contracts there is freedom of contract, *see* section 322 subsection 1:

> The provisions of the present Chapter do not apply in so far as anything to the contrary follows from the contract, practice established between the parties, or custom of the trade or other usage which must be considered binding upon the parties.

The major exception (in subsection 2) is that for 'voyage chartering in domestic trade in Norway and in trade between Norway, Denmark, Finland and Sweden' section 347 prevails. This section says that for cargo damage and delayed delivery of cargo the rules in Chapter 13 apply – in short: the Hague-Visby Rules (however with some additional protection for the cargo owner).

It should be noted that section 325 is an important exception from the general statement that freedom of contract prevails in chartering. This section states that if the carrier issues a bill of lading (*see* paragraph Nos 127 and 131 as to whether he is obliged to do so) such bill of lading – a so-called tramp bill of lading – 'shall govern the conditions for the carriage and delivery of the goods as between the carrier and a third party holder of the bill of lading'. In other words: the mandatory rules in Chapter 13 may be applicable.

Another important exception follows from section 325: When a bill of lading is issued under a voyage or time charterparty the bill of lading relationship may be subject to the mandatory rules in Chapter 13 (*see* Chapter 6 (paragraph Nos 133 et seq.) below).

II. Voyage Charters

123. The stipulations regarding voyage chartering are grouped under the following headings:

- Introductory Provisions (sections 326–329).
- Loading Time (sections 330–335).
- Loading (sections 336–338).
- The Voyage (sections 339–342).
- Discharge and Delivery of the Goods (sections 343–347).

- Breach of Contract and Hindrances on the Part of the Contract Carrier (sections 348–351).
- Breach of Contract and Hindrances on the Part of the Voyage Charterer (sections 352–357).
- Termination of Chartering Agreements (sections 358–361).

III. Quantity Contracts

124. This type of contract was for the first time regulated in the 1994 MC sections 362–371. The scope of application is defined as follows:

> The provisions relating to quantity contracts apply to carriage by ship of a definite quantity of goods divided into several voyages within a given period.

However, if it has been agreed that the voyages are to be performed consecutively by a specific ship, the provisions do not apply.

The statute outlines the mechanism for deciding the actual quantities to be carried: If latitude is allowed as to the total quantity to be carried, it is the charterers who may choose. A latitude regarding the quantity to be loaded on the individual voyage is, however, subject to the owner's decision: He is entitled to determine the exact quantity of cargo to be taken on board.

Furthermore, there are stipulations regarding the major elements of the ordinary quantity contract, such as:

- Shipment Schedules (section 364).
- Notice of Shipment (section 365).
- Nomination of Ships (section 366).
- Performance of Voyages (section 367).

Sections 368–370 aim at regulating the consequences of some typical contractual breaches by the parties:

> If the charterers fail to give proper notice of a shipment, and the carrier fails to give proper notice of a ship, a new reasonable time limit should be given. But if a delay gives reason to expect significant delays regarding subsequent shipments, the other party may rescind the whole contract. In other words, the statute aims at applying the general principle that a substantial breach of contract gives right to cancel. The principle of substantial breach applies also if the charterer fails to honour his obligation to pay freight and demurrage etc. The carrier is also entitled to 'suspend the performance of the contract' in case of delayed payment; in this respect there is no 'substantial breach' requirement.

IV. Time Charterparties

125. Time chartering is regulated under these subtitles:

- Delivery of the Ship (sections 372–377).
- Performance of the Voyages (sections 378–387).
- Redelivery of the Ship (sections 388–389).
- Time Charter Hire (sections 390–392).
- Termination, etc. (sections 393–394).

The 1994 MC builds to a large extent on the previous legislation on time chartering, but efforts were made to reflect the general development, practical and legal, which had taken place since the previous code was revised.

MC section 374 states that if the vessel is delivered at sea, and a subsequent survey shows that the vessel was not in conformity with the charter party, 'freight shall not be paid for the time lost in making the defects good.' If the defects are so serious as to entitle the charterer to cancel the charter party, then the owner shall also lose his claim for hire from the time of delivery to the survey-port.

Section 379 introduces a mutual obligation to inform: The carrier shall inform the charterer of all matters of importance relating to the ship and the voyage, the charterer shall tell carrier of planned voyages.

Normally, the time charterer's liability towards the owner for damage to the vessel is based on negligence (section 385), but with a stricter liability if the vessel is damaged as a result of charterer's orders to proceed to a port which is not safe. If damage is caused to cargo during loading/discharging and the owner is held responsible by the cargo owner he has a recourse claim against the charterer unless the damage was due to the participation of the master, the crew or other circumstances for which the owner is responsible (section 381).

For losses arising from damage to the engines as a consequence of fuel not meeting the agreed specifications, the time charterer is responsible (section 380).

The payment of the charter hire is, of course, the paramount obligation of the time charterer. The MC in this respect has provisions regarding two practical situations. The charterer's right to set-off hire payments with alleged claims, and the owner's right to withdraw the vessel if the time charter hire is paid too late.

MC section 390 stipulates that a time charterer cannot set-off with a disputed claim if the owner offers to provide security for such claim. This would, e.g., prevent the charterer from legally withholding money for a disputed cargo claim if the owner offers a letter of guarantee from the P&I underwriters.

Regarding payment of hire instalments, the MC section 391 has introduced a grace period, viz. seventy-two hours after notice of default has been given by the owner. Thus, the owner cannot withdraw the ship, i.e., cancel the time charter party, until after such time lapsed. In the meantime, the owner may, however, suspend performance of his obligations under the charter party, e.g., refuse to load or sign bills of lading. The owner is also entitled to 'default interest' on the instalment, from the due date until it is paid.

§3. The Duties of the Shipowner

I. General

126. The contract will decide the relationship between the parties. It should have rules on how expenses and risks should be divided between the parties, and on who should have the right to give the necessary instructions relating to ship and cargo under the various stages and situations of the voyage. The regulation will be different for the various types of charter parties (voyage, time and bareboat charter parties), but may also differ considerably within each group, depending upon the cargo and voyage in question. It is therefore difficult to give a full description of the respective rights and duties of the owner and the charterer. A brief outline must suffice.

II. Voyage Charterparty

127. The first main obligation of the shipowner under a voyage charterer will be to present the agreed vessel at the right place/port within the right time, after having given proper notices. If a particular ship has not been named, the owner must find and offer a vessel within the agreed category. If the vessel arrives too late, the charterer will normally have a right to cancel. Obviously, the owner's obligation may commence some time before giving notice of readiness to receive the cargo: The vessel has to be operated so that it can reach the agreed port in time. And at the time when loading commences the vessel has to be in such a condition that it can safely load and carry the goods to the port of discharge. In other words, the shipowner must ensure that the vessel is seaworthy when tendering it. Seaworthiness' includes *inter alia* that the vessel has a full and competent crew and necessary equipment, including charts and navigational instruments (MC section 327).

The vessel must be in berth for a given loading time which includes laytime and time on demurrage (MC section 330). When cargo is being delivered at the ship's side, the carrier shall take it on board (MC section 330), but very often it has been agreed that loading is a matter for the charterer – then under the supervision of the master and to some extent with the assistance of the crew.

The voyage shall then be performed with due dispatch and otherwise with due care (MC section 339).

At the port of discharge, the cargo shall be delivered to the person who 'demonstrates authority as receiver'. If cargo is delivered to an unauthorized party, the shipowner may incur liability.

If the goods carried have suffered damage or have been lost while in the shipowner's custody, MC section 347 stipulates that the owner/carrier shall be liable unless he can show that the loss was not due to his fault or neglect or that of his servants. This section makes the rules in liner trade applicable also in voyage chartering (for these rules, *see* Chapter 6 below).

According to MC section 338, the owner is obliged to issue a bill of lading when the cargo has been loaded.

III. Time Charterparty

128. As the name indicates, this type of contract is concluded for a certain period of time. The period may be linked to the duration of two or more defined voyages, a so-called trip timecharter; then there will be several similarities between the time charter and in particular charters for consecutive voyages.

Normally the charter period will be described in terms of months or years. During this time – from 'delivery' to 'redelivery'- the shipowner will have undertaken to 'perform the voyages ordered by the time charterer in accordance with the chartering agreement' (section 378). The ship must comply with the (often very detailed) description given in the charter party and generally be in a 'seaworthy' condition. In MC section 372 subsection 2, it is said that the shipowner 'shall, when delivering the ship, ensure that its condition, mandatory certificates, manning, provisions and other equipment satisfy the requirements of ordinary trade in the trading area stipulated in the chartering agreement'.

If there are defects in the ship, the owner must remedy these, and no charter hire is paid for the time so lost (*see* section 392 on off-hire); are the defects substantial the charterer may even decide to cancel the charter party.

The owner must continue to keep the vessel seaworthy and in a condition as stipulated in the contract throughout the term of the charter (MC section 384). If this obligation is not observed and delays or other losses arise the charterer may claim damages when the failure is due to fault or negligence on the part of the owner. Should the breach have as a consequence that the purpose of the contract is frustrated, the time charterer may also cancel the contract (MC 384).

The master may have a delicate task when the vessel is on time charter. He shall to some extent serve both the owner and the charterer. In carrying out the charterer's orders, he must also bear in mind the interests of his owner. Thus he may have to refuse to follow the charterer's orders if they, in the master's opinion, threaten the safety of the vessel. This conflict may appear in connection with the nature of the cargo: is it dangerous and consequently to be excluded? If this is not so: how should it be loaded and secured onboard the vessel? Another example is the charterer's order that the vessel shall go to a specific port or berth: Will complying endanger the safety of the ship – physically or politically?

MC section 383 places a liability in negligence with reversed burden of proof on the owner for cargo damage occurring while the cargo is in his custody. However, if the damage results from loading, stowing, trimming, securing, discharging or delivery of cargo, the charterer must indemnify him, provided the loss is not due to the 'participation of the crew or other circumstances for which the [shipowner] is responsible' (section 381).

IV. Bareboat Charter party

129. Since there are no stipulations regarding this type of charter party, neither in 1893 MC nor in 1994 MC, Scandinavian law on this subject must be found in case law and legal theory when the contract does not give precise answers. Today, the relationship will basically depend on the in practice detailed terms of standard bareboat charter parties.

The main obligation of the shipowner would then simply be to deliver the unmanned vessel before an agreed deadline to the charterer, the vessel then being as described in the charter party. In this context, 'delivery' is delivery in its true meaning: a physical transfer of possession from owner to charterer. The standard forms provide that the owner may have economic responsibility for latent defects in the vessel which are ascertained within eighteen months from delivery (Barecon A and Barecon 89). Otherwise, the owner would have few obligations in connection with the ship after delivery. The further control and operation are taken over by the charterer.

An important matter is insurance of the vessel, in particular providing funds for repair expenses after grounding, etc., and protecting the investment in general. What kind of insurances should be arranged, who shall see to it that this is done and who shall pay for it, is usually regulated in detail in the contract.

§4. The Duties of the Charterer

I. Voyage Charterparty

130. An important obligation of the voyage charterer is to arrange for delivery of the goods in accordance with the charter party. This means that the nature of the goods must be as described. If a cargo of grain is agreed, the charterer cannot deliver, e.g., coal. The quantity (x tonnes, y standards, z containers, etc.) is often given with margins, usually in the charterer's favour, but when the quantity is described as 'a full and complete cargo', the owner has the final word.

The cargo must be delivered within the stipulated time and is nowadays usually loaded by the charterer. For the loading operation a certain time is allowed: the laytime. The laytime may be fixed in a number of ways, e.g., four working days (typical for dry cargo) or seventy-two hours (typical for tankers: the pumps are working day and night). The starting point for laytime will usually depend upon whether the vessel has reached the agreed place in a proper condition for receiving the goods and has served a notice of readiness. The factors for deciding commencement and length of laytime may vary, and the interpretation may often seem somewhat surprising.

If the loading is not completed within the laytime, the vessel comes 'on demurrage'. The laytime is included in the freight, but when the vessel comes on demurrage the charterer has to pay an extra compensation, e.g., USD X per day. For the laytime there may be exceptions, e.g., that time shall not count when bad weather interrupts the loading process. When the vessel is on demurrage, however, such exceptions do not ordinarily operate ('once on demurrage, always on demurrage').

The charterer cannot be forced to deliver the cargo, but if he fails in delivering any cargo he is liable towards the owner for the loss he has suffered. Such liability may be avoided if there is a force majeure incident which prevents delivery, e.g., an export ban is introduced in the agreed loading port (MC section 352).

The paramount obligation of the charterer is to pay the agreed freight. The conditions for earning it are often specifically regulated in the contract (e.g., freight to be earned cargo and/or ship lost or not lost). Lacking contractual rules the main requirements for earning freight is that the cargo arrives at the agreed port of discharge, but not necessarily in a perfect condition. MC section 344 states that 'freight cannot be claimed in respect of goods which no longer exist at the end of the voyage.' However, the cargo may 'exist' even if its commercial value is substantially reduced, e.g., grain damaged by sea water, which may only be used as animal feed. There is some case law on where to draw the line, but no precise criteria have yet been developed.

MC section 357 states that the voyage charterer is liable for damage to the ship caused by the goods if the damage is due to fault or negligence on the part of the charterer or anyone for whom he is responsible.

Cargo with a dangerous nature that has not been made known to the shipowner may, according to the circumstances, be destroyed or otherwise disposed of by the carrier without incurring any liability (MC section 342).

When a bill of lading is issued, section 338 subsection 3 says that if the bill contains 'other terms than those stated in the chartering agreement, and this increases the voyage liablility of the carrier, the voyage charterer shall hold the voyage carrier harmless'.

II. Time Charterparty

131. The paramount obligation of the time charterer is to pay the hire on time. Strictly speaking, he may not be obliged to do anything else, inasmuch as he has no obligation to trade the vessel.

However, if the time charterer chooses to operate the vessel (utilize it commercially) – which is, of course, the normal situation – he must make a number of decisions and perform a number of tasks. Thus it is for him to decide which voyages the vessel shall carry out – involving three main elements: from where to where, at what time and with what type of cargo? These decisions must, of course, be within the limits of the agreement (e.g., a geographical limit: 'wide world trading where no extra insurance premium is incurred'), *see* MC section 378.

It is the time charterer that shall arrange the loading and discharge of the cargoes, and pay for these operations (MC section 381). He shall also arrange for stowing of the cargo onboard the ship. However, 'the cargo must be stowed so as to ensure that the ship is stable and the cargo is secure' (MC section 381). If the master is of the opinion that the suggested stowing may endanger the safety of the vessel, the time charterer shall follow the instructions of the owner regarding the handling of the cargo. For losses incurred through bad stowage, the time charterer is normally responsible, unless the damage is caused by the contributory neglect of those for whom the owner is responsible.

The expenses incurred in calling at the ports (port dues, pilotage, towage, etc.) as well as other voyage expenses (bunkers, canal dues) are also for the charterer's account (MC section 387). When supplying bunkers the charterer must ensure that the fuel ordered and received is in accordance with the specifications stipulated in the charter party.

According to MC section 382, the shipowner shall issue bills of lading for the goods. Should the owner thereby incur greater liability towards the cargo interests or bill of lading holder than he has contracted under the terms of the charter, the time charterer must indemnify him.

When the charter party period ends, there shall normally be an off-hire survey (MC section 388), defining first of all the end for payment of charter freight. Also the condition of the vessel is ascertained, and if it is found (from comparing with the description in the 'on charter survey') that the vessel has suffered damage during the time charter period, and these damages have been negligently caused by the charterer or his servants, the charterer is (as indicated above) liable for the repairs (MC section 385).

III. Bareboat Charterparty

132. Under this form of charter, the charterer assumes practically all the functions of an owner. The bareboat charterer shall employ master, officers and crew, and has the obligation to keep the vessel, engines and equipment fully maintained. He will sometimes – depending upon the duration of the charter – even be responsible for the classification of the vessel. The insurance of the vessel is important, and the arrangement in this respect will usually reflect the distribution of the maintenance obligation/risk in case the vessel is damaged.

Chapter 6. Transport under Bill of Lading or Sea Waybill

§1. Definitions and Functions of the Bill of Lading

133. The bill of lading (b/l), which is the typical transport document in liner trade, is defined in MC sections 292 and 296. It is a document which contains:

- an acknowledgement that goods of a certain nature and quantity have been received, either for shipment or loaded on board;
- a promise to transport the goods to a named destination; and
- a promise to deliver the goods at the destination against the return of the document. If the document is issued to A or order, he who demands delivery must also appear to be entitled to the goods based upon the endorsements.

The document is signed by the shipowner/the line or by an agent. Often, it is signed 'on behalf of the master' (or actually by the master himself) – which has raised the question: Who does the master represent when the vessel is on charter – does he bind the contracting carrier or the shipowning company? The answer was finally given in MC 295: 'A bill of lading signed by the master of the ship carrying the goods is regarded as having been signed on behalf of the carrier.' The bill of lading is given to the person who has delivered the goods to the ship (the shipper). Usually, the bill is not signed by the other party (the sender/cargo owner/shipper).

The holder of a bill of lading, relying upon its text in good faith, is by law protected to such an extent that the document is considered 'a negotiable document'.

134. Prior to the issuing of a liner bill of lading, some sort of contractual relationship will naturally exist between the line and the cargo owner. The cargo owner will have contacted the line and inquired about transport of the goods and the conditions that would apply. If the cargo owner is satisfied, an agreement may be reached. The terms of the agreement are evidenced by a so-called booking note, which is signed by both parties.

During the period between the signing of the booking note and the issuance of the bill of lading, the seller may wish to withdraw from his contract with the carrier. This may happen if, for example, he has difficulties with the buyer. Conversely, the line may encounter problems or wish to undertake the shipment at a different time. The question then arises of whether the booking note is binding. The main rule is that it is binding on both parties. In many cases, however, there will be so many reservations that liability can only arise in special situations.

When the goods are delivered, for instance to the line's shed, the shipper may demand a 'received for shipment bill of lading'. The shipper is entitled to have an 'onboard bill of lading'; but a previously issued 'received for shipment' bill of lading must then be returned.

§2. Various Types of Bills of Lading

135. | As stated, the bill of lading can be 'shipped' or 'received for shipment', depending on whether the goods are described as loaded on board a named ship, or as received for shipment (MC section 294 subsections 1–2, and MC section 296 subsection 2). The bill of lading can be either for carriage by one ship (ordinary bill of lading) or it can be a 'through' bill of lading, i.e., the document provides that a part of the transportation distance shall be performed by someone other than the carrier who received the goods from the shipper (MC section 293).

Quite often, the carrier – the one who has given the promise of transportation – leaves the actual transportation task to another. Such sub-carriage is accepted by MC to the extent it is permitted in the individual contract. At the time X contracts to perform the relevant carriage, it may be self-evident that the carriage will be performed by another party. This may be the case when a booking note is signed indicating that the cargo will be carried by a ship which the line has on time charter, or, more common, the carrier is described as a 'timechartered owner'. Most frequently, however, the contract of carriage contains a reservation: In principle, it is stipulated that the carrier (the contracting party) will perform the carriage himself, but that he reserves the right (has the option) to use tonnage belonging to another party, i.e., to allow the carriage to be performed wholly or partly by another party. This is often expressed in a so-called liberty clause, which may have varying degrees of detail. But even if use of a sub-carrier is permitted under the contract, the parties are not necessarily free to decide the consequences of this. The MC regulates the consequences in sections 285–287, basically in this way.

The main rule is that the contracting carrier 'remains liable according to the provisions of this Chapter [MC Chapter 13] as if the carrier had performed the entire carriage him- or herself' (section 285 subsection 1). The carrier may, however, make a reservation in case sub-carriage is 'expressly agreed' (subsection 2). In case the cargo is damaged while in the custody of the sub-carrier, the sub-carrier is liable 'pursusant to the same rules as the carrier' (section 286 subsection 1). When both carrier and sub-carrier are liable there is joint liability (section 287).

Should there be no entitlement to use a sub-carrier, and a sub-carrier nonetheless is entrusted with (part of) the carriage, this will be considered a serious breach of contract, treated in a similar way as illegitimate (unreasonable) deviation.

§3. Charterparty and Bill of Lading

136. Even when a ship is time chartered or fixed on a voyage charter, bills of lading will normally be issued for the cargo. The shipper may need the bill of lading in connection with the performance of the underlying sale. Pursuant to MC section 322 subsection 3 the shipper has a right to demand a 'shipped bill of lading' in the trades specified in section 252. Whether the shipper is the charterer under the charterparty (e.g., in connection with a CIF sale), or whether he has no interest in the charter relationship (e.g., in connection with a FOB sale) is irrelevant.

137. If the shipper is the same entity as the charterer, it would be illogical for parties, who may already have been through tough negotiations about the contents of the charter, to seek to change their contractual relationship by using a bill of lading containing clauses that conflict with the charterparty. This is the background to the important rule that the bill of lading in the hands of the charterer is not a transport document (but *see* paragraph No. 139 below on incorporation clauses). Instead, the terms of the transport are regulated by the charterparty (unless it has been clearly agreed otherwise, compare the clause 'the bill of lading to supersede the charterparty'). Nonetheless, the bill of lading is a receipt in which the owner acknowledges the type of cargo and quantity received. This information supplements, rather than conflicts, with the charterparty. However, it should be noted that the carrier is entitled to present contradictory evidence – a possibility which is denied when the bill of lading is transferred to a part that in good faith has relied upon the description (MC section 299). Furthermore, in order to get delivery of the goods the carrier may insist upon redelivery of the bill of lading (section 304). For these reasons, the bill of lading is still relevant.

138. When the shipper has transferred the bill of lading to a third party (sold or pledged) and the document is in the possession of such third party, the importance of the document increases significantly. The transfer (with endorsement(s) in case of a 'to order bill of lading') changes the legal character of the document (cf. section 325 first paragraph and section 292 third paragraph). The terms of transport in the bill of lading (with additions and modifications as per MC) will now be decisive. For instance, should the goods be damaged, the claim from the person who has received the goods after handing in the bill of lading will depend upon the terms applicable to the bill of lading. Another example is that the bill of lading may set payment of freight and other items as conditions for delivery. Another important change relates to the function of the bill of lading as a receipt. Section 325, compare section 299 subsection 3, has the effect that evidence contradictory to the information in the bill of lading cannot be brought against a third party who has obtained the bill of lading in good faith in reliance on the correctness of information therein (*see* above).

139. Normally, it is undesirable to have different terms in the charter party and the bill of lading. First of all, because different terms may unsettle the balance of rights and obligations in the charter party and lead to indemnity claims (recourse actions).

A simple way of ensuring that the documents have identical terms is to have a reference in the bill of lading to the charter party (ref. section 325 subsection 1 compared to section 292 subsection 3). In this way, the charter party, or at least parts thereof, will be considered part of the bill of lading. This is achieved by a so-called incorporation clause, e.g.,: 'All the terms, conditions, liberties, and exceptions of the Charter are herewith incorporated.' It should be added that this technique is used for reference to a voyage charter, almost never to a time charter party.

Incorporation clauses have traditionally been treated with a certain amount of scepticism by the courts. This is primarily because it is difficult for the bill of lading holder to grasp his legal position and it therefore seems natural to protect the cargo interests against unexpected and often burdensome clauses. This explains why some incorporation clauses, in addition to the general reference to the charter party, say for example 'including the exemption clauses'. The same applies to arbitration clauses in the charter party. This was of particular importance previously because, pursuant to the Civil Procedure Act of 1915 section 452, an arbitration agreement had to be in writing. The courts interpreted this requirement quite stringently so that an arbitration clause in a bill of lading did not bind the bill of lading holder. The present act on arbitration of 2004 has not maintained the writing requirement in commercial relationships.

When a bill of lading is an independent contract in the manner described above, it is not unusual for the owner to be subject to greater liability pursuant to the bill of lading than would be the case if the charter party rules had been applied. This may be due to the terms of the bill of lading or to mandatory legislation governing the bill of lading relationship. In both instances, the owner and the charterer are free to agree on indemnity arrangements, see for example Baltime clause 9 on the charterer's obligation to 'indemnify the Owners against all consequences or liabilities arising from the Master, Officers or Agents signing Bills of Lading'. Also, MC section 338 subsection 3 has rules on indemnification, but only in respect of increased liability as a consequence of different terms; increased liability due to the operation of mandatory law is outside the scope of this provision.

§4. Hague Rules/Hague-Visby Rules, Hamburg and Rotterdam Rules

I. National Incorporation of the Hague-Visby Rules. The Hamburg and Rotterdam Rules

140. The Hague Rules of 1924, giving the cargo owner a minimum, mandatory protection and on the other hand the carrier some rights to limit liability, were implemented in Norway in 1938. According to Norwegian principles, a ratified convention like the Hague Rules is not automatically binding for carrier and cargo owner: A statutory law is required. This opens for two possibilities: An act stating that the convention is formal law, or transforming the convention rules into Norwegian law.

When Norway ratified the Hague Rules the first possibility was chosen: We got an act of 1938 which was for all practical purposes a translation of the Hague Rules. At the same time 1893 MC was amended, and the substance of the Hague Rules was made applicable for domestic trade, however, expressed in conformity with the traditional Norwegian law language. This double track-system was criticized, and when the time came in 1973 to implement the Visby Rules of 1968, modifying the Hague Rules, the total Hague/Visby set of rules were formalized in MC.

The next step in the development of rules was the Hamburg Rules of 1978. Norway has not ratified this convention, but when 1893 MC was revised and substituted by 1994 MC the rules were formulated as closely as possible to the Hamburg Rules, without necessitating formal termination of the Hague/Visby obligations.

The Hamburg Rules have not been a success, and therefore a new convention – the Rotterdam Rules of 2009 – has been worked out. The Norwegian Maritime Law

Committee has in 2012 given a report (NOU 2012: 10), recommending implementation of the rules and proposing the necessary legislative amendments. As per 2018, no corresponding legislation has been proposed by the Government.

II. Freedom of Contract, Choice of Law and Jurisdiction

141. Under Norwegian Law, the parties to a contract are normally free to decide how and where they wish to settle possible disputes. The parties may, for example, agree to have a dispute settled in London under English law. This possibility is often used, and MC section 253 acknowledges that under *charterparties*, the parties may agree as they deem fit in respect of applicable rules, law and forum (with some reservations for domestic trade, see below). However, when it comes to a dispute arising under a bill of lading, whether issued under a voyage/time charter or not, the position is different. As already indicated here, there are mandatory rules regarding the carrier's liability (the rules are discussed below). The carrier is not allowed to contract out of this liability simply by stipulating in the bill of lading that disputes shall be decided in countries and under laws which do not recognize these mandatory rules.

The scope of the mandatory legislation is defined in section 252 subsection 2 Nos 1-5 (on subsection 1 for Scandinavian and domestic trade see below). In short, subsection 2 says that the mandatory rules apply:

- to export from and import to Norway;
- where the loading port is in a Convention State (i.e., a state bound by the Hague-Visby Rules);
- where the bill of lading is issued in a Convention State;
- where the bill of lading contains a Paramount clause, i.e., the bill of lading is subject to the Convention or convention-based legislation.

The question of whether it is permissible to have a case, in principle falling within the scope of the mandatory rules, decided in another way than by litigation in a Norwegian court is dealt with in MC sections 310–311. The main rule in section 310 is that you can have no valid agreement in advance (typically in the bill of lading) unless:

> the plaintiff at his own discretion can bring an action before the Court where:
>
> a. the defendant's principal place of business is, or
> b. the contract was concluded, or
> c. the place of receipt for carriage is, or
> d. the place of agreed or actual delivery is.

Section 311 permits, however, a written agreement on arbitration, provided: (i) that arbitration can be instituted 'at the discretion of the plaintiff in one of the States where a place as mentioned in section 310 paragraph one is located' and (ii) that the tribunal shall apply the rules of MC Chapter 13.

In case of tramp bills of lading incorporating the terms of the charterparty, it should be noted that the arbitration clause of the charterparty cannot be invoked against a third part who has acquired the bill of lading 'in good faith', i.e., without knowledge of the arbitration clause (section 310 subsection 3).

Regarding domestic trade, see description in paragraph No. 160 below. For such transportation and also inter-Scandinavian trade the mandatory rules are applicable (section 252 subsection 1, cf. section 254 subsection 1), and this is so even if the contract of carriage is contained in a voyage charter party (section 322). On sea waybills, *see* paragraph Nos 163 and 164.

III. The Liability Period

142. Under the 1893 MC, the carrier, as is the case today, had various duties of care for the cargo. These duties naturally apply from the time the cargo was received until delivery. Nonetheless, liability could be excluded for damage to the cargo prior to loading and after discharge. This was often done in a clause in the bill of lading headed 'period of responsibility'. Practically speaking this meant that liability period was 'from tackle-to-tackle', and that the transport of the goods from the warehouse to the side of the ship was not subject to mandatory rules. At the port of discharge, the effect of the clause was that the duty of care ceased when the hook was released after the goods had been placed on the dock.

Nordic case law, however, extended the period during which the carrier was subject to mandatory liability at the port of discharge. Some cases held that liability extended until the goods were located in a secure place after completion of discharging.

In 1994 MC, the 'tackle-to-tackle' principle is abandoned. This follows from section 274, which defines the period of responsibility. Subsection 1 describes this period as the time the carrier has the cargo in his possession at the loading and discharging ports and during the voyage. Subsections 2–3 clarify this.

143. In the loading port, the period of responsibility will normally begin when the carrier or someone on his behalf receives the cargo from the shipper (irrespective of whether the shipper is the sender or not). For example, the crates or bags may be discharged from the shipper's truck and brought into the carrier's warehouse, or the container may be placed within the carrier's domain in a location designated by him. Sometimes an official institution at the loading port has to take charge of the goods in the first instance. In such a case, the carrier's period of responsibility will not begin until the goods have been delivered from such institution.

The third paragraph specifies the point at which the carrier can no longer be deemed to have the cargo in his possession. The period of possession and thus the period of responsibility typically ceases when the goods are delivered to the receiver (or someone acting on his behalf). Ordinarily, the receiver will present the bill of lading and receive the cargo from the warehouse or alongside the ship. When the receiver does not pick up the cargo in time, the cargo may be warehoused 'on the account of the receiver', and then the carrier's liability ceases when the cargo has been brought to the warehouse. The same is true if the cargo has been delivered 'to any authority or other third party to whom the goods must be delivered according to law or regulations applicable at the port of discharge'.

144. The FIO-clause (FIO = free inn and out) is quite common. It transfers the loading and discharging operations from the carrier to the shipper/receiver: The cargo shall be loaded and discharged by the shipper/receiver – the organization of these operations and the costs involved are on the cargo side. This clause (and similar clauses) needs further consideration: Do they have any impact upon what has been stated above on the mandatory liability period? The question is often formulated in this way: Do the rules define the scope of the contract service? If the answer is yes, the carrier will be liable even when the damage is caused by stevedores employed by the shipper/receiver. Or are the rules defining 'the terms on which service is to be performed'? If so, the carrier is not responsible for damage due to acts or omissions flowing from the shipper/receiver's performance of the obligations under the FIO-clause.

MC does not give a clear answer, nor is there any authoritative court decision. However, the general understanding, confirmed by an arbitration decision (ND 1988 288), is in favour of the latter alternative. This is subject to an important qualification: The obligation on cargo side to do the loading/discharging does not relieve the carrier of all obligations relating to supervision and care of the goods. Examples are the Supreme Court decisions in ND 1967 24 and ND 1992 386 on the duty to interfere when stowing is negligently performed.

IV. The Cargo and Excepted Cargo

145. The MC pertains to all kinds of cargo. However, there are special stipulations regarding dangerous cargo, live animals and deck cargo. The questions relating to deck cargo will be dealt with under V (paragraph Nos 149 and 150) below. An adequate definition of 'dangerous cargo' is difficult. Where, for example, a barrel containing lubrication oil, syrup or another sticky substance springs a leak other cargo stowed nearby may easily be damaged. However, this is not sufficient for the barrel and its contents to be categorized as 'dangerous cargo'. There must be more than an everyday risk, i.e., the potential for damage must be significant (e.g., a barrel containing corrosive substances which could attack the steel in the cargo holds). Such damage will typically occur quickly and dramatically, but this is not always the case (e.g., poisonous gas gradually leaking out of steel flasks). Further complications follow from the fact that a cargo which usually is innocuous may become dangerous in contact with other types of cargo, or in special temperature or humidity conditions. Guidance can be obtained by referring to lists of dangerous cargoes which are prepared by the authorities. The parties can, of course, include a detailed definition in the contract by, for example describing certain cargoes as dangerous.

In the case of carriage of general cargo, the cargo is usually described by the shipper and the question that then arises is whether the carrier knew, or should have known, that it was dangerous. Naturally, the cargo owner has a special duty of disclosure when dangerous cargo is transported, so that the carrier may take precautionary measures. Often, it is sufficient to make the carrier aware of the type of cargo, e.g., dynamite. The carrier will then know how to act or how to acquire the necessary information for safe carriage. In other cases, where such information is not available, the shipper must describe the properties of the cargo and how it should be handled.

146. MC section 257 contains special rules on dangerous cargoes which, in accordance with the above principles, place the duties on the sender. The goods must be marked as dangerous pursuant to the applicable public regulations, and reasonable advance notice must be given concerning dangerous characteristics and safety measures which may be necessary (subsection 1). This obligation to provide information may be more wide-ranging than what follows from public regulations, and goods may be deemed dangerous in relation to section 257 even if they are not so defined in the public regulations. Moreover, pursuant to subsection 2, the sender must inform the carrier if he otherwise is aware that the cargo is of such nature that the carriage 'may involve danger or significant inconvenience to persons, ship or cargo'.

As stated above, the duty is imposed on the *sender*. If the sender is not the same person as the shipper, the sender must ensure that the shipper marks the goods as required and provides the necessary information. The sender will be liable if shipper fails to do this.

If the cargo appears to be dangerous and the carrier has not undertaken to transport such cargo, the carrier can refuse to take it on board. Should dangerous cargo have been loaded and the sender has failed to inform the carrier that it is dangerous and the carrier has not otherwise become aware of the situation, then section 291 subsection 1 gives the carrier, depending on the circumstances, the right to discharge the cargo or destroy it or render it innocuous. Such measures can be taken by the carrier without any risk of liability. However, if he has taken the cargo onboard knowing the danger, these rules do not apply – *see* subsection 2 ('assumption of risk').

Subsection 3 contains a broad provision regarding the carrier's right in all cases (also where neither the sender nor the carrier knew of the dangerous properties at the time of loading): When the cargo proves to be 'a danger to persons or property', he may without liability 'discharge, render innocuous or destroy' it. This rule allows the destruction of the cargo, even where the carrier has received information about its dangerous nature, but a pre-condition is that the risk relating to the dangerous nature of the cargo must be imminent.

147. In addition, section 291 imposes strict liability on the sender for damage caused by dangerous cargo when the cargo is delivered without information about its dangerous characteristics and necessary safety measures. This may include physical damage to the carrier's ship (e.g., fire or explosion damage), extra expenses associated with the removal of dangerous cargo, expenses relating to the carrier's liability to third parties for damage to their cargo, etc. A pre-condition to the imposition of strict liability is that the carrier was not 'otherwise aware' of the dangerous properties. Liability under section 291 only applies in relation to the carrier. The extent to which other owners of cargo on the same ship can prevail in a tort claim is outside the scope of section 291.

148. In the case of carriage of live animals, the system now is that the carrier is in principle liable under the ordinary rules, but he is not liable for damage or loss resulting from the 'special risks' involved in such carriage – *see* section 277 subsection 1. The carrier avoids liability if he can establish that the damage or loss resulted from one of these 'special risks'. The burden of proof is eased by rules in subsection 2. Thus if the carrier has followed the instructions given and can establish that the loss or damage resulted from one of the 'special risks', he is not liable, unless the cargo owner can establish that the loss or injury was 'wholly or partly caused by the fault or neglect of the carrier personally or of someone for whom the carrier is responsible'.

V. Deck Cargo

149. The risks associated with deck cargo have traditionally been considered so great that the placement of the cargo on deck without a contractual basis has been considered a serious breach of contract, perhaps sufficiently serious for the carrier to lose his various rights to limitation of liability. Carriage of cargo on deck has thus been equalled with unlawful (geographical) deviation. Particularly in view of the modern container trade this strict attitude has been softened. This is reflected in 1994 MC with fairly extensive rules on when a cargo may be legitimately carried on deck (section 263), and on the carrier's liability if deck cargo is damaged (section 284).

MC section 263 establishes that carriage of cargo on deck is lawful in the following three instances: (1) deck carriage is agreed; (2) deck carriage is usual in the trade or usual on the relevant route; or (3) loading on deck is required by regulations based upon statutory rules (e.g., in the case of particularly flammable goods). For goods to be carried on deck pursuant to an agreement such agreement should appear from the transport document; if this is not the case, the carrier has the burden of proving that such an agreement exists. The consequences of the omission are more severe when the transport document is a bill of lading: The deck carriage agreement cannot be pleaded against a third party who has acquired the document in good faith.

If cargo placed on deck in accordance with these rules is damaged or lost the ordinary rules on liability apply. In other words, the parties are not allowed to agree on more lenient rules for deck cargo than for other cargo.

150. If cargo is loaded unlawfully on deck – i.e., in violation of the provisions of section 263 (including the situation where an agreement regarding loading on deck cannot be invoked against a third party) – special rules on the carrier's liability in section 284 apply. The basic rule is that the carrier is strictly liable for losses which would not have arisen if the cargo had been carried under deck. For example, if a container placed on deck is washed overboard, the carrier cannot avoid liability by showing that neither he nor his servants were negligent with respect to the lashing of the container. Nor can he avoid liability by showing that the damage resulted from a navigational error unless the error would also have affected the container if it had been placed under deck. Thus if the ship runs aground and sinks, it is generally irrelevant whether the container was stowed on or under deck. As a further illustration, if the contents of a container on deck are damaged by rain or sea water, the damage is borne by the carrier.

The carrier can invoke the unit limitation rules in sections 280–283. However, pursuant to section 284 subsection 2 the carrier loses this benefit if the loading on deck took place despite an express written or oral agreement on under deck carriage.

VI. Liability for Cargo Damage and Delay

151. The main rule on the carrier's liability for damage and loss of the goods is found in MC section 275 subsection 1 and for delay in section 278. Sections 275 and 278 impose in general a *liability in negligence (fault)* by the owner and his servants for damage, loss and delay. The burden of proof rests on the carrier (reversed burden of proof). Certain *general exceptions* from liability apply according to section 276, and there are some special rules for dangerous cargo, deck cargo and animals (dealt with in paragraph Nos 141–144).

The cargo owner must prove that the goods have been damaged or delayed while in the carrier's possession and that he has suffered an economic loss. Usually, this is done by comparing the condition of the goods as discharged with the description in the bill of lading. The carrier must thereafter face the burden of proof in order to escape liability: He must 'show' that neither he nor a person for whom he is responsible has negligently caused the damage or delay. The Court of Appeal has clarified that 'show' (Norway: '*godtgjøre*') means that 'somewhat more than preponderance of probability is required' (ND 2003 374). Practically speaking, in order to avoid liability the carrier has to explain how the damage or delay occurred and that he is not to be blamed for what has happened.

It should be added regarding *onus of proof* that there are few restrictions in Norwegian law on the admissibility of evidence; generally, the judge will base his decision on the fact he finds most believable, whether the information comes from the carrier or the cargo owner. The burden of proof becomes relevant when the judge concludes that one part's version of the facts is as likely as the other's. However, we have seen that the burden placed on the carrier is a qualified one: 51% probability for a no-blame conclusion is not sufficient.

152. Section 275 states that the carrier has a duty of care – the cargo shall not suffer damage or loss from 'fault or neglect'. This duty covers the total period the goods are in the possession of the carrier, regardless of whether the goods are ashore prior to loading, onboard the vessel or ashore at the place of discharge waiting to be picked up by the receiver (however, undue delay on the part of the receiver may change this). Furthermore, the carrier is responsible for the acts or omissions of a number of persons taking part in the performance of the transportation: master and crew, stevedores in charge of the loading and discharging operations, the pilot and the tug and some others as well. How wide the circle should be drawn is to some extent uncertain under Norwegian law. It seems, however, to be common ground that the carrier is not responsible for errors committed by the repair yard, provided that he has chosen a reputed yard, given proper instruction and has not failed in supervising and checking the work done. Some guidance can be obtained from MC section 151 defining the vicarious liability of the shipowner in tort. It is clear that the circle is just as wide and in some respects wider, in contractual relationships.

The standard of care required will depend upon a number of factors: the nature of the cargo, the voyage and the weather and temperatures to be expected on the voyage, etc. The sender/shipper is the one who best knows the cargo; he can and ought to give information and instruction to the carrier on how to handle the cargo, and the carrier has, of course, to pay due regard to this. If no information is given the carrier must rely upon his knowledge of the cargo in question, depending upon the circumstances supplemented with what can be found from handbooks and manuals, etc.

In respect of cargo onshore, the cargo has, if necessary, to be protected, e.g., against rain and snow, sun and frost – some cargo may safely be placed on the Quayside, others should as soon as possible be taken into the shed. Another factor to be considered is the risk of theft or vandalism.

An especially risky phase is loading/discharging. In many instances, this work is performed by stevedores – with, practically speaking, little possibility for the master (on behalf of the carrier) to intervene. However, as stated above, if the cargo is damaged by what is considered a faulty operation, the carrier is nevertheless responsible (unless we have a FIO-clause, *see* above paragraph No. 144).

The vessel should be fit for safe reception, carriage and discharge of the cargo and voyage in question. First of all, the vessel should be in such a condition that it can reasonably be expected that the voyage will be properly fulfilled: The ship itself is in a good condition with satisfactorily working engines, a competent crew and sufficient navigational aid. The requirements for carriage of bananas and tractors are obviously different, and tractors which are safe with brakes drawn in coastal trade may need solid lashings for a mid-winter crossing of the Atlantic. A further example: Cleaning a tank for wine and for solvents are different matters. These demands are often described so that the vessel should be seaworthy (or 'cargoworthy' in order to distinguish the more technical concept of seaworthiness). We shall revert to the seaworthiness concept below.

During the voyage, both ship and cargo may require attention; the cargo may need airing or additional securing, and if the ship is damaged repairs should be carried out.

Under III. above, the period of mandatory liability is described. However, avoiding damages during this period may require, as the examples above demonstrate actions on the part of the carrier prior thereto: The ship should be in a fit condition when loading commences, which may e.g., require extensive repairs.

153. Obviously, the time element is of importance. Delayed delivery of the cargo may result in cargo damage: The fruit is rotten on arrival. And liability of the carrier depends on the principles explained above. But even if the cargo is undamaged delay may cause considerable loss for the cargo owner: The cargo is raw material for his factory and late arrival causes production problems, the cargo has been resold and late arrival results in non-fulfilment of the re-sale contract, etc. The liability of the carrier is in this respect based upon the same principles as applicable to cargo damage. In short: the carrier is liable if he or anyone for whom he is responsible (vicarious liability) can be blamed for the late arrival – MC section 278.

Whether there is delay is often a matter of dispute. It is very seldom that a contract specifies the delivery date. The contractual time for delivery depends in most cases upon the test of due diligence: Has the cargo arrived at the time to be expected when the concrete circumstances are taken into consideration and it is assumed that the carrier has acted prudently? The performance of other carriers is of importance; if 'our' carrier is slower this will be to his prejudice unless he is able to show that there are reasonable grounds for his performance.

154. In a commercial sense, there is in most instances one route that is followed from the port of loading to the port of discharge. Other cargo commitments may lead to deviation from this route, and this is typical in liner trade: A's cargo is not carried directly to the port of discharge. The liner vessel may go to a number of intermediate ports, some on the direct route (seen from A's perspective), some quite a distance off route. Such calls at intermediate ports may cause late delivery of A's cargo and they may expose his cargo to risks different from those usually encountered along the direct route. This type of deviation is, however, a part of liner business that A should have taken into consideration. But there is a limit. In 1893 MC section 98, it was stated: 'Deviation is only permitted in order to rescue life or salvage ship or goods or on any other reasonable ground.' In this context, deviation was defined as deliberate deviation from the natural route for other reasons than nautical ones. And it followed that in uncontractual (unreasonable) deviation a very strict liability regime applied. When MC was revised the attitude was that these rules might be appropriate in chartering, but that modern liner trade required somewhat more flexible rules. The result was MC section 275 subsection 2:

> The carrier is not liable for losses resulting from measures to rescue persons or reasonable measures to salvage ships or other property at sea.

The liability regime implies, probably, that in respect of minor breaches the general rules on liability are decisive, compare section 275 subsection 1 (with exceptions in section 276). In case of a serious breach it is very likely that there is strict liability, with no right to plead the exemptions in the Code.

VII. Exemptions

155. It follows from the Hague-Visby Rules and also from MC sections 275 et seq. that the carrier is protected against liability in certain instances and that, when he is liable, he is entitled to limit his liability. We will first discuss the exceptions (Nos 156–157); the rules on calculation of the loss are dealt with in paragraph Nos 158–160.

The Hague-Visby Rules have in Article 4.2 listed a number of situations where the liability of the carrier is clarified in relation to the main rule on liability based on negligence with a reversed burden of proof. The Norwegian attitude has been that letters a and b contain true exceptions (dealt with in paragraph No. 156 below), while the remainder of the list (the 'catalogue') is superfluous: Basically it expresses what follows from the main rule. Accordingly, in respect of Article 4.2 the MC reproduces only what is contained in letters a and b, *see* MC section 276.

156. MC section 276 subsection 1 has two important exceptions regarding cargo liability (Nos 1–2) – applicable to physical damage as well as loss due to delay (in the latter respect, *see* section 278 referring to section 276). These exemptions are, however, subject to an important seaworthiness requirement (which is dealt with in paragraph No. 157).

No. 1 exempts the carrier from liability for loss, damage or delay which is caused by 'fault or neglect in the navigation or management of the ship'. A pre-condition is that the fault or neglect is committed by the ship's 'master, crew, pilot or tug or others performing work in the service of the ship'. Thus the carrier is not protected against damage caused by his own fault or the fault of senior management personnel (owner's privity). If the damage can be attributed to equipment acquired by the technical inspector who should have realized that the equipment was inadequate, or the damage is due to unqualified personnel hired by a manager who should have realized their incompetence, then the exception does not operate. The exemption from liability depends on whether the negligence relates to the navigation or management of the ship.

The first category, navigation of the ship, covers steering and manoeuvring the ship (including use of lanterns, signals and navigational equipment, as well as responses to signals from other ships and marks, etc.). For instance, if the first mate fails to recognize a lighthouse or misjudges a distance, with the result that the ship runs aground and the cargo sustains damage, the carrier is exempted from liability.

The second category, management of the ship, relates to the ship's condition, manning and equipment. A shoddy repair job on the engine would be considered a fault in the management of the ship. However, acts related to the cargo is outside the exemption (for instance: regulation of the temperature in the cooling chambers, cleaning of the holds before loading grain in bulk, securing cars on the cargo deck). However, the borderline between 'management of the ship' and acts related to the cargo (often characterized as an 'error in the management of the cargo' or a 'commercial error') may be difficult to draw. For example The stowage concerns primarily the safety of the cargo, but bad stowage may also endanger the safety of the ship (cargo starts shifting with capsizing as the final outcome). The guiding principle is: Was the act or omission primarily in the interest of the cargo or the ship? Where a deckhand intended to fill the ballast tank but erroneously connected the hose to the cargo hold, so that the cargo became damaged, this was considered as an error relating to the management of the ship – ND 1975 85 Supreme Court.

Just as important as the exemption relating to navigational error is the exemption for fire contained in MC section 276 No. 2. The carrier is not responsible for the consequences of 'fire not caused by the fault or neglect of the carrier personally'. The exemption is drafted in a similar way to that for navigational errors, i.e., it applies to fires caused by persons for whom the carrier is responsible. However, if the carrier himself or one of his managers can be blamed, liability will be imposed according to the general rule in section 275. For example, the carrier will be liable if adequate fire procedures have not been developed, especially if the carrier or his senior management have failed to take corrective measures after receiving reports that fire protection is inadequate.

157. For both exemptions in section 276 there is an important qualification in subsection 2:

> The carrier is nevertheless liable for losses in consequence of unseaworthiness which is caused by the carrier personally or a person for whom the carrier is responsible failing to take proper care to make the ship seaworthy at the commencement of the voyage. The burden of proving that proper care was taken rests on the carrier.

For example, a grounding causing damage to cargo on board would have been avoided if the vessel had been equipped with updated charts or the navigational equipment had functioned properly. If such defects existed when the voyage commenced, then the vessel is unseaworthy, and if say the master can be blamed for not remedying them before departure, the exception does not apply. Or, if the fire warning and fire extinguishing equipment were in bad shape prior to commencing the voyage, the vessel was not seaworthy, and the thus fire exemption does not apply if someone on the carrier's side can be blamed for not having rectified this in time. However, sometimes an improper condition may be fixed before a dangerous situation arises. A typical situation is securing the hatch covers; the vessel may leave the port with open hatches when it reasonably can be expected that proper closing will take place before the vessel reaches the open sea (ND 1919 364 Supreme Court).

A more recent Supreme Court decision in ND 2011 125 concerns watchkeeping on the bridge during the night. The master's acceptance of inadequate routines amounted to unseaworthiness at the commencement of the voyage, and as the cargo damage – following a collision – would have been avoided by proper watch on the bridge, the carrier was held liable.

VIII. Extent of Liability

158. If the carrier is liable for cargo damage or delayed delivery of the cargo under the rules we have examined, the next issue to consider is the extent of liability.

The general principle in contract law is that the injured party is entitled to compensation for his actual economic loss. However, the MC contains rules which to some extent deviate significantly from ordinary legal principles. The main rule is that damages are *standardized.* MC section 279 says:

> Damages for loss of or damage to the goods are calculated on the basis of the value of goods of the same kind at the place and time when the goods were or should have been delivered according to the contract of carriage.

The value of the goods is determined on the basis of the market price. If there is neither an exchange price nor a market price, the value shall be determined according to the current value of goods of the same kind and quality.

Thus, the actual loss, i.e., the particular cargo owner's loss due for instance to the loss of a favourable re-sale contract, does not appear to be relevant, and the same applies, for example, to loss of profits due to lack of raw materials in the cargo owner's factory. Case law shows, however, that there are exceptions to these rules, see in particular ND 1987 160 Supreme Court: A fishing vessel received bunkers in Arctic waters from a supply ship. The bunkers had been contaminated under the transport so that the fishing vessel got engine problems and suffered loss of income. The repair bill had clearly to be covered by the supplying vessel, but also the loss of income was considered recoverable.

159. In addition to the limitation following from the principles in section 279 the Code has – in conformity with the Hague-Visby Rules – limitation rules based upon the units damaged. Section 280 subsection 1 provides:

> The carrier's liability shall not exceed 667 SDR for each package or other unit of the goods or 2 SDR for each kilogram of the gross weight of the goods lost, damaged or delayed. The limit of liability which results in the highest liability shall be applied. By SDR is meant the unit mentioned in Section 505.

Thus, if the carrier is liable for the loss of a container with machine parts worth 100,000 SDR he will satisfy the claim by paying 667 SDR (on kilogram limitation, *see* below). Where the contents are damaged, the result is similar. The unit concept is not in all respects clear, *see,* e.g., ND 1970 281 Supreme Court, where the questions arose how one should classify bundles of copper wire where each bundle contained seven coils. The Court concluded that each bundle was one unit. A container may contain a number of cases, drums, etc. Here the basic rule is that the description in the bill of lading is decisive: If 'one container containing 200 cases' is lost the carrier may be liable for 667 SDR x 200 (+ 667 SDR in respect of the container itself). Some of these classification questions are solved in section 281, within particular a view to modern methods of handling cargo – typically through the use of pallets and containers.

The alternative to the unit limitation is the rule on *kilogram* limitation, whereby the liability is limited to 2 SDR per kg of damaged or lost goods. The cargo owner can choose between the two alternatives, which means that the rule on weight is used where the lost or damaged unit weighs more than 333 kg.

The carrier loses his right of unit or kilogram limitation if he 'personally caused the loss wilfully or through gross negligence and with knowledge that such loss would probably arise' (section 283).

IX. Domestic Trade

160. In domestic trade, there are some special rules. The basic rules on liability are the same, but there are two important exceptions.

First, it follows from MC section 276 subsection 3 that the exemptions for 'fault or neglect in the navigation or the management of the ship' and for 'fire' (section 276 subsections 1–2) do not apply to contracts for 'carriage by sea in domestic trade in Norway'. If the cargo is damaged e.g., by fire, the question of liability for the carrier has to be decided in accordance with the general rule: The carrier is held liable, unless he can show that neither he nor anyone for whom he is responsible has acted negligently.

Second, when the carrier is liable the unit and kilogram limitation rules in MC section 280 subsection 1 do not apply. But according to subsection 2 he is entitled to limit his liability to '17 SDR for each kilogram of the gross weight of the goods lost or damaged'. This is in conformity with the road carrier's liability. In case of delay, the liability 'shall not exceed the full freight according to the contract of carriage'. The underlying consideration is that in domestic trade it is, because of the usual options in the contract of carriage, often difficult to say beforehand whether the goods will be carried by sea, by truck or rail.

It is 'domestic trade' where the place of loading and the place of discharge are in Norway. A shipment from a Norwegian port to a port abroad is not domestic trade, even if it is clear that the vessel will call at one or more Norwegian ports before leaving Norwegian waters; a damage occurring in Norwegian waters is in such a case not within the domestic rules. A second example: The owner of a consignment coming from abroad, which is transferred in a Norwegian port to a local liner and is damaged on the Norwegian leg cannot be awarded damages on the basis of 17 SDR per kg.

X. The Description of the Goods in the Bill of Lading

161. The shipper is entitled to get a bill of lading from the carrier (MC section 294). In paragraph No. 129 above, the three main functions of this document have been stated. Further rules regarding the contents of a bill of lading are found in section 296. According to subsection 1 the bill of lading shall give this information:

(1) the nature of the goods, including dangerous features, and necessary marking, units numbers and the weight or otherwise expressed quantity of the goods, all as furnished by the shipper;
(2) apparent condition of the goods and its packing;
(3) name and principal place of business of the carrier;
(4) name of the shipper;
(5) the receiver, if stated by the shipper;
(6) port of loading and the date the carrier received the goods there;
(7) port of discharge and any agreement on time for delivery there;
(8) number of counterparts, if the bill of lading is issued in more than one counterpart;

(9) the place where the bill of lading is issued;
(10) the amount of freight and other conditions for delivery, if same are to be fulfilled by the receiver;
(11) that the carriage is subject to the Hague-Visby Rules;
(12) that the goods may or shall be carried on deck;
(13) the upper amount of limitation for the carrier's liability if an increased liability is agreed.

Some of the items are more or less self-explanatory. The following will be confined to some comments on items Nos 1-2.

No. 1 concerns the nature and the quantity of the goods. The description must be more specific than, e.g., steel plates, animal skins, lumber. The bill of lading must refer to, e.g., the type of steel plates, the type of lumber, etc. If the cargo consists of cars or other machinery, the description must state the type, model and registration or production number. If the cargo has been packed, the type of packaging material should be mentioned (e.g., wooden crates, cardboard boxes, sacks, containers). It is possible to give a brief description and provide the details by referring to the underlying invoice '–as specified by invoice' (e.g., serial numbers for machinery and electrical appliances). No. 1 also requires the inclusion of necessary identification marks, typically letters and numbers stamped on the packaging to distinguish between the individual units. If the goods have properties that are dangerous, these must be specified in the bill of lading (this also is required by public regulations).

In addition, the bill of lading must provide information regarding quantity: number of units or items (e.g., one container, fifty sacks or seventeen bundles/coils) and weight (e.g., 500 kg or 3 tonnes) or quantity expressed in a different manner (e.g., 200 m cable/iron pipe, 20 standards or 80 m^3 lumbers, etc.). In other words, the carrier has a duty to include two types of data – the number of units or items, plus either weight or quantity. On this point, there has been an alteration in relation to the 1893 MC (which was based on the Hague-Visby Rules Article 3 No. 3), which required the inclusion of either the weight of the goods, their measurements or the number of items. The present rules are in accordance with the Hamburg Rules Article 15 No. 1 letter (a).

Information about the cargo will, of course, initially come from the shipper – *see* section 296 No. 1 (cf. section 301 on the responsibility of the shipper for information supplied). The necessary information must be available in time for the carrier to ascertain whether the cargo received accords with the shipper's description. The carrier has a duty to carry out investigations, but he is also obliged to reserve his position if he has not had a reasonable opportunity to check the accuracy of the information – *see* section 298.

No. 2 requires information regarding the apparent condition of the goods and the packaging. The carrier's servants must check the cargo sufficiently to allow a proper description to be made. If the cargo appears to be in good order, the carrier will typically note this with the words 'in apparent good order and condition'. However, if damage is apparent or there are other factors that may be relevant to the receiver, these must be described. If, for example, the steel plates are rusted, this must be noted. If the packaging is defective, this must also appear on the bill of lading '15 bags torn'. If the bags have been used previously, this should also be mentioned –'used bags'.

There is an important distinction between the on board bill of lading (or: shipped bill of lading) and the received for shipment bill of lading. The former, which can always be demanded (section 294), shall give the name of the ship on which the cargo is loaded, the nationality of the ship, the place of loading and the date that loading was completed (section 296 subsection 2).

In the hands of the shipper the bill of lading is a receipt for goods received and a confirmation of the contract of carriage (previously contained in a booking note). Such a receipt may have important evidentiary effect when there is disagreement as to whether the cargo has been damaged while in the custody of the carrier (section 299 subsection 1). However, when the bill of lading is transferred it may have acquired a fundamentally different status, *see* MC section 299 subsection 3:

> If a third party in good faith has acquired a bill of lading in reliance on the accuracy of the statements in it, evidence to the contrary according to paragraphs one and two is not admissible. If the carrier knew or ought to have understood that a statement concerning the goods was incorrect, the carrier cannot invoke a reservation as mentioned in Section 298, unless the reservation expressly states that the information is incorrect.

If, e.g., a statement regarding the quantity is incorrect – one crate was loaded, but the bill of lading says two – then the carrier is precluded from proving that only one was loaded. The difference is presumed to be a loss during the carriage, and the liability of the carrier depends upon the ordinary cargo damage rules ('implied transport liability'). However, here it will be impossible for the carrier to show how the 'loss' occurred and that he or his 'servants' are not to be blamed. In short, the carrier has a strict liability: He has to pay according to the rules for cargo lost, with the right, however, to plead the usual unit or kilo limitations.

However, MC section 300 subsection 1 provides an alternative remedy:

> If a third party incurs a loss by acquiring a bill of lading in reliance on the accuracy of the information it contains, the carrier is liable if the carrier understood or ought to have understood that the bill of lading was misleading for a third party. No right of limitation of liability under this Chapter applies.

The liability of the carrier is here determined on the basis that the third party (the buyer) shall be put in the position he would have been in if the information had been correct – which in many cases would mean that he had not paid the purchase price but cancelled the underlying sales agreement. If the market price of the goods has dropped, the buyer will usually be better off with the application of section 300 – in particular, it should be noted that this type of liability is not defined as transport liability and consequently the unit/kilogram limitation rules in section 280 cannot be pleaded by the carrier.

In situations where both sections 299–300 are applicable, the cargo owner is entitled to choose.

XI. The Right of Action

162. The bill of lading is a contract primarily between carrier (the contracting carrier, distinguished from the performing/actual carrier) and the sender. When the bill of lading is traded, the rights accrued in the hands of the sender are transferred to the new holder of the bill of lading. Often the cargo will be acquired in this way, i.e., by purchasing the document representing the goods. Thus, it will be the holder of the bill of lading that will have the right to sue when goods are damaged or lost. The question then remains against whom he may commence proceedings.

The cargo owner may sue the contracting carrier (MC section 285) and the contracting carrier is liable for the acts and omissions of the performing carrier. The cargo owner may also sue the performing carrier, i.e., the owner of the vessel actually carrying out the transport, based upon tort rules. The lawmaker has, however, decided that the contractual rules shall apply, *see* MC section 286 on corresponding application of sections 282 and 283.

The rules in sections 285–286 have the effect that the contracting carrier is liable for the acts of the performing carrier, but not vice versa. Their liability will be joint and several (section 287 subsection 1), but the total liability cannot exceed the limitation amount – practically speaking: the cargo owner will not obtain the unit limitation amount twice by suing both the contracting and the performing carrier.

For combined or intermodal transports involving a vessel, *see* Part III. Chapter 4 below (paragraph Nos 349 et seq.).

§5. The Sea Waybill

163. The sea waybill is defined in MC section 308. It is a non-negotiable document which:

(1) is (like a bill of lading) evidence of a contract of carriage by sea – *see* section 292 subsection 1;
(2) contains an acknowledgement that the goods have been received. This also corresponds to the definition of a bill of lading – *see* section 292 subsection 1. The acknowledgement may either be to the effect that the goods have been received at the terminal for purposes of loading, or that the goods have been loaded on board the ship; and
(3) contains an undertaking by the carrier to deliver the goods to the receiver named in the document. On this point, the sea waybill is clearly different from the bill of lading – *see* section 292 subsection 2 on delivery of goods in exchange for the bill of lading.

There is no requirement that the document actually be designated as a sea waybill or waybill. The document must, however, satisfy the above-mentioned requirements, and have the contents stated in section 309:

(a) information about the goods which have been received for carriage (*see* below);
(b) the name of the sender, the receiver (List(3) above) and the carrier;

(c) the terms of carriage – in practice, the sea waybill may be an extensive document with many clauses similar to those in a liner bill of lading. A simple reference to the MC rules is, however, sufficient; and
(d) specification of the freight and other expenses to be paid by the receiver.

The MC expressly stipulates three consequences of issuing a sea waybill:

> As mentioned, the sea waybill must specify the receiver. Pursuant to Section 308 subsection 2 this does not mean that the sender has relinquished his right in relation to the goods (right to modify the contract for carriage). The sender is still entitled to instruct the carrier to deliver the goods to another party, unless he has 'waived this right as against the carrier or the receiver has already asserted his right.'

The sea waybill is evidence of the contract for carriage and of receipt of the goods as described in the document (section 309 subsection 2).

The fact that a sea waybill has been issued pursuant to section 308 subsection 3, does not extinguish the right of the shipper to demand a bill of lading, *see* section 294. However, if the sender has waived his right to name another receiver, the shipper (irrespective of whether or not he is the sender) can no longer demand a bill of lading.

164. Whether a sea waybill is preferred to a bill of lading will depend on the agreement between sender and carrier, but generally, the choice will be determined by the custom of the trade. In certain areas, and in connection with the carriage of certain types of goods, sea waybills are traditionally used and the carrier will thus issue such document as a matter of course, perhaps based upon his standard terms containing a reference to a named sea waybill form. Such a procedure is not unreasonable in relation to the sender who, as we have mentioned, can demand the issue of a bill of lading even if a sea waybill exists.

It is the sender who has a right to demand a sea waybill from the carrier, but the sender may accept that the shipper receives the sea waybill directly from the carrier. In practice, the sender will be the shipper.

Chapter 7. Piloting

§1. Introduction

165. Due to its long coast, piloting has always played an important part in navigation in Norwegian waters. Indeed, there are enactments about piloting going back to the early eighteenth century.

For a long time, piloting was left to the initiative of the individual pilots, based on the principle that the pilot who first came on board the ship in question was entitled to pilot her into the harbour. Gradually this changed, and today the Norwegian state has taken responsibility for arranging piloting along the coast. The Ministry of Transport and Communications is the authority responsible, but much of the administration has been delegated to the Norwegian Coast Directorate.

§2. Statutory Provisions

166. Piloting is now regulated by the *Act on Piloting* of 15 August 2014 No. 61, covering the inner waters and the sea territory as well as the Svalbard area. The Ministry is empowered to give regulations on the type of vessel where the use of pilot is obligatory and to define areas where this duty applies. The obligation is met by the use of a person holding a pilot's certificate – usually a state employee. There is, however, an important alternative in the fairway certificate system: Such a certificate may be issued to the master and other navigators on the vessel, and it gives the right to sail without a certified pilot in areas where piloting is obligatory. The typical example is the local liner where the master and his officers on the bridge know all about the trading area.

§3. Duties of the Pilot

167. Section 8 of the Act states that the pilot shall in a safe manner guide the master, or the person having command in his place, in the navigation and manoeuvring of the vessel (subsections 1 and 2). During the piloting, the pilot shall be on the bridge, or on such position from which the piloting is best performed (subsection 3).

§4. Liability of the Pilot

168. The Act section 10 stipulates that 'the pilot is deemed to be in the service of the vessel during piloting', which is in conformity with MC section 151. This means that if the vessel causes damage to third parties and the damage is attributable to the pilot, the pilot's actual employer, the state, is not liable for it. The pilot himself is liable for damage in accordance with the Tort Act section 2-3, but his liability may be reduced and/or lifted. He may also have a recourse to the shipowner for such sums paid to the injured party which the shipowner ought to have paid.

Chapter 8. Towing and Pushing Contract

§1. Introduction

169. A maritime towing contract is simply a contract whereby a person or a company agrees to perform a towing service at sea against a remuneration. The towing contract should be distinguished from charter parties, salvage contracts and the use of towing vessels for other purposes than towing, e.g., laying out cables on the sea bottom or performing supply services. However, towing contracts do not only apply to towing of vessels. They include, e.g., towing of barges, timber, rafts, and oil rigs and platforms. They also apply to contracts where the vessel in question does no drag but pushes.

There have been towages of huge petroleum installations in Norwegian waters. The Troll platform (concrete gravity base structure with integrated processing, drilling and accommodation units), which was tugged from Stavanger to its site in the North Sea in 1997, had a ground area of about 165,000 m^2 and was 370 m high (water depth on location 330 m), and had a value at about NOK 39 billions.

The longest device that has been towed in Norwegian waters is a 1,246 m long unit forming part of the floating bridge section of a major bridge project in northern Norway.

§2. Statutory Provisions

170. There are few statutory provisions relating to towage. The one that is of importance is MC section 151, which will be mentioned in §3. below.

§3. Liability and Limitation of Liability

171. Liability for the tug owner and the vessel towed may take many forms.

The tug may cause damage to the vessel (or unit) it is towing. The latter may cause damage to the former, or one or both vessels may cause damage to third parties by collision with other vessels or with property ashore.

Questions will then arise as to whether liability has been incurred at all, and if so, which of the two parties – the owner of the tug or the owner of the towed vessel (or both) – shall be liable, and whether recourse from one party to the other is possible. Ultimately, the question arises as to whether the liability established may be limited.

172. In the absence of statutory provisions, the legal relationship between the tug owner and the towed unit must be judged in the first instance from the stipulations in the contract between the parties. Normally this is based on a standard tow contract, such as the one prepared by the Scandinavian Tug Owners' Association (STA of 1985) or the Towage Agreements ('Towcon' or 'Towhire', latest edition of both 2008) prepared and recommended by the BIMCO.

173. In the absence of clear stipulations in the contract about liability, general Norwegian contract and tort law will apply. This will result in liability for the tug owner if negligence on his part (or from his servants) may be established. For contractual liability, it appears that the tug owner may face a liability in negligence with a reversed burden of proof. Likewise, if the owner of the towed vessel can be said to have been negligent, they may be jointly liable for the damage incurred.

On the tug owner's part, negligence will mainly be found in navigation during the towage. However, the tug owner will normally also be considered to be responsible for fulfilling certain duties *before* the towage starts. Thus the tug owner will be liable for the fitness of the tug boat for the operation in question. The tug must be seaworthy and have a capacity and crew capable of executing the task undertaken.

The tug owner must also take care to ascertain the weather conditions for the time in question. The more unusual and therefore the more precarious the forthcoming towage is considered to be, the more important it is that the tug owner shows due diligence in respect of ascertaining the weather, and does not commence the towage if the weather forecast is unfavourable.

Third, the tug owner should be well-acquainted with the sailing route and the dangers connected therewith. This, of course, is particularly important when the tug is in command of the towage operation.

If negligence is established on the tug owner's part, he will be liable towards the owner of the towed vessel, unless the latter has also shown contributory negligence, or the contract exempts the tug owner from liability. This is the case both in STA and in the Towcon. In the former, the tug owner is only liable for damage to the towed vessel if this has been caused by the management of the tug-owning company.

In Towcon clause 18, it is stated that the hirer shall bear the loss or damage of whatsoever nature and howsoever caused to or sustained by the tow.

174. Regarding liability towards third parties, the main principle is that if they have suffered damage they will have a claim in tort against the tug if the tug has been negligent. In such a case, the third party will also have a claim against the owner of the towed vessel under the rules of MC section 151 on vicarious liability, as the tug is considered as a servant acting in the service of the vessel. If the damage has been caused solely by the tow, the owner of the latter will be the sole party responsible.

Chapter 9. Salvage and Assistance

§1. Definition

175. MC section 441 litra (a) contains the following definition of salvage:

> any act the purpose of which is to render assistance to a ship or other object which has been wrecked or is in danger in any waters.

This definition is, however, not exhaustive, as it follows from MC section 445 subsection 2 that salvage may also involve the saving of human life. Moreover, the prevention or limitation of environmental damage may be an element of an ordinary salvage operation, *see* section 446 litra (c).

§2. Statutory Provisions

176. Norway has adopted the International Convention on Salvage of 1989 and has incorporated its rules into MC Chapter 16. The following will therefore to a large extent be explanatory notes to these rules, which first of all determines when assistance is deemed to be an act of salvage entitling the salvor to a salvage award.

Typically, the assistance is rendered to a 'ship'. MC section 441 litra (b) defines a ship as 'any ship or vessel and also any other construction capable of navigation'. The reference to 'any other construction capable of navigation' is intended to apply in particular to drilling platforms and similar floating installations (MC section 507 subsection 2 expressly makes MC Chapter 16 applicable to floating drilling platforms and similar installations which are not otherwise considered to be ships). Since it follows from the definition of 'salvage' that 'other object' can also be salved, there is no need for the term 'ship' to be narrowly defined.

177. The term 'object' is defined in MC section 441 litra (c). As a general principle, all items of property can be subject to salvage. The 1989 Convention appears to expand the definition considerably in comparison with the 1910 Convention. However, as in the past, salvage mainly concerns goods which are, or have been, on board a ship. The ship's cargo is, of course, of primary interest, but other property on board – ship equipment, bunkers, stores, etc. – will also be subject to salvage. In the case of property outside the vessel, the statutory text places various limitations on what can fall within the definition. Property which is permanently attached to the shoreline, e.g., a floating dock (MC section 441 litra (c)), permanent installations or pipelines for petroleum activities or property which is considered a cultural artefact (cf. MC section 442 subsection 4), fall outside the scope of the Chapter.

178. The saving of human life does not in itself give rise to a right to a salvage award (cf. MC section 445 subsection 2 first sentence). Thus a salvor of human life will not be entitled to a salvage award if the salvage operation of the ship has failed. If human life is salved in addition to property, this will be taken into account when the salvage award is assessed (cf. MC section 446 litra (b)).

179. The salved property must be 'wrecked' or 'in danger'. This requirement follows from the definition of salvage in MC section 441 litra (a). As regards the concept 'in danger', the first issue to examine is the type of danger that must be present. The answer is straightforward in principle: there must be a risk of fairly extensive *physical damage* to the ship and/or object. Thus, if there is a risk that the ship or object will be a total loss, the salvage rules clearly apply. An example would be a ship which has sprung a leak and will sink in deep water if it is not assisted. However, a salvage situation will also arise where a ship is in danger of sinking in a place where it can be raised later. The salvage operation will prevent the damage caused by the sinking and save the expense of raising the vessel. On the other hand, a risk simply of *delay* has not been considered relevant. If a ship were in danger of being frozen in, without there being a risk of property damage, a salvor would not be entitled to a salvage award, even though the shipowner might save considerable time.

The second question is how serious the danger to the disabled ship must be before there is a legitimate salvage situation. This question concerns the requisite *degree* of danger. It is difficult to set clear criteria. In general, the danger must be more severe than the ordinary perils of the sea. In practice, there is not always a need for a clear definition, since the degree of danger influences the size of the salvage award. A factor which may affect the degree of danger is the availability of assistance from sources other than the potential salvor. Generally, a disabled ship in well-frequented waters is less in danger than a ship in similar difficulties far away from shipping routes. Nevertheless, this consideration will usually only be relevant in assessing the size of the award and not in determining the existence of a bona fide salvage situation.

An odd issue arises where both the salvor and the salved believe the ship to be in danger, but where it later becomes clear that this was not actually the case. The Norwegian Supreme Court (NSC) has dealt with this issue three times in recent years, *see* ND 1996 238 NSC, ND 1999 269 NSC and ND 2004 383 NSC. The law now seems to be settled: The ship receiving assistance must objectively be in danger for a salvage situation to be present.

A ship is *wrecked* following the occurrence of an accident of some significance. For example, the ship may have sunk after a collision or grounding. Such a ship will also often be 'in danger'; a grounded vessel may, for example, disengage and sink. Since the MC has 'wrecked' and 'in danger' as alternatives, the former term will only be of relevance when a ship is not simultaneously in danger. The alternative –'wrecked'– is not found in the 1910 or 1989 Conventions.

§3. Salvage Award

180. A salvor can only claim an award if the salvage operation has been successful. This 'no cure no pay' principle is implied in MC section 445 subsection 1, which states that the salvage award must not exceed the value of the salved property.

The parties may agree to set aside the 'no cure no pay' principle. However, there must be a clear and express agreement to this effect, since it represents a deviation from the general rule in statute, convention and case law.

A claim for a salvage award does not depend on the salvage having been undertaken on the basis of a contract. In practice, however, a contractual relationship will normally be established between the salvor and the disabled ship. Standard contracts containing wide-ranging provisions are often used. Internationally, Lloyd's Standard Form of Salvage Agreement (in practice, Lloyd's Form or LOF), is used extensively. In Scandinavia, a similar form known as the 'Skandinavisk bjergningskontrakt' (1994) is also used.

Salvage agreements usually state that the salvors are to work on a 'no cure no pay' basis (subject to exceptions relating to environmental damage). If the parties cannot agree on the size of the award, there will be an arbitration. Under LOF, the arbitration will take place in London, subject to English law.

181. The MC contains no absolute rules regarding the size of the salvage award, aside from the limitation in MC section 445 subsection 1, second sentence, that the award shall not exceed the value of the salved property. In other words, the salvage award can be anywhere up to 100% of the salved property's value. An important factor to be taken into account when assessing salvage awards is the necessity of providing an incentive for salvage operations, compare MC section 446 subsection 1 first sentence. The salvage award should be assessed generously, especially in the case of complex and risky salvage operations. The amount of remuneration should be significantly higher than if the work had been performed on a time or project basis. The factors to be considered are specified in MC section 446 litras (a) to (j). The factors are not in any order of priority, and the list is not exhaustive.

The value of the salved property (litra (a)) is normally taken to be the value immediately after the salvage operation is completed, which means that it is necessary to determine the market value of the ship, taking into account the cost of repair. It is the value of the ship itself that is determinative, which means that the fact that the ship is on a charter party will not be relevant. The award should take into account the salvor's expertise and endeavours during the salvage, in other words, the 'quality' of the operation, see litras (b) and (c). Other important factors are the extent to which the salvage operation has succeeded (litra (d)), and the type of danger and the degree of risk to the disabled ship (litra (e)). The speed of the salvage response is also relevant (litra (g)). The salvor's expenses in connection with the operation are a significant factor (litra (f)). They should in principle be fully covered by the award, but if high expenses result from a poorly implemented operation, an exception will have to be made. A related factor is the degree of risk involved in the salvor (litra (h)). Finally, there are two factors of particular importance to professional salvors (litras (i) and (j)), entitling them to extra remuneration compared with other salvors.

Under certain conditions, the salvors may lose their claim for a salvage award, wholly or partly, compare MC section 450 subsection 3. Three scenarios may be pointed out: (1) The salvors have caused the danger which necessitates the salvage operation, typically a collision, where the ship at fault afterwards salves the innocent ship. (2) The salvors have damaged the disabled vessel during the salvage operation. (3) The salvors have acted dishonestly by, for example, stealing cargo or equipment on board the disabled vessel or by withholding salved property.

182. A central feature of the 1989 Convention was the desire to provide incentives to prevent or limit damage to the environment. An important innovation was that the salvor has a right to so-called *special compensation* where salvage operations are carried out to avoid damage to the environment, irrespective of whether such efforts succeed or not. The relevant rules are found in MC section 449. Pursuant to subsection 1, the right to special compensation is conditional on the performance of a salvage operation in respect of a vessel, which in itself or through its cargo threatens environmental damage as defined in MC section 441 litra (d).

The amount of special compensation shall as a starting point correspond to the expenses incurred by the salvor in the salvage operation, ref. subsection 1 first sentence. MC section 449 Subsection 3 determines what costs should be considered 'salvor's expenses'. As a general principle, the salvor can claim actual expenses reasonably incurred in connection with an action which directly or indirectly was intended to prevent or minimize damage to the environment. If the salvor receives reimbursement for his expenses through an ordinary salvage award, he is only entitled to claim special compensation for the part of the expenses which was not covered, ref. subsection 1 second sentence.

If the salvage operation successfully prevents or minimizes damage to the environment, but the disabled ship is not saved, the amount of special compensation may be increased so that the salvor receives more than his actual expenses, ref. MC section 449 subsection 2. The amount may increase by up to 30% of the salvor's expenses, but when it is found reasonable, the amount can be increased by up to 100%.

MC section 51 provides a maritime lien in the salvaged vessel for salvage claims.

§4. Reward of the Crew

183. MC section 451 sets out the rights of the crew in relation to a salvage award in considerable detail:

> When a ship registered in Norway has salvaged something on a voyage, the salvage reward shall first compensate any damage that the ship, cargo or other property on board may have sustained in the salvage operation, and also expenditure for fuel, wages and food for the master and crew incurred in connection with the salvage.

The remainder, the net salvage reward, shall be apportioned according to the following rules:

(1) The owner shall receive three fifths. Of the remainder, the master shall receive one third and those belonging to the genuine crew two thirds. The share of the crew shall be apportioned in proportion to their respective wages. The share of the master shall nevertheless always be at least twice that of the most highly

paid crew member. A pilot on board a salvaging ship participates in the distribution of the share of the crew even if the pilot is not in the employment of the owner, and shall in the event receive a share corresponding to the wages of the senior mate.

(2) If the salvage was carried out by a fishing or catching vessel in use as such, four fifteenths shall be distributed equally between the members of the crew, including a pilot on board, compare No. 1 sentence five. Of the remaining, one further crew member's share is due to the master seiner, and to the master in total two single crew member shares but at least two-fifteenths of the net salvage award. The rest goes tot he owner. The provisions of this number do not apply to vessels in use in pelagic whaling.

(3) If the salvage was performed by a Norwegian state-owned ship in use for purposes of a public law nature, the state shall receive three fifths. The remainder shall be distributed among those on board according to rules laid down by the King. The state may refrain from claiming salvage rewards without incurring liability towards those on board.

(4) When there are particular reasons indicating a different apportionment, exceptions can be made to the apportionment rules of Nos 1, 2 and 3.

A master or crew member cannot waive his or her rights according to this Section unless they have signed on a salvage vessel specially equipped for salvage, or the waiver was made in connection with signing on and relates to a particular salvage operation. In such cases as mentioned in subsection 2 No. 2, deviating rules as to apportionment can be agreed by collective agreement. [The Supreme Court has accepted that the waiver to claim salvage remuneration need not be express, but could normally be implied through employment on board a salvage vessel, *see* ND 1980 190 NSC].

As soon as the salvage reward has been fixed by agreement or final judgment, the shipowner shall send each person entitled to a share of the salvage reward notification of the amount of the reward and a plan for its distribution. Claims according to subsection 2 No. 4 or other objections to the distribution must reach the shipowner no later than three months after the notification was sent.

If the ship is not registered in Norway, the laws of the State in which it is registered shall apply.

184. The crew onboard a vessel in distress will normally not be entitled to a salvage remuneration, because they have done only what they had a duty to do, compare MC section 450 subsection 1. However, the section leaves an opening for allowance of a salvage award when 'the services rendered exceed what can be considered as due performance of the contract.' Such 'excess performance' may be that the master and/or chief engineer stay on board a burning ship and thereby, through their actions, significantly contribute to extinguishing the fire and the vessel's subsequent salvage.

§5. Liability and Limitation of Liability of Salvors

185. The salvor has an obligation to 'perform the salvage operation with due care' (MC section 444 subsection 1 litra (a)). MC section 444 further specifies that the salvor must co-operate with other salvors when this is reasonably requested by the owner or master, and seek the assistance of other salvors when this is reasonable under the circumstances. MC section 444 subsection 2 litra (b) stipulates that the salvor is bound to 'take due care during the salvage operation to prevent or limit environmental damage'.

Failing to observe his obligations, the salvor may incur liability. He may also be liable for the acts of his servants, in particular of course the master and crew.

Should the need arise, a salvor would be entitled to limit his liability (*see* Chapter 4 above). This right to limitation is explicitly stated in MC section 171 subsection, 1 second sentence.

§6. Removal of Wrecks

186. If a vessel sinks or strands, the owners and/or their underwriters may find it unprofitable to salvage it. It becomes a wreck, perhaps with cargo on board. Before 2007 there were no international conventions relating to wrecks and wreck removal. That year the IMO adopted the Nairobi convention on wreck removal, which came into force in 2015. Norway has adopted relevant legislation for accessing the convention, see Act 20 December 2018 No. 115 on modifications to the MC, etc. (removal of wreck). The act will come into force when the necessary regulations have been adopted.

The new MC Chapter 10 a has the heading 'Liability for costs for locating, marking and removal of wrecks according to The international Nairobi-convention on removal of wrecks, 2007 (wreck removal convention)'. The chapter applies first and foremost to wrecks located in Norwegian territory or territorial waters or in Norwegian economic zone, see MC section 210 h. The registered owner has strict liability for the costs for locating, marking and removing wrecks under the rules of the convention, see MC section 210 a. Rules on channeling of liability and limitation of liability are set out in MC section 210 c. Acording to MC section 210 d the owner must have insurance which covers his potential liability and a certificate to confirm that insurance is in place.

187. In Norwegian law, there are currently two other sets of regulations on wreck removal in force, the *Harbour Act* of 17 April 2009 No. 19 section 35 and the *Pollution Act (PA)* of 13 March 1981 No. 6 section 37. It seems that in practice the rules of the PA are those most often used as a basis for the removal of a wreck. The rules in the Harbour Act and the PA on wreck removal will still be applied when the new rules in MC Chapter 10 a come into force.

The PA section 28 first paragraph prescribes that no waste material or ship wreckage which can have a disfiguring effect or cause damage or harmful consequences to the environment can be left behind. Under section 37 second paragraph owners of shipwrecks may be ordered by the authorities to remove such ship wreckage

188. Previously, it was unclear whether MC section 172 a entitled the owner of a wrecked ship to limit the scope of his liability for the obligation to take measures under the PA section 37. The issue was whether the owner could avoid any of the obligations he had been ordered by the authorities in the event that the overall cost would exceed the ship's limitation amount. A Supreme Court decision from fall 2017 resolves the question: The owner is not in a position to limit his liability for such an obligation and accordingly will have to cover the full costs of the wreck removal operation.

Chapter 10. General Average

§1. THE CONCEPT OF GENERAL AVERAGE

189. The rules on general average have their basis in the fact that during a voyage, the ship, cargo and freight form part of a common venture. The principle underlying the rules is simple. If the common venture comes under threat during a voyage, then extraordinary sacrifices and expenditure necessary to prevent the loss of the venture must be apportioned according to the values of each respective interest. In this form, general average has ancient origins. Roman law (*Justinian's Digesta*, Book 14, Title 2, dating back to about 530 A.D.) recognized that 'if in order to lighten a (sinking) ship merchandise is thrown overboard, that which has been given for all shall be replaced by the contribution of all'. The rules on general average have developed over time from this simple principle, which is generally referred to as the *principle of common safety*. The most significant development has been that today, general average expenses may include extraordinary expenses incurred for the benefit of the venture, even where this was not necessary for the avoidance of danger. This may be referred to as the *principle of common benefit*, although this is rather imprecise, as it encompasses only a few special situations.

190. As far as sources of law are concerned, the general average rules have a unique position in maritime law. The main legal source is the so-called York-Antwerp Rules (YAR). The first version dated from 1877, with revisions in 1890, 1924, 1950, 1974 (with an amendment in 1990), 1995, 2004 and 2016. The rules are drafted and adopted by the Comité Maritime International (CMI), a private organization, and are not founded on an international convention.

191. General average has been under attack for many years. It is not only criticized as being cumbersome and costly, but also as being unnecessary, since most of the interests involved are, or can easily be, insured. However, the concept has proved to be extraordinarily robust, partly no doubt because strong interest groups have an economic interest in maintaining the system. In this regard, it is worth mentioning that an UNCTAD report in 1991 advocated either abandoning the rules or at least thoroughly revising them. Despite this, the latest editions of the YAR (1994, 2004 and 2016) contain only minor alterations compared with previous editions.

192. The YAR 2016 consist of seven general rules (the so-called lettered rules) and twenty-three casuistic rules (the so-called numbered rules). In addition, there is a 'rule paramount' which establishes that expenditures or sacrifices must have been 'reasonably made or incurred', and a rule of interpretation – the *Makis* rule – which establishes that, in the event of conflict, the rule paramount and the numbered rules have priority over the lettered rules. The rules are not structured in a systematic or logical way, which makes it difficult to acquire a complete understanding of their content.

§2. Statutory Provisions

193. MC Chapter 17 bears the title 'General Average'. It contains seven sections with various stipulations about the preparation of a general average statement, and about the education and qualification of general average adjusters. The main rule is laid down in MC section 461:

> Unless otherwise agreed, allowance in general average of damages, losses and expenses and the apportionment thereof shall be governed by the York-Antwerp Rules. The King decides which version of the York-Antwerp Rules shall apply according to the foregoing sentence, and shall publish the rules in their English wording and in a Norwegian translation.

A Royal Decree from 2018 prescribes that the YAR 2016 shall apply as from 1 January 2019.

§3. Definition and Application of the YAR 2016

I. The Principle of Common Safety

194. The principle of common safety is set out in YAR Rule A, which states:

> There is a general average act when, and only when, any extraordinary sacrifice or expenditure is intentionally and reasonably made or incurred for the common safety for the purpose of preserving from peril the property involved in a common maritime adventure.

Although the wording seems clear, the rule only indicates the general requirements for a general average act, and must be read in conjunction with the qualifications and exceptions contained in the other YAR rules. The most important rules in this respect are Rules X and XI, which contain the common benefit rules.

For the requirements of Rule A to be fulfilled, the property must first of all be in *danger*. This means danger either of total loss or of physical damage of some significance. In any event, the danger must be more severe than the ordinary perils of the sea. The criteria are quite similar to those which apply under the salvage rules. The second requirement is that the danger must form a *common danger for the ship and cargo*. Thus, a danger which exclusively threatens the ship or the cargo – e.g., where the cargo is threatened by decay following a breakdown in the refrigeration system – is irrelevant. Third, there must be an *intentional, extraordinary* sacrifice or expenditure. There will thus only be a general average act if the danger is met with a conscious and extraordinary action. Finally, the action taken must have been *reasonable*. This means that the action must have been appropriate in the circumstances, even if it was not successful.

Situations encompassed by the common safety principle include jettisoning cargo to refloat a grounded ship or to prevent the ship from capsizing (*see* Rules I and II);

extinguishing a fire on board (*see* Rule III); voluntary stranding (*see* Rule V); salvage assistance and the cost of a salvage award (*see* Rule VI); damage to machinery and boilers, including expenses in connection with refloating a grounded ship (*see* Rule VII and Rule VIII); and the use of ship materials and stores for fuel (*see* Rule IX).

II. The Principle of Common Benefit

195. If a ship has had to seek a port of refuge because of danger to the ship and cargo (e.g., the cargo has shifted and threatens the ship's safety), then certain expenses will already be admitted in general average under the common safety principle. The expenses were necessary to bring the common venture to safety. YAR Rules X and XI expand the applicability of general average where a ship seeks a port of refuge. Even expenses not necessary for bringing the ship and cargo out of danger will be compensated. These expenses could, for example, include the cost of unloading, handling, storing and reloading cargo while the ship is repaired, or wages incurred during the ship's stay in a port of refuge. Such expenses are admitted in general average because they have been incurred for the benefit of the ship, cargo and freight; they make the continuation and completion of the voyage possible. In other words, the principle of common benefit is applied. The call at a port of refuge, and the enforced stay there, are extraordinary events and it seems unfair for the carrier to incur such expenses without any right to compensation.

At the same time, it is unreasonable for the carrier to be completely released from his duty under the contract of affreightment to bring the cargo to its destination. In such a case, general average brings about a compromise: the carrier's duty to look after the cargo interests is maintained, but he receives partial compensation for the expenses incurred.

The common benefit principle, as it is expressed in Rules X and XI, is structured casuistically and does not allow for generous interpretation. In practice, however, there is considerable room for manoeuvre. An important reason for this is Rule F. This establishes that an extra expense which is incurred instead of another expense which would have been allowed as general average, shall be deemed to be a general average expense ('substituted expenses'). This principle applies regardless of what is thereby saved by the other interests, but limited to the amount saved in general average. Rule G is also relevant: It refers to the so-called non-separation principle, which establishes that forwarding the cargo from the port of refuge to the destination with other means, does not cause the common adventure to end. Together, Rules F and G make it possible to avoid the limitations of Rules X and XI by awarding compensation in general average for alternative ways of approaching the problem.

III. The Danger Is Caused by One of the Participants

196. The need for a general average act may result from the fault of one of the parties to the venture – most commonly the carrier. For example, the ship was unseaworthy when the voyage commenced; this was known to the crew, and, as a result, salvage assistance had to be requested during the voyage. Should there be a general average adjustment, or should the expenses be covered solely by the party at fault? Rule D establishes that a general average adjustment must take place, but emphasizes at the same time that this shall 'not prejudice any remedies or defences which may be open against or to that party in respect of such fault'. MC section 289 expands on this: 'The provisions of sections 274–288 relating to the liability of the carrier for loss of or damage to goods apply correspondingly to the right of the receiver to refuse to pay a general average contribution and to the obligation of the carrier to reimburse the receiver for any general average contribution or any salvage award which the latter may have paid.' In practice, this means that if the carrier claims a general average contribution from the cargo owner, he can refuse to pay. If, on the other hand, the cargo owner is claiming a general average contribution from the carrier or, alternatively, his share of a salvage award, the carrier will be able to invoke the exemptions and limitation rights set forth in MC sections 276 and 280, *see* ND 1993 162 NSC.

§4. The General Average Adjustment

197. Settlement of general average disputes is normally handled by an *average adjuster*– an expert in general average adjustments. In a general average adjustment (ref. MC section 462), the adjuster (1) conducts an investigation to determine if the conditions for general average have been fulfilled, (2) calculates which losses, damages and expenses are eligible for general average adjustment, (3) determines the property values the contributions of the three interests (ship, cargo and freight) shall be based on and (4) calculates the respective contributions.

MC section 467 stipulates who can be average adjusters, the conditions for obtaining a licence to practice as such and the knowledge and qualifications demanded from the possible candidates.

§5. The Contributing Fund

198. The losses, damages and expenses allowed in general average must be divided among the interests involved on the basis of their respective values. It is therefore important to determine how these values are to be established. According to Rule G, the relevant figure is the value at the end of the voyage – not the value at the time the general average act takes place. For example, if a ship is re-floated after a grounding and then collides with another ship and is further damaged, this damage must be taken into account when the ship's contribution is determined.

Other provisions regarding the determination of the respective values are found in Rule XVII. This rule sets out the important general principle that general average compensation potentially recoverable by one of the interests must be added to that interest's value. Thus, if part of the cargo is jettisoned, the compensation the cargo owner will receive in general average is added to the value of the remaining cargo.

The discussion above has assumed that the freight is one of the interests in the common venture, and as such, subject to contributing in general average. MC sections 260 and 344 establish the general principle that freight is not payable if the cargo is not intact at the end of the voyage. If the freight is pre-paid, it must be returned if the carrier has no rightful claim to it. In other words, the carrier's claim to freight is at risk until the voyage is completed. This also means that the carrier has a vested interest in completing the voyage after an accident. Quite frequently, the parties will agree that the freight is pre-paid with final effect, i.e., the freight is paid before departure and cannot be reclaimed regardless of whether the ship and/or cargo are lost. In such cases, the freight does not appear as an individual interest in general average, but is included in the value of the cargo (Rule XVII). Thus, when the cargo's value is determined, the result will be higher if the freight has been paid with final effect.

§6. The Receiving Fund

199. The YAR contain principles for calculating compensation for loss of or damage to the ship and cargo, or loss of freight, respectively. The rules (Rules XVIII, XIII, XVI and XV) provide that the injured party shall be fully compensated, but the adjustment is to some extent standardized. Moreover, the rules must be viewed in the light of the general principle in Rule C, that only loss, damage and expenses which are a direct consequence of a general average act shall be allowed in general average. However, the YAR do not contain more specific rules for determining the extraordinary expenses admissible in general average, but Rules A and C, as well as Rule VI on salvage remuneration and Rules X and XI on port of refuge expenses provide reasonable guidelines for determining which expenses are allowable.

Once the general average expenses have been determined and the values of the different contributory interests calculated, the general average contributions can be established. For example, if general average expenses total NOK 100,000 and the value of the contributing interests total NOK 1,000,000, the general average percentage will be 10%. This means that each interest must pay 10% of its value as a general average contribution.

The shipowner is personally liable for the ship's contribution when there is a maritime lien on the ship, ref. MC section 51 subsection 1 No. 5. In contrast, the cargo owner is not personally liable for his general average contribution, ref. MC section 465 subsection 1, but liability attaches to the cargo itself, and there is a maritime lien on the cargo, ref. MC section 61 No. 1. To ensure that the cargo's contribution is actually made, MC section 465 subsection 2 provides that the shipowner must not release the cargo to the cargo owner unless the cargo owner accepts personal liability and provides security.

§7. Proceedings

200. MC section 463 stipulates that a request for a general average adjustment should first come from the owner. However, if he fails to demand such statement within two weeks after the event, any person 'having a legal interest in the general average' may present a request for such adjustment.

MC section 464 imposes a duty on all persons having a legal interest in a general average adjustment 'to disclose without undue delay any information and produce any documents in his possession' which the adjuster may demand.

In MC section 466, certain rules are laid down as to how a party being dissatisfied with a general average adjustment may proceed in order to try to set it aside as incorrect. Such proceedings may be brought 'in the jurisdiction where the general average adjuster has his or her permanent place of business'.

Claims for contribution under a general average adjustment become time-barred one year after the date of the adjustment (MC section 501 No. 10).

Chapter 11. Particular Average

§1. GENERAL CONCEPTS

201. As we have seen, a general average is based upon the condition that one or more of the parties under a voyage has made a *sacrifice* in order to save as much as possible of the economic interests involved. A 'particular average' is, in contrast, an average where the damage has hit a particular interest – a cargo or a vessel.

As a general principle, the loss caused by such damage would lie where it falls. Unless there is a tortfeasor who has caused the loss by negligence (say by a collision), there would normally be no one to whom the owner of the property may turn to in order to receive compensation. Considering the seriousness of such losses, it becomes essential to seek protection of the risks through insurance. In order to achieve cover, there are certain pre-requisites which must be fulfilled:

(1) there must be a binding insurance agreement;
(2) the conditions must cover the incident and the perils involved; and
(3) the insured must not have forfeited his rights by his own behaviour.

202. In Norwegian law, several legal sources come into play in respect of the above. There is, first, the Act of 16 June 1989 No. 69 on *Insurance Agreements* (the IA Act). However, according to the IA Act section 1-3 subsection 2 letters (c) and (e), the stipulations of the statute are not mandatory when the insurance relates to a vessel which must be registered or to goods under an international transport.

Second, and more importantly, the NP of 2013 Version 2019 sets out the general conditions upon which insurances of vessels are undertaken. NP (which replaces the previous Norwegian plan of 1996) stipulates the perils insured against, the duties of the insured, the liability of the insurer, the settlement of claims and other related items in great detail. Although these terms in principle only represent standardized insurance conditions, NP has in many ways the impact of a statute. Both the systematic structure, the wording of the rules and the fact that NP has been prepared by and agreed to beforehand by representatives of both underwriters and shipowners, puts this codification of the marine insurance conditions in a unique position. As for cargo insurance, the *Conditions relating to Insurance for the Carriage of Goods* (CICG) (1995/amended 2004) have the same standing and serve the same purpose as NP does for the insurance of vessels.

Third, special terms will often be introduced in the individual insurance agreements. The premiums and the insurance amounts will also be stipulated in these agreements.

§2. Particular Average on Vessel

I. Definition

203. Particular average is a term which is used in general average statements, and it simply means that the expenses and losses caused by the 'average' in question are not recoverable in general average. However, this is a 'negative' description. Normally 'particular average' will be synonymous with *damage*. This latter word is also chosen as headline for NP Chapter 12, which deals with 'particular averages'.

Damage should be distinguished from total loss of the vessel. There is an actual total loss when the ship is lost without there being any prospect of it being recovered or when the ship is so badly damaged that she cannot be repaired, *see* NP section 11-1.

Damage and total loss are intertwined when the damage is so serious as to give the assured a right to claim that the ship be condemned. According to NP section 11-3, the conditions for condemnation are met when the damage is so extensive that the cost of repairing the ship will amount to at least 80% of the insurable value. Since there is no *actual* total loss, but only a total loss in an *economic* sense, the term 'constructive total loss' (CTL) is also used in such cases. NP Chapter 11 contains rules for the procedure and the pre-requisites for claiming condemnation and therefore the full insured value of the vessel.

II. Insurance

204. The purpose of insurance is to secure indemnification of the assured for losses suffered due to an average. The insured should preferably be placed in the same position as if the damage had not occurred. This is also the general principle in Norwegian law. The IA Act section 6-1 stipulates that the 'insured shall have full compensation for his economic loss'.

In NP, the main rule regarding damage is set forth in section 12-1 subsection 1: the insurer is liable for the costs of repairing the damage in such a manner that the ship is restored to the condition it was in prior to the occurrence of the damage. The costs encompass not only the actual repair yard invoice but also associated expenses which are necessary to have the repairs performed.

205. It follows from the main rule that the assured has a *right* to repair the vessel and have the costs of the repair covered. He cannot be forced to take a cash payment. However, it follows from NP section 12-2 subsection 1 that the assured may claim compensation in cash for the damage when the insurance period expires. Such a cash compensation is calculated on the basis of the estimated reduction in the market value of the ship due to the damage at the time of expiry, but shall not exceed the estimated costs of repair, *see* NP section 12-2 subsection 2. For practical purposes, the estimated costs of repairs will normally be decisive.

206. NP Chapter 12 contains three provisions, section 12-3, section 12-4 and section 12-5, regarding types of loss which are not covered if the ship is damaged. These rules operate in addition to the rules in the general section of NP regarding limitations on the recoverable losses, ref. especially section 4-2. Of the three provisions, section 12-3 is most important and most complicated. The section establishes that where a part or parts of the hull, machinery or equipment is in a defective condition as a result of listed perils – inadequate maintenance, wear and tear, corrosion, rot and the like – the insurer is *not* liable for the costs of renewing or repairing the relevant part or parts. In the case of a casualty, one must examine whether the parts to be repaired or renewed were in a defective condition prior to the casualty. Parts which were in sound condition prior to the casualty, shall be compensated, even where the breakdown of a part which was in defective condition was the actual cause of damage to these other parts. 'Inadequate maintenance' comprises primarily the situation where there has been negligence from the crew over a longer period of time which again has caused damage through wear and corrosion. The situation will not be considered inadequate maintenance where a part has been damaged or destroyed by a single omission or negligent act – the lack of supervision must have extended over some time. When it comes to the delimitation of the term 'part', the approach must be based on a technical/economic evaluation, where neither the size nor value of the relevant part will be of central importance. If a screw or bolt in the machinery has rusted to pieces and if it could have been changed without particular difficulty, only the expenses of renewing the screw or bolt will be excepted from cover. However, if it is technically or economically sensible to renew a larger component of the machinery, and not just the smaller part which itself was defective, it will be the relevant component which comprises a 'part' in the provision. Insofar as the evaluation of whether one or several parts were in 'proper condition' is concerned, the classification societies' minimum requirements will provide useful guidance.

NP section 12-4 regulates the insurer's liability where the relevant damage can be traced back to error in design or faulty material. The insurer is not liable for the costs of renewing or repairing the part or parts of the hull, machinery or equipment unless the part or parts in question has been approved by the classification society. The term 'faulty material' covers situations where the material has been of inferior quality, for example, due to a casting error. Error in design covers the situation where the ship has been given unsuitable form or inferior strength. It is irrelevant whether anyone can be blamed for the condition. Error in design is thus different from faulty workmanship, i.e., errors made by the last performing link in the production chain. Damage due to such error is not subject to any special rules regarding cover.

NP section 12-5 is considerably less complicated than section 12-3 and section 12-4. The provision contains a straight-forward listing of particular types of losses which the insurer will not cover in a damage situation, where the solutions to a considerable extent would already follow from an application of the main rule in section 12-1 subsection 1.

Because the exceptions in section 12-3 and section 12-4 are formulated so as to require causation (*see*, for example, section 12-4: 'if the damage is a result of error in design or faulty material'), the ordinary apportionment rule in NP section 2-13 will become applicable if the damage to the part in question is partially caused by a peril covered by the provisions (e.g., inadequate maintenance) and partially due to a peril which is covered by the insurance (e.g., adverse weather).

207. When it comes to actual *performance of repairs*, there are rules in sections 12-7 to 12-14. The damage will normally be surveyed by the insurer and the assured as quickly as possible, ref. NP section 12-10. The purpose of the survey is to determine, so far as possible, when and how the ship's damage arose, and at the same time evaluate the cost of repair. The incurred damages may be treated in different ways. If the damages are small, without affecting the ship's technical and operational safety, the assured will often find it most practical to postpone repair until the ship goes to a repair yard for maintenance work, class survey or the like. The assured may also find it sensible to delay permanent repair of more significant damage, in order to save valuable time. In such a case, it may be necessary to carry out temporary repairs, so that it can continue in service, ref. NP section 12-7 subsection 2.

In normal circumstances, tenders will be obtained from different repair yards, before final repair takes place, ref. NP section 12-11. The assured has the right to decide which yard shall be used, but the insurer's liability for the costs is normally limited to what it costs to carry out the repairs at the cheapest yard, ref. NP section 12-12 subsection 2.

It is not uncommon for the assured to make use of the time at the repair yard to carry out works not within the liability of the insurer. Such work may involve ordinary maintenance or repair of smaller damage which do not exceed the deductible. If expenses have been incurred which are common to both repair work for which the insurer is liable and work which is not covered by the insurance, NP section 12-14 establishes as a main rule that the expenses shall be 'apportioned on the basis of the cost of each category of work'.

The hull insurance only covers the assured's interest in the asset value of the ship, not its loss of earnings. The NP has, however, imposed on the hull insurer a duty to compensate the assured for part of the loss of time he would have avoided by selecting a more efficient (= faster) repair yard than the most inexpensive (= slower) yard, and by way of using time saving techniques and more costly methods. The rules regarding the cover of a portion of the assured's loss of time in connection with the choice of repair yard is found in NP section 12-12 subsection 2, while section 12-8 regulates the situation where the assured expedites the repair work by way of extraordinary measures so as to limit the loss of time. The borderline between ordinary measures, which are subject to full cover by the insurer, and extraordinary measures, for which he is only partially responsible, is difficult to establish, since one also has to take into account technological advances. NP section 12-7 subsection 2 applies the same solution in relation to temporary repairs which are not necessary to ensure the vessel's technical and operational safety. NP section 12-11 subsection 2 also contain a certain amount of cover for loss of time suffered by the assured. The actual loss of time suffered by the assured (or saved by special measures) under all the above-mentioned rules is assessed to 20% per annum of the hull valuation. Per day this amounts to 0.55 thousands of the hull valuation.

III. Settlement

208. NP Chapter 5 contains fairly complete rules regarding 'Settlement of Claims'. These rules are common for settlement of all marine insurance claims, and are not only applicable to hull insurance.

NP section 5-1 establishes the duty of the assured to provide 'such information and documents as are available to him'. Since it is the assured who has the burden of proof in establishing that he has a valid claim under his insurance policy, the aforementioned duty of providing documents may, at first sight, be thought to be obvious. The purpose is, however, to establish an obligation on the assured to give *all* the relevant information he may possess, and not only the material which supports his own claim. Indeed, according to NP section 5-1 subsection 2, 'the insurer is only liable to the extent he would have been liable if the assured had fulfilled his duty' in the said respect. When the material is collected 'the insurer shall issue the claims adjustment as promptly as possible' (NP section 5-2). However, in the meantime, the insured may need money to pay for obligations falling due in connection with repairs, etc. NP section 5-7 subsection 1 establishes a duty for the insurer to make payments in advance '[i]f the assured … proves that he has incurred, or will in the near future incur, major expenses or losses which are covered by the insurance.' However, the aforesaid 'rules do not apply if the insurer has reasonable doubts as regards his liability', *see* subsection 2.

209. The issuing of the claims adjustment is of importance in several respects. The main effect follows from NP section 5-6: 'Compensation is payable four weeks after the date when the claim adjustment is or should have been issued.' While the insurers are obliged to credit the assured with interests (CIBOR/NIBOR/STIBOR + 2% or LIBOR + 2%) from one month after the date on which notice of the casualty was sent to the insurer (NP section 5-4), this duty may be more severe after claims adjustment has been made. The insurer's obligation is then regulated by the separate *Act on Interest on Overdue Payments* of 17 December 1976 No. 100, if the interests stipulated therein are higher than CIBOR/NIBOR/STIBOR or LIBOR plus 2%.

There must be a separate adjustment for damage stemming from different averages. There are several reasons for this. A deductible is normally applicable for each incident. The re-insurers may be different under the various policies. The insurance sum is the limit for the insurers' liability for all losses flowing from one average. The insurers have a right to set-off in the settlement. This does not only apply to premiums due, but for any claim for which the assured is liable. However, in relation to a co-insured mortgagee, the right to set-off is limited to claims solely related to the insurance contract of the ship in question (NP section 7-4 subsection 6).

'The assured loses his right to claim compensation if notice of the casualty is not given to the insurer within six months of the assured, the master or the chief engineer of the ship becoming aware of it' (NP section 5-23 subsection 1). In any event, the assured loses his right to claim compensation other than for hull damage below the light waterline if notice of the casualty is not given to the insurer within twenty-four months of the date of the casualty, ref. NP section 5-23 subsection 2.

In addition, separate rules on limitation of claims are found in NP section 5-24. There is a separate time limit of three years, after which the claim becomes time-barred. The limitation period commences at the end of the calendar year during which the assured acquired the necessary knowledge of the facts on which the claim is based. In any event, the claim becomes time-barred at the latest ten years after the end of the calendar year during which the casualty took place. In all other respects, the rules contained in the *Limitations Act* of 18 May 1979 No. 18 will apply.

§3. Particular Average on Cargo

I. Definition

210. The cargo may be damaged or lost or there may be a shortage of quantity. Where the economic loss is not compensated via a general average adjustment(*see* paragraph Nos 189 et seq.), there is a particular average on cargo.

II. Insurance

211. An owner of cargo will normally expect that the cargo under transport will arrive safe and sound and in due time at its destination. If this does not happen, he may expect that the shipowner will be liable for the economic loss suffered.

However, as we have seen, a shipowner is not always liable for damage to or destruction of cargo. To be on the safe side, many cargo-owners therefore take out a separate insurance. Such policies may be entered into for one voyage only or for goods to be shipped in the course of a longer period, say during a year. In both cases, the main thing is that there be a binding insurance agreement, that the terms are adequate and that the right person or company is the beneficiary. In Norway, there are agreed standardized terms for insurance of goods, *CICG* (1995/amended 2004). Rules regarding the interests comprised under the insurance are found in CICG section 9. The provision takes as its starting point the person effecting the insurance. The insurance is to the benefit of this person and various others who have acquired a right to the goods from him, namely subsequent owners and secured parties who are assignees of the transport document for the goods, ref. CICG section 9 subsection 1. The scope of the insurance will thus depend on whether the seller or the buyer has effected the insurance. The structure of CICG section 9 causes the insurance to apply to the benefit of several parties over time, as well as simultaneously. If a casualty occurs, however, the insurer shall nonetheless only be liable for one sum insured per incident.

Cargo insurance is first and foremost property damage insurance which covers three types of loss, namely total loss, shortage and damage.

212. *Total loss* applies where the entire consignment of goods covered by the relevant insurance has been subjected to a particularly serious casualty, ref. CICG section 35 subsection 1. First of all, a total loss has arisen where the entire consignment of goods has been destroyed (No. 1). This will be the case where it is destroyed by fire, disintegrates, evaporates or is otherwise completely physically destroyed. Total loss also applies where the insured has been deprived of the entire consignment of goods without there being any possibility of retrieval (No. 2). The insured 'is deprived' of the goods, for example, where they have sunk, been stolen, confiscated or the like. There is no requirement that they be physically destroyed or damaged. The requirement regarding 'impossibility' can, on the other hand, not be considered to require certainty with respect to whether the insured will recover the consignment. If he has been deprived of the goods for a certain period of time without there being any indication that he will be able to retrieve them, they must be deemed a total loss. The length of time necessary will have to be determined in each individual case, taking into account the length of the transport and the locations involved. Total loss also applies pursuant to No. 3 where the transport has been abandoned in accordance with CICG section 27 or section 28. Finally, No. 4 contains a CTL rule: There is a total loss where the entire consignment has been so severely damaged that at least 90% of the value must be deemed lost.

In the case of a total loss, the insured can claim the sum insured so long as it does not exceed the insurable sum of the goods, ref. CICG section 35 subsection 2 first sentence. No deduction shall be made for damage incurred by the goods during the insurance period regardless of whether this damage is covered by the insurance or not, ref. CICG section 35 subsection 2 second sentence.

Shortage applies where a part of the insured consignment of goods is lost in the manner described in CICG section 35, ref. CICG section 36 subsection 1. In such an event, the insurer shall be liable for such proportion of the sum insured of the entire consignment as corresponds to the goods that have been lost, ref. CICG section 36 subsection 2 first sentence.

213. If the goods have been *damaged* during the transport, the insurance settlement and thus to some extent the scope of the insurer's liability will be affected by the insurer's decisions. The insurer may require that the damage be repaired in return of the costs of repair as they are incurred, ref. CICG section 37 subsection 1 first sentence. However, the insurer cannot require repair if this results in unreasonable loss or inconvenience for the assured, ref. CICG section 37 subsection 1 second sentence. A number of factors will be relevant in this evaluation, for example, the expected repair time and the type of goods involved. For so-called brand name articles intended to be sold to consumers, repair may seem unreasonable both because such repair would cause uncertainty regarding the damaged consignment as well as with regard to the 'brand name' itself. In such cases, the circumstances may very well allow the assured to collect compensation for total loss because the goods can no longer be sold and therefore do not have any value.

If the insurer does not or cannot require that the damage be repaired, CICG section 37 subsection 2 contemplates a cash payment established on the basis of a damage percentage. Such percentage shall reflect the final reduction in the value of the damaged goods; i.e., the relationship between the sales value in sound condition and damaged condition at destination.

If the damage percentage is assessed at 50% or more for goods intended for resale, the insurer has the right to demand that the damaged goods be sold and decide the sale procedure, ref. CICG section 37 subsection 3 first sentence. If the goods are perishable, the same applies even where the damage percentage does not exceed 50%, ref. CICG section 37 subsection 3 fourth sentence. In these cases, the compensation shall be fixed at the difference between the insurable value, or the sum insured if that is lower, and the price obtained from sale of the goods, ref. CICG section 37 subsection 3 second sentence. The sale must be requested without undue delay after the final survey report has been made available, ref. CICG section 37 subsection 3 third sentence, and the insurer's right to demand sale is subject to him taking reasonable account of the assured's interests, ref. CICG section 37 subsection 3 fifth sentence, which refers to CICG section 52.

III. Settlement

214. If the assured claims compensation for damage, or alternatively compensation for total loss because the consignment is more than 90% damaged, the goods shall be surveyed if either the insurer or the assured so requests, ref. CICG section 47 subsection 1. Such a survey shall be undertaken jointly by a representative of the assured and a representative of the insurer. As set forth in CICG section 47 subsection 2 second sentence, the survey shall provide a basis for determining the cause of damage, time of the occurrence, scope of damage, etc. and thus facilitate the determination of whether the damage falls within the scope of the insurer's cover and the amount recoverable. The report from the surveyors will also provide a basis for determining the insurer's right to require repair, ref. CICG section 37 subsection 1 and what damage percentage shall apply.

Prior to the survey, the goods shall as far as possible be grouped according to the nature and extent of the damage, ref. CICG section 47 subsection 2 first sentence. The grouping has direct relevance in relation to the compensation rules in CICG sections 35–37, because an individual damage percentage will be set for each group, as opposed to a collective damage percentage for the entire consignment of goods. Thus, if the damage percentage in individual groups exceeds 90%, it will allow the insured the right to a total loss compensation for the goods in the particular group pursuant to the rules on shortage in CICG section 36.

If the insurer pays a claim for total loss or shortage, he will be subrogated to the rights of the assured to the relevant goods, unless this right has been waived by the insurer when payment was made, ref. CICG section 52 subsection 1. The taking over of the property rights to the goods imposes certain obligations on the insurer, for example, he may be subjected to expenses relating to removal or destruction of the goods. When rights are taken over in relation to the goods, the insurer will also have to take into account the interests of the assured when disposing of the goods, ref. CICG section 52 subsection 2.

IV. Extra Expenses and Financial Losses

215. The owner of the goods may incur extra expenses if the goods are damaged or damage threatens. Under CICG section 25, with the title 'Duty of the Assured to minimise losses', the assured shall do what may reasonably be expected of him to avert or minimize the loss, if there is imminent danger that loss or damage will occur, or has occurred, ref. subsection 1 first sentence. If the insurer issues specific instructions, the assured is obliged to follow them, unless he must understand that they are based on incorrect or incomplete factual information.

The insurer shall be liable for the assured's salvage charges in accordance with the relevant rules in Insurance Contract Act (ICA) section 6-4, ref. CICG section 39 first sentence, unless the provisions of CICG section 40 on general average are applicable. In case of an international transit, however, the insurer shall not be liable for the assured liability for loss caused to a third party.

Chapter 12. Collisions

§1. Definition

216. MC Chapter 8 on collisions is first and foremost applicable when there is actual physical contact between two ships. It is irrelevant whether the ships are both underway or one of them is moored. It is also irrelevant whether the collision is caused by a ship which is moving under its own power or because of wind or currents. MC section 163 makes the provisions of MC Chapter 8 applicable also in cases 'when a ship by its manoeuvres or in similar ways causes damage to another ship or to persons or goods on board although no collision takes place between the ships' – typically: vessel A has to change course and is consequently damaged, because of vessel B's manoeuvres which are not in conformity with the Rules of the Road.

The term 'ship' should be read in the usual way. However, MC section 507 subsection 2 makes the rules of MC Chapter 8 applicable also to mobile drilling rigs and similar installations which are not otherwise considered to be ships.

§2. Statutory Provisions

I. Incorporation of Treaty Law

217. The rules covering collisions are found in MC Chapter 8. This chapter is based on the international convention from 1910. The convention, as well as MC Chapter 8, is based on the concept of fault as a condition for liability. The shipowner will only be liable to the other ship if he, or someone he is responsible for under MC section 151, is at fault.

The rules on collisions exclude the application of strict liability as developed by the Norwegian courts in other areas and they deviate from general Norwegian tort law in other respects as well. If an issue is not expressly dealt with by Chapter 8 rules, the rules must, however, be supplemented with general principles of Norwegian tort law.

II. The Basic Rules on Liability

218. A collision is often caused by the fault or neglect of one ship, while the other cannot be blamed. In such a case, the ship at fault is required to compensate the damage or loss thereby caused under MC section 161 subsection 1. Compensation must be provided for losses resulting from the collision, such as damage to the other ship, its cargo and passengers.

Nearly as frequently, both ships are at fault – a so-called both-to-blame collision. In such cases, the losses will be allocated in proportion to the amount of blame accorded to each ship or, to use the words of MC section 161 subsection 2 first sentence: 'in proportion to the faults committed on each side'. The total loss caused by the collision is thus determined and this loss is allocated based on an assessment of the degree of fault attributable to each ship.

The allocation of fault is discretionary, with the courts assigning liability on the basis of facts in each individual case. The customary proportions used are 1/2–1/2, 1/3–2/3 and 1/4–3/4. MC section 161 subsection 2 second sentence, however, establishes that the losses should be divided equally if the facts do not support any specific allocation.

Collisions between three or more ships are not regulated directly by MC section 161, but it is natural to apply its provisions by analogy where this is helpful. If only one ship is at fault, this ship will be wholly responsible for the total losses suffered by the other ships. If two ships are at fault, they will together be liable for the damage suffered by the third ship. There is an indication in case law that the ships at fault will be jointly and severally liable to the damaged ship. However, there is still no definite answer to the issue.

If the collision results from an unavoidable accident, meaning that neither ship is to blame, then each ship must bear its own losses (MC section 162 and ND 1971 36 NSC). This is also the case when the question of blame is left in doubt. The rule seems therefore to establish that the injured party has no claim for damages if there is no proven negligence on the part of the colliding ship.

The rules in MC Chapter 8 regarding the basis of liability must be supplemented by the ordinary tort rules on necessity, which in turn are based on the Torts Act section 1-4. Under these rules, a tortfeasor is obliged to compensate for losses caused through attempts to save his own property from imminent danger. The idea is that the act of damage is deliberate although justified or excused from punishment otherwise imposed under criminal law.

219. There are no special rules regulating collisions between ships and other structures, such as bridges and docks. The liability of a shipowner in such circumstances must be determined under ordinary tort rules. If such a collision is caused by the shipowner's fault, or by someone he is liable for under MC section 151, the shipowner will normally be liable. This is also the case if the collision can be traced to an act of necessity covered by the Torts Act section 1-4. The more difficult question is whether the shipowner also may become liable under the rules on strict liability established in case law. In two instances, the Supreme Court has imposed strict liability on shipowners whose ships collided with a bridge and a dock respectively, following technical problems with the reverse engines (ND 1921 401 NSC and ND 1952 320 NSC). The courts, however, have not been willing to impose strict liability in cases where docks, bridges, etc. have been damaged by ships without there having been technical failure (ND 1958 587 NCA). If a ship has collided with a structure other than a bridge, dock, etc., the courts have not imposed strict liability, even in the presence of technical failure or impropriety (ND 1973 348 NSC, where a submerged submarine ran into and damaged the trawl of a trawler).

III. The Evaluation of Fault

220. The provisions of MC provide little guidance concerning the evaluation of fault, except for MC section 161 fifth paragraph: 'When determining the question of fault, the court shall especially consider whether or not there was time for deliberation.' However, this is only of slight assistance, because the question of time would, in any case, be central to the evaluation of fault.

The evaluation of fault must be approached in the same way as questions of negligence in ordinary tort law. The judge must decide whether the act or omission which was a cause of the collision can be considered reasonable or acceptable in the light of what could be expected from a normally insightful person in such a situation. In reaching his decision, the judge will be assisted by written rules of conduct in the particular field, as found in legislation or public regulations, or in acknowledged customary rules. He will also have to evaluate the risks involved in the act or omission, in other words how great a risk there was that the accident might occur, and how serious the damage in such a case could be expected to be. Whether or not there were sufficient time and possibility to prevent the accident will also be an important factor. In principle, the assessment of fault is objective, and subjective individual elements – such as the crew's tiredness, inexperience, age, etc. – will normally be disregarded.

221. Imperative to the determination of negligence are the *International Rules for Preventing Collisions at Sea* (COLREGs; the *Rules of the Road*), which were adopted as a convention of the IMO in 1972.

The SSSA section 14 subsection 2 litra (a) provides a legal basis for the Ministry to promulgate rules for safe navigation, including Rules of the Road. This authority has been delegated to the Maritime Directorate, which has promulgated regulations of 1 December 1975 No. 5, wherein the international Rules of the Road were incorporated into Norwegian law.

The Rules of the Road have much in common with traffic rules on land. They attempt to regulate travel at sea by setting up rules of action, for example when navigating in reduced visibility. If a collision results from a violation of one of the rules, fault will normally be established.

Special mention should be made of some of the rules. Rule 17 requires the stand-on vessel to maintain its course and speed. It has, however, a right to make precautionary manoeuvres to avoid collision if the ship obliged to yield does not appear to be doing so. The right to take precautionary action becomes a duty, if the ships are so close that a collision cannot be avoided solely by precautionary action by the ship obliged to give way, see as examples ND 2001 157 NSC and ND 1967 180 NSC. Rule 19 imposes duties on both ships when navigating in restricted visibility, see as an example ND 2000 515 NSC. Rule 5 imposes a duty to maintain 'adequate lookout', see as an example ND 2001 254 NCA. Rule 6 requires a vessel to proceed at 'safe speed' at all times, so that it can manoeuvre correctly and effectively to avoid collision and be stopped at a distance which is appropriate to the prevailing circumstances and conditions, see as an example ND 2006 417 NCA. In order to simplify the evaluation of a safe speed, the rule also lists a series of factors which must be considered. These include visibility, traffic density, manoeuvring ability, stopping distance, weather and current conditions, etc. There are also special rules for ships equipped with radar.

222. Violation of other public regulations may also be relevant in the determination of negligence. The *SSSA* and associated regulations contain rules regarding the safety of ships, and violation of these rules can result in a finding of negligence (fault). An example would be where a collision has been caused by a ship's poor manoeuvring ability resulting from overloading in regard to SSSA section 12 and associated regulations. Another example would be where the crew is not sufficiently trained or competent, *see* SSSA section 16.

IV. Liability for Cargo Claims

223. In a collision between ship A and ship B, the cargo on board A may be damaged. If A is solely to blame, the cargo's claim against A will depend upon the rules in MC sections 275 et seq., and in most cases, this leads to non-liability based upon the exemption for navigational faults in section 276 subsection 1 No. 1. If B is solely responsible for the collision the cargo's claim against B will depend upon the rules in MC Chapter 8.

224. The situation is more complex when both ships are to blame. Where there are several tortfeasors, the rule under general Norwegian tort law is that they are all jointly and severally liable to the injured party, ref. Torts Act section 5-3. In other words, the injured party may sue any of the tortfeasors for the whole amount of his loss. However, the collision convention and MC resolve the question differently. MC section 161 subsection 3 first sentence imposes liability pro rata, i.e., each ship is only liable for damage in proportion to its own degree of fault.

The pro rata liability rule, together with the fact that there can often be no cargo claim against the carrying ship (*see* above), makes the cargo owner's legal position rather weak compared to what it would be under general tort law: The cargo on board ship A can only get a partial compensation from ship B. The best rationale for this solution is that joint and several liability would result in complicated recourse and indemnification claims.

V. Liability for Personal Injury

225. If there has been personal injury and both ships were to blame, 'they are jointly and severally liable', ref. MC section 161 subsection 3 second sentence. An injured passenger on vessel B can thus sue ship A for full damages, although ship A may only be partially to blame for the collision. Social policy considerations and protection of personal injury claims underlie this deviation from the pro rata liability applying to cargo claims. The extent to which the injured passenger on ship B can pursue ship B will be determined by the rules relating to carriage of passengers in MC Chapter 15 or similar rules in other jurisdictions.

The degree of fault is therefore only relevant where a party presents a recourse claim. Section 161 subsection 4 first sentence establishes that there is a right of recourse where a party has paid more than his share. This means that there is no basis for a recourse claim unless one of the parties has covered a greater portion of the injured party's claim than that which corresponds to the amount for which it was to blame. If the ships are equally at fault, ship A only has a claim against ship B if it has covered more than half the total damage. A cannot demand a contribution simply because he has covered his proportion of damage, while B, for whatever reason, has paid nothing.

MC section 161 subsection 4 second sentence places a few restrictions on recourse demands. The party from whom a contribution is sought may 'invoke the same right to exemption from or limitation of liability as it would have been entitled to in relation to the injured party by virtue of the law applicable to the relation between it and the injured party, or by virtue of any valid contractual exemption clause'. The latter applies only to the extent that it does not result in exemption or limitation of liability beyond the mandatory rules on liability for passengers in MC Chapter 15 or corresponding rules in foreign law, *see* MC section 161 subsection 4 third sentence. This means that the colliding ship may be required to pay a greater portion of damages than that which follows from the extent of its fault. This would be the case, for example, when the transporting ship can invoke the limitation rule in MC section 422 against the injured passenger.

VI. The Determination of Damages

226. The MC does not contain specific rules for determining damages, except for the rules on limitation of liability (MC sections 171 et seq.). Thus, general tort law principles must be considered in determining what damages are recoverable. These principles establish that an injured party has a claim for compensation provided that the loss is sufficiently proximate. In practice, a series of complex problems arise which necessitate careful consideration. Most of these problems have parallels in non-maritime law.

Questions may arise as to *who* may claim damages (e.g., is the charterer entitled to present a claim for delay suffered through a collision) and *how* the claims should be calculated, both in connection with what items may be included (a shipowner loses a favourable time charter after a collision) and practical questions regarding the calculation (e.g., how the time lost should be established in a given situation).

VII. Procedure

227. Most shipowners have insurance which covers their liability in relation to collisions. Hull insurance, which is primarily insurance covering property damage, covers (with a few significant exceptions) a shipowner's tort liability resulting from a collision, ref. NP 2013 version 2019 section 13-1, to the amount for which the ship is insured, ref. NP 2013 version 2019 section 13-3. The most important exceptions in the hull insurance policy will be covered by the shipowner's ordinary liability insurance – his P&I insurance.

Most shipowners and many cargo-owners have insurance which covers loss or damage to their ship or cargo. On payment of a claim under the insurance, the insurer is subrogated to the assured's claim against third parties, ref. for cargo claims CICG 2004 section 53 subsection 1 first sentence. The insurer steps into the shoes of the assured. After settlement with his insurer, the assured will therefore often have little economic interest in pursuing claims against the liable party. It will mainly be the insurers who are interested in possible recourse claims. Although formally acting in the name of the assured, it will, in fact, be the underwriters who are behind and who direct the litigation following a collision.

228. Their first consideration will then be where it will be possible to commence proceedings. There may be several alternatives: First of all, one may start proceedings in the state(s) where the vessel(s) are registered, i.e., the flag state. Second, a case may be opened in the state in whose territorial water the collision took place. However, it may also be relevant where the vessels' managements are situated. If liability for cargo and passengers are involved, their respective home countries may also enter the picture.

In choosing between the alternatives, practical questions also arise. How is the legal system developed in the various countries, what will it cost to litigate and what are the prospects of being awarded costs?

The most important issue usually will be to establish the *law* governing the dispute and where such law most likely will give a favourable result. Perhaps the claim is already time-barred under the law of one of the states to be considered. But even after litigation has started, the law to be applied may be an open question: this is due to the fact that in many collision cases, the court will apply foreign law, according to the principles of international private law.

The NSC stated in a maritime case that 'a case should preferably be decided according to the law of that country to which it has its strongest links' (ND 1923 289 NSC). In the case, two Norwegian vessels collided in English territorial water. The collision was partly due to an error made by a compulsory pilot. The question came up as to whether the liability for the pilot's mistake should be based on English or Norwegian law. The Supreme Court decided in favour of the latter.

229. The Norwegian insurance companies or P&I clubs will normally be reinsured to a larger or minor extent. If the underwriters for both the vessels have reinsured in the same market, it may be the re-insurers who decide whether proceedings should be commenced, and/or continued. It was reportedly English re-insurers who decided that the matter should be settled and further litigation stopped, after the tragic collision between the Swedish passenger vessel *Stockholm* and the Italian cruise vessel *Andrea Doria* in 1953.

230. The victim of a collision has reasonably good security for his claim. Tort claims against the shipowner are secured by a maritime lien on the ship (MC section 51 Nos 3–4).

VIII. Limitation of Liability

231. The shipowner is entitled to limit his liability incurred by a collision. This applies both to liability for personal claims, e.g., passengers, and to physical damage. The rules are set out in Chapter 4 above.

Chapter 13. Marine Pollution

§1. Introduction

232. During the last fifty years, there has been increasing awareness of the importance of avoiding environmental pollution. There are now rules, both at a national and international level, designed to protect the environment on land and at sea. First, there are rules aimed at avoiding incidents which may cause pollution. Second, there are rules dealing with such incidents, so that pollution is avoided, or at least minimized. Finally, there are rules which ensure that liability can be ascertained and compensation paid for damage, loss and expenses incurred as a result of pollution or threatened pollution.

Shipping is a serious source of pollution. Environmental problems arise primarily in connection with oil spills and the discharge of other substances. These discharges are to some extent associated with the daily operations of a ship. However, discharges also occur as a result of accidents such as groundings, collisions, fires and explosions.

§2. Statutory Provisions: Sources of Law

233. The main piece of Norwegian legislation concerning pollution is the *PA of 13 March 1981 No. 6*. This Act is essentially all-encompassing and applies to all types of pollution without regard to source. In addition to the PA, there are individual rules dealing with particular sources of pollution. In case of conflict, these specialized rules will generally have priority; but such rules may be supplemented by the PA unless the specialized rules are designed to preempt the particular issue.

Central in the efforts of overcoming the pollution problems in the shipping industry is the International Convention for the Prevention of Pollution from Ships of 2 November 1973, as amended in 1978 (*MARPOL 1973/78*). MARPOL 1973/78 is incorporated into Norwegian law through the *SSSA of 16 February 2007 No. 9* Chapter 5, *see* Regulation of 1 June 2004 No. 931 (with later revisions) regarding the Limitation of Pollution, Chapters 20–23 and the general provisions in Chapter 41. This regulation implements important parts of the convention.

The following presentation focuses primarily on the rules regarding liability for oil pollution arising from ships (§3.I. below). Most important in this respect is on the one hand the Liability Convention (CLC) 1992 and the Fund Convention 1992, together with the Supplementary Fund Protocol 2003, all applying to ships carrying oil in bulk, and on the other hand, the Bunker Convention from 2001, applying to any seagoing vessel. These conventions/protocols have all been incorporated into Norwegian law through *MC Chapter 10*.

In *MC Chapter 11*, rules on liability where damage is caused by HNS have been introduced (§3.II. below). The rules are based on the HNS Convention 2010 and will come into force when the convention is put to force.

As regards other environmental damage caused by ships, the ordinary maritime rules presented in Chapter 4 will apply. However, these rules are modified by the provisions of the PA of 13 March 1981 No. 6 (§3.III. below).

As regards pollution from the offshore petroleum activity on the Norwegian continental shelf, the *Petroleum Act* of 19 November 1996 No. 72 Chapter 7 regulates the liability questions (§3.IV. below).

§3. Sources of Pollution and Related Liability

I. Oil pollution from Ships

234. The Torrey Canyon disaster in 1967, when 120,000 tonnes of oil escaped and caused major pollution on the coasts of England and France, provoked a quick response from both the public and private (shipowners and oil companies) sectors. Directly or indirectly, it resulted in the creation and subsequent adoption of four international conventions, all of which were ratified by Norway.

235. First, attention should be given to MARPOL 1973/1978. The most important substantive rules contained in the convention can be found in six very detailed annexes with related appendices. The titles of the annexes are as follows:

- Regulations for the prevention of pollution by oil.
- Regulations for the control of pollution by noxious liquid substances in bulk.
- Regulations for the prevention of pollution by harmful substances carried by sea in packaged form, or in freight containers, portable tanks or road and rail tank wagons.
- Regulations for the prevention of pollution by sewage from ships.
- Regulations for the prevention of pollution by garbage from ships.
- Regulations for the prevention of air pollution from ships.

236. Second, the 1969 'Intervention' convention should be noted. This gives the coastal states involved a right to take necessary steps where an accident on the high seas causes pollution. This convention is now incorporated into PA section 74 subsection 5 and the appurtenant regulation dated 19 September 1997 No. 1061.

Third, a convention on questions of liability for the polluter was agreed to; the so-called CLC Convention of 1969.

Finally, the Fund Convention 1971 aimed to establish an international liability fund.

In December 1992, new protocols to the CLC and Fund Conventions were approved, replacing the unratified 1984 protocols. The revised conventions are called the *Liability Convention* (CLC) 1992 and the *Fund Convention* 1992. They have been ratified, *inter alia*, by the Nordic countries, and came into force on 30 May 1996.

In addition to the aforementioned conventions, Norway has also adhered to the *Ospar Convention* of 22 September 1992. This convention is a merger of the two previous Oslo and Paris conventions. Its purpose is to prevent pollution in the North-Eastern Atlantic. There are five annexes to the Ospar Convention. These regulate land-based outlets, dumping and incineration, offshore activities, supervision and ecosystems and biological diversity. Norway ratified the Ospar Convention on 8 September 1995, and it was implemented on 25 March 1998 (*see* §3.V. below).

Recent experiences have demonstrated that bunker pollution from non-tankers can cause considerable local pollution. Previously such pollution was not covered by the international rules, but the Bunker Convention 2001, which came into force in 2008, has changed this position.

237. As for oil pollution damage from laden tankers, the relevant rules in Norway are found in MC Chapter 10.II, sections 191–209.

According to MC section 191 subsection 1 first sentence, a shipowner who transports oil as bulk cargo is *strictly liable* for oil pollution damage. Under MC section 192 subsection 1, the shipowner is exempted from liability in three force majeure situations:

(1) if he can prove that the damage was caused by an act of war or a similar action in an armed conflict, civil war or insurrection or by a natural phenomenon of an exceptional, inevitable and irresistible character (litra (a));
(2) if he can prove that the damage was entirely caused by an act or omission by a third party with intent to cause damage (litra (b)); and
(3) if he can prove that the damage was entirely caused by the negligence or other wrongful act by a public authority in connection with the maintenance of lights or other navigational aids (litra (c)).

If the injured party has deliberately or negligently contributed to the damage, the liability may be reduced in accordance with general tort law (MC section 192 subsection 2). The concept of 'oil pollution damage' is defined in MC section 191 subsection 2. In addition to the actual loss or damage caused by the pollution, the concept also encompasses expenses, damage and loss arising as a result of reasonable measures taken to avoid or limit damage after the occurrence which has caused imminent and significant risk of such damage.

238. The party strictly liable pursuant to MC section 191 is the shipowner. Shipowner means the entity listed as owner in the ship registry, ref. subsection 5. Consequently, a bareboat charterer will not be considered as owner even if he nautically operates the vessel.

The owner can only be made liable for oil pollution damage according to the provisions of MC Chapter 10, *see* MC section 193 subsection 1. An injured party cannot, therefore, pursue the shipowner under a different basis of liability if his loss is not covered by the convention-based rules.

Convention-based liability for oil pollution damage is essentially channelled to the owner of the ship. MC section 193 subsection 2 prevents the injured party from pursuing other potentially responsible parties, for example, where the pollution was caused by their negligent conduct. The rationale for channelling liability is that the interests of the injured party are protected by the extensive and well-secured strict liability imposed on the shipowner. Another factor is the uncertainty that possible exposure to liability would cause for other parties involved, as well as the need for insurance that would arise. The protection provided by the MC, however, is not complete. The injured party is free to sue parties other than the owner if the damage resulted from their personal act or omission, committed with an intent to cause such damage, or through gross negligence and with knowledge that such damage would probably result.

The protected parties are: a member of the crew, anyone employed by the owner, and others the owner will be liable for (litra (a)); the pilot or any other person performing services for the ship (litra (b)); the ship operator ('reder') or manager (when these entities do not own the ship), and any charterer, sender, shipper, owner or receiver of cargo (litra (c)); any person performing salvage operations with the consent of the owners or under instructions from a public authority (litra (d)); any person taking preventive measures to avoid or limit damage or loss as mentioned in section 191 (litra (e)); and, finally, any person who is either employed by persons mentioned in litras (b)-(e) or for whom these persons are liable (litra (f)). The scope of the protected group is based on the provisions of the CLC, with the exception that the Convention does not mention the sender, shipper, owner or receiver of the cargo. The tortfeasors protected from direct claims from injured parties are also protected from indemnity claims from the shipowner, with one exception, ref. MC section 193 subsection 3: persons mentioned in litra (c) are not protected against recourse actions.

239. Special limitation rules apply to convention-based liability for oil pollution damage from tankers. The owner's liability is limited to 631 SDR per tonne for all liability arising in connection with the same event, but with minimum and maximum amounts, ref. MC section 194 subsection 1. The minimum amount of liability, which is 4.51 million SDR, applies to ships not exceeding 5,000 tonnes. The maximum amount of liability is 89.7 million SDR. The reference to tonnage means gross tonnage, calculated in accordance with the International Convention on Tonnage Measurement of Ships of 1969, ref. MC section 194 subsection 4 second sentence. There is no limit on the owner's liability for interest and legal costs (MC section 194 subsection 2, second sentence).

The owner is not entitled to limit liability if the pollution which caused the damage resulted from his personal act or omission, committed with an intent to cause such damage, or through gross negligence and with knowledge that such damage would probably result (MC section 194 subsection 3, second sentence).

If the owner wishes to limit liability in accordance with MC section 194, he must establish a limitation fund in the court at which the action has been brought or can be brought, ref. MC section 195 subsection 1 first sentence. Thus, a fund may be constituted even if a claim for compensation has not been raised in court. The fund must be for the full amount of potential liability pursuant to MC section 194, ref. MC section 232 subsection 3.

240. The owners of a ship carrying more than 2,000 tonnes of oil as bulk cargo are required to have approved insurance or similar security covering liability under the convention rules, ref. MC sections 197–200. Normally, this requirement will be satisfied through the owner's P&I insurance. A certificate must be issued confirming that the compulsory insurance or other security is in place.

The injured party has an unconditional right to bring his claim under the convention-based rules directly against the insurer (MC section 200 subsection 1 first sentence). The insurer may rely on the same defences that are available to the owner, ref. MC section 200 subsection 1 third sentence; in addition, the insurer can limit his liability pursuant to MC section 194, even if the owner has lost his right to limitation, ref. MC section 200 subsection 1. In contrast, the insurer cannot defend a claim on the basis of defences available in the insurance contract with the owner, except if the damage was caused by wilful misconduct by the owner himself, ref. MC section 200 subsection 1 fourth sentence.

241. Payments from the international compensation funds may be triggered in situations where the damage caused by pollution is covered by the convention-based rules on liability for tankers. The MC does not contain any rules relating to the liability of the compensation fund, but the Fund Convention 1992 and the Supplementary Fund Convention 2003 are given direct legal effect in Norway, ref. MC section 201 subsection 1 second sentence.

The two funds can become liable to parties who have suffered damage or loss in connection with oil pollution and who have not received full compensation for their loss under the rules in MC sections 191–196 and 200, ref. MC section 201 subsection 1 first sentence. For the funds to be liable, damage caused by pollution must have arisen in the territory (including the territorial sea) or the economic zone of a state which has ratified the Fund Convention 1992, or measures must have been taken to prevent or minimize such damage.

Liability to injured parties can arise in three situations:

(1) where the shipowner is not liable because of the exceptions in MC section 192;
(2) where the shipowner and his insurer are financially not able to cover the liability; and
(3) where the damage exceeds the owner's limitation on liability pursuant to MC section 194.

The funds are nonetheless exempt from liability if it can be proved that the damage was caused by an act of war or in a warlike situation or if the injured party cannot prove that the damage was caused by the discharge of oil from one or more vessels.

The compensation fund covers amounts up to 203 million SDR per incident. If the injured parties have not been fully compensated by the compensation fund because the damage exceeds its limitation amount, the supplementary fund will cover amounts up to 750 million SDR.

242. The Bunker Convention 2001 has been incorporated in MC Chapter 10.I (sections 183–190). The rules apply to any seagoing vessel or seaborne craft, ref. MC section 183 subsection 3, with the exception that the rules do not apply to pollution damage which is covered by MC section 191 subsection 2, i.e., pollution damage falling within the scope of the rules regarding convention-based oil pollution liability for tankers, ref. MC section 183 subsection 10.

MC section 183 subsection 1 first sentence establishes that the 'shipowner' is liable for pollution damage caused by bunker oil regardless of fault. However, the rules regarding exemptions from strict liability are the same as in connection with oil pollution liability for tankers, ref. MC section 184, which refers to section 192.

The term 'shipowner' is defined in MC section 183 subsection 5, stating that it is to be interpreted as the owner, including the registered owner, the 'reder', the bareboat charterer, the managing owner or others responsible for central functions relevant to the running of a ship.

As regards channelling of liability, it follows from the reference in MC section 185 second sentence to the rules in MC section 193 subsections 2 and 3 that the rules on channelling there will apply to a bunker oil spill as well. However, an important exception should be noted: To the extent persons covered by the rules in MC section 193 subsections 2 and 3 also fall within the definition of a 'shipowner' in MC section 183 subsection 5, the rules regarding channelling of liability do not apply to them. In other words, they will be liable for the claim in the ordinary course.

When it comes to limitation of liability, MC section 185 subsection 2 expressly establishes that the shipowner has a right to limit pursuant to the rules in MC Chapter 9 – the so-called global limitation rules. The higher limitation amounts in MC section 175a, compare section 172a, will normally be relevant.

243. According to MC section 186, an insurance obligation is imposed on the registered owner regarding his liability for bunker pollution. Others who are encompassed by the term 'shipowner' are not obliged to carry insurance. It is also a requirement that the ship must have gross tonnage in excess of 1,000 tonnes. The insurance shall cover liability up to the liability limits established in the Limitation Convention of 1976, as modified by the Protocol of 1996. The fact that Norway has established higher limitation limits for wreck removal, *see* MC section 175a, has no impact on the scope of the insurance obligation. In practice, this does not create problems as long as the ship carries an ordinary P&I insurance. Such P&I insurance will normally cover any excess portion of the liability under MC section 175a. The claimant has an unfettered right to pursue his claim for damages under the convention-based rules on bunker pollution liability directly against the insurer, *see* MC section 188 subsection 1 first sentence. The insurer can invoke the legal defences available to the registered owner, *see* MC section 188 subsection 2 first sentence, and may limit liability pursuant to MC Chapter 9, even where the registered owner has lost his right to limitation, *see* MC section 188 subsection 1 second sentence. However, the insurer cannot invoke insurance-related defences against the claimant which he could have invoked against the registered owner, *see* MC section 188 subsection 2 second sentence. There is one exception: The insurer can invoke the defence that the damage was caused by the wilful misconduct of the registered owner personally, *see* MC section 188 subsection 2 third sentence.

II. HNS Liability for Ships

244. HNS carried as cargo on board ships can be the cause of many kinds of loss and damage. Some substances are highly inflammable or explosive, others exude poisonous gases and others still can cause damage to the environment if they escape from the ship.

In 1996 the IMO adopted a separate convention concerning liability and compensation for damage in connection with the carriage of HNS the HNS Convention. There were difficulties, however, in achieving international acceptance of the Convention and thus it never came into effect. IMO chose to produce a protocol to the Convention which modified it in individual points. The protocol was adopted in 2010 and together with the 1996 Convention was called the HNS Convention 2010. As of January 2019 the Convention has not come into force.

Norway passed legislation based on the amended HNS -convention in 2015 (new Chapter 11 in the MC). The legislation will come into force together with the HNS convention itself.

245. The legal scope for the rules concerning HNS liability in MC Chapter 11 are contained partly in the definitions in section 211 and partly in individual provisions in section 212.

The provisions in MC Chapter 11 are to apply in the case of a ship undertaking transport by sea carrying hazardous goods (HNS substances). The concept of a ship is wide and includes 'any seagoing vessel or other mobile seagoing craft', see section 211 subsection 2. With regard to what is meant by the concept 'hazardous goods' the answer is to be found in subsection 1. It varies between goods which are being carried in bulk, called HNS in bulk, see letters a) to c) and letters e) to h) and goods which are being carried in packaged form, called packaged HNS, see letter d). HNS in bulk includes oil, noxious liquid substances, hazardous liquid substances, liquified gases, liquid inflammable substances, solid bulk cargoes with particular chemical characteristics and residues of substances from previous carriage of those substances.

The geographical scope of the rules concerning HNS liability in MC Chapter 11 are to be found in MC section 227.The rules are more complicated than the corresponding rules for oil pollution liability in MC section 206, primarily because the HNS rules deal with all kinds of damage whereas the oil pollution liability rules deal only with pollution damage.

246. The owner of a ship which carries hazardous goods has strict liability for damage caused by the goods insofar as the damage can be attributed to the hazardous characteristics of the goods, *see* MC section 212 subsection 1 first sentence. However, In the same way as with liability for oil pollution and for bunker oil pollution there are three exceptions, *see* MC section 213 subsection 1, which gives the rules in section 192 equivalent application for HNS liability. In addition MC section 214 subsection 2 has its own exception. The shipowner is exempted from liability if he can prove that he was not given information about the goods' HNS characteristics and that the absence of information has led to him not obtaining the insurance required by MC section 218.

Strict liability applies to the damage caused. MC section 212 subsection 2, amplified in subsection 3 sets out what is included in the concept of damage. There are four different categories. The first concerns loss of life or personal injury, *see* letter a). In this instance it is in principle immaterial whether the damage has occurred on or off the ship, but see the reservation in subsection 3 letter c). The second category concerns loss of or damage to property, *see* letter b). It is only property not on board the ship which is relevant, but the reservation in subsection 3 letter c) will apply here as well. The third category is loss or damage caused by pollution of the environment, *see* letter c). The fourth category, *see* letter d), are the expenses of reasonable measures taken to avoid or minimize the damage referred to in letters a) to c). If it cannot be shown clearly whether damage has been caused by HNS goods or by some other means then in principle all of the damage will be regarded as caused by the HNS goods, *see* subsection 4.

247. The responsible person in respect of the strict liability under MC Chapter 11 is the shipowner, *see* MC section 212 subsection 1. The definition of the shipowner in MC section 211 subsection 4 tallies with the definition in § 191 subsection 5. Claims for compensation against the shipowner can only be made validly under the rules in MC Chapter 11, *see* section 214 subsection 1.

HNS liability is channelled to the shipowner to a significant extent. In the same way as with the bunker oil pollution rules, MC section 214 subsection 2 gives the provisions in section 193 subsections 2 and 3 corresponding application for HNS liability. There is a significant exception, however: The shipper, consignee, owner or receiver of the cargo are not protected against claims for compensation, *see* subsection 2 second sentence, nor against claims for recourse from the shipowner, *see* first sentence.

248. There are special limitation rules for HNS liability, *see* MC section 215. The rules differ according to whether the damage is caused by HNS in bulk or by packaged HNS. The owner's liability in respect of HNS in bulk is limited to 1500 SDR per ton for ships under 50,000 tons and to 360 SDR per ton for bigger ships. The minimum liability for ships under 2,000 tons is 10 million SDR, *see* subsection 1, whereas the maximum liability for all ships is 100 million SDR, *see* subsection 2. The limitation amounts for packaged HNS are somewhat higher, *see* subsections 3 and 4: the liability for ships under 50,000 tons is 1725 SDR per ton, for bigger ships 414 SDR per ton, the minimum liability is 11.5 million SDR and the maximum 115 million SDR. The limitation applies to all HNS liability in connection with the same incident or series of incidents with the same cause, *see* subsection 5 first sentence. Legal costs and interest for delays on the limited amount must be paid in full, *see* second sentence.

The right to limit liability is lost if the owner himself has caused the HNS damage deliberately or by gross negligence and with knowledge that such damage would probably arise, *see* subsection 6.

If the owner wishes to limit his liability, he must establish a limitation fund. The fund must be set up in the court where the claim is being or can be brought, *see* MC section 216 subsection 1. The fund must correspond to the amount of liability pursuant to MC section 215, *see* MC section 232 subsection 5. The fund must be divided pro rata between all claims arising out of the same incident, *see* subsection 2. There is one important exception to this, however: A claim in connection with loss of life or personal injury is preferential, although only within a framework of two-thirds of the total amount of the fund.

249. Under MC section 212 the shipowner is obliged to have obtained insurance or established other security which covers his HNS liability up to the limits which follow from MC section 215, *see* MC section 218 subsection 1 first sentence. It is not a precondition for the obligation to insure that the ship has in fact hazardous goods on board. Pursuant to the third sentence a certificate must be issued which confirms that the necessary insurance or other security has been effected. The ship is not entitled to sail under Norwegian flag without such a certificate, *see* fourth sentence.

A claim for compensation in respect of HNS damage can be made directly against the insurer, *see* MC section 220 subsection 1 first sentence. As regards the insurer's tort law and insurance law defences, these are the same as in an injured party's direct claim against an insurer under MC section 200, *see* third sentence. It is expressly stated in the first sentence that the insurer is entitled to limit liability even in circumstances where the owner has no such right.

The insurer can establish a limitation fund with the same effect as if it had been established by the owner, *see* subsection 2.

250. In addition to compensation which an injured party can obtain from the shipowner or the insurer, he has an entitlement also to make a claim against the HNS fund to the extent that it is necessary to cover his loss or damage. No provisions concerning the liability of the HNS fund have been incorporated into MC, instead section 221 subsection 1 establishes that Chapter 3 of the HNS Convention is effective as Norwegian law.

The liability of the fund is designed in the same way as that in the compensation fund for oil pollution. The combined liability of the owner and the HNS fund on an individual incident totals 250 million SDR. If this is not sufficient to cover all the claims which have been presented, the amount will be divided pro rata between the injured parties. The preferential right for claims arising out of death and personal injury in the owner's limitation fund is the same, however.

The HNS fund is financed by duties from receivers of HNS goods, *see* MC section 222. The rules are complicated and not easy to grasp. The main principle arises out of subsection 1: Receivers of more than 20,000 tons HNS in bulk in any one calendar year are obliged to pay a duty to the fund. The obligation to pay the duty applies to both national and international carriage. The size of the duty is set by the HNS fund organization. The main rule will lapse if one of the special rules in subsection 2 or 3 comes into effect. It should be noted that receivers of packaged HNS are not subject to duty. Duty will only be demanded by the fund after an incident has occurred which requires payments out of the fund.

III. Other Environmental Liability

251. In the case of other environmental damage, the basis for decisions are the ordinary maritime rules on tort liability presented in Chapter 4 above. However, these rules are modified by the provisions of the PA of 13 March 1981 No. 6 (PA) Chapter 8.

252. The PA section 53 subsection 4 establishes that PA Chapter 8, which deals with liability for damage caused by pollution, applies to cases of pollution and garbage-dumping from ships insofar as the question of liability is not specifically regulated in other legislation. Within the geographic scope of the Chapter, *see* section 54, any party who performs activities which cause pollution damage, i.e., generally the shipowner, will be strictly liable for such damage, *see* PA section 55 subsection 1. Others who have contributed to the damage are also potentially liable if they have acted wilfully or negligently, *see* PA section 55 subsection 2. In other words, there is no channelling of liability. The identity of the parties who can claim compensation and the extent of such compensation is set out in PA sections 57–58. These rules are probably more extensive than has normally been the case in Norwegian law in respect of the interests protected.

PA Chapter 8 is based on the premise that liability under the Chapter is unlimited. In the case of ships, there is a reservation in PA section 53 subsection 1 that the special limitation rules in MC Chapter 9 will be applicable. The parties who, pursuant to the MC section 171, are entitled to global limitation, will thus be able to limit their liability.

IV. Pollution from Sea-Bed Activities

253. The *Petroleum Act* of 29 November 1996 No. 72 Chapter 7 contains rules regulating liability for oil pollution, insofar as damage caused by pollution occurs or is threatening in connection with exploration or exploitation of petroleum reserves. Section 7-3 subsection 1 first sentence sets the main rule: 'The licensee is liable for pollution damage without regard to fault.' The liability is in principle unlimited, but if it is demonstrated that an inevitable event of nature, act of war, exercise of public authority or a similar force majeure event has contributed to a considerable degree to the magnitude of damage under circumstances which are beyond the control of the liable party, the liability may be reduced to an extent that is considered reasonable, *see* section 7-3 subsection 3.

254. The rules contained in the Petroleum Act regarding liability for oil pollution may modify the provisions of MC Chapter 10. MC section 209 subsection 1 establishes that the provisions in MC Chapter 10 do not in any way restrict the liability of a licensee under the Petroleum Act Chapter 7 regarding damage caused by pollution. In other words, the Petroleum Act has priority in relation to the liability of the licensee. MC section 209 subsection 2 establishes that if the licensee is liable under the Petroleum Act Chapter 7, claims pursuant to MC sections 207–208 can only be invoked with such limitations as follow from the Petroleum Act sections 7-4 and 7-5. These sections contain channelling provisions for direct liability and for recourse liability, and significantly restrict the liability of third parties in relation to damage caused by pollution covered by the Petroleum Act rules.

MC section 209 subsection 2 does not refer to MC section 206, which regulates the scope of application of the Liability Convention. This is intentional. In situations where liability is covered by both the Petroleum Act Chapter 7 and MC section 206, it follows from Norway's obligations under the Liability Convention that the shipowner cannot be exempt from liability which extends beyond that flowing from the rules of the convention itself. Injured parties will thus still have a right to claim against the shipowner, while at the same time the licensees will be fully liable under the Petroleum Act. The overlap, however, is not particularly great. Given the scope of application of the convention-based rules and the Petroleum Act, this situation will only arise where measures are taken to prevent or limit damage caused by pollution on Norwegian or other signatory states' territory or economic zone following pollution from a tanker loading at an offshore installation, *see* section 7-1 subsection 2 third sentence.

V. Dumping and Incineration of Wastes

255. Article 4 of the Ospar Convention obliges the parties 'to take all possible steps to prevent and eliminate pollution by dumping or incineration of wastes or other matter'. The contents of this obligation are specified further in Annex II to the convention. Article 2 of Annex II simply states: 'Incineration is prohibited'. Article 3 also starts with a general prohibition of dumping of all wastes but allows thereafter certain exceptions.

These stipulations have been made Norwegian law by regulation 1 June 2004 No. 931 (pollution regulation) Chapter 6.

Chapter 14. The Arrest of Ships

§1. Sources of Law

256. The general rules on enforcement of monetary claims are found in the Enforcement of Claims Act of 26 June 1992 No. 86 (EC Act). These rules include attachments and forced sale of attached, pledged or mortgaged property. The rules on the interlocutory remedies injunction and arrest are laid down in the ACL in Civil Matters of 17 June 2005 No. 90 (ACL) Chapters 33 and 34, supplemented by Chapter 32. Here we shall outline the rules regarding the latter: the temporary security for a monetary claim.

The main principle in Norwegian law, as embodied in the ACL, is that a creditor with a monetary claim, due or not due, may demand arrest of assets belonging to the debtor, provided that there is a ground for arrest as defined in ACL section 33-2. However, the possibility of arresting property belonging to the debtor is limited when it comes to arrest of ships. This is due to the *Brussels Arrest Convention* of 1952 (1952 Convention) to which Norway adhered in 1993; the convention rules are implemented in MC Chapter 4.

§2. The Procedure for Conservatory Arrest

257. The rules on the judicial procedure for arrest are contained in the ACL. According to section 32-5 the procedure starts with a petition for arrest, preferably in writing, stating the claim and the ground for arrest. The petition should be presented to the Court of First Instance ('tingretten') in whose district the debtor has his ordinary venue (for a company where the registered main office is located). Section 32-4 goes on to say that also the Court in whose district the debtor has assets, or where it is expected that the debtor will have 'chattels' (which include ships) in the near future, is competent.

The possible *grounds for arrest* are stated in section 33-2 subsection 1:

> Assets can be arrested if the debtor's conduct gives grounds to fear that enforcement of the claim would otherwise be evaded or considerably impeded or would have to take place outside the realm.

For ships there is a further possibility: An identified ship can be arrested even if none of the mentioned grounds exist, provided that the claimant has a claim due that is secured by 'pant' in the ship – and 'pant' includes a maritime lien, an execution attachment and a contractual mortgage on the ship.

The general rule is that the claimant has to make his claim and the grounds for arrest probable (section 33-3), which is an easier burden than in an ordinary litigation. An arrest decree may, in the discretion of the Court, be subject to the claimant putting up security for the loss the debtor might suffer from the arrest. The Court has also the power to decree arrest where the claimant has not made his case 'probable', if delay 'poses a risk', but this can be done only on the condition that security is provided by the claimant.

The Court's arrest decree may state (identify) the arrest object, but this may be left to the enforcement officer who implements the arrest decree (section 33-5).

The arrest decree may be appealed to the Court of Appeal, and then – with some restrictions – to the Supreme Court.

The effect of an arrest, stated in section 33-7, is first of all that the debtor loses the right to dispose of the asset to the disadvantage of the claimant, but the arrest does not prevent claims of other creditors of the shipowner from attaching to the arrested asset. The arrest is not an enforcement ground: The arrest is not sufficient basis for having the asset sold according to the EC Act, but the arrest may serve as a priority reservation for a later attachment (and the attachment will, when registered, give a basis for demanding a forced sale).

258. The above rules apply also to arrest of vessels, but with some modifications in MC Chapter 4.

MC section 95 says that a decision to arrest a ship can only be taken if the ship is in or is expected to arrive in the district of the enforcement officer if it is his task to 'select the object of the arrest'. An arrest can always be implemented if the ship is in Norway. There is a geographical extension for the continental shelf: An arrest can always be granted and implemented if the ship is engaged in activities on the Norwegian continental shelf.

Important modifications follow from the 1952 Convention, as incorporated in MC Chapter 4.

The convention defines in Article 1(2) arrest as 'detention of a ship by judicial process to secure a maritime claim'– however with an important exception for 'the seizure of a ship in execution or satisfaction of a judgment'. This exception is formulated in MC section 91 subsection 2 letter c. The 1952 Convention rules incorporated in sections 92–94 and 96 do not apply to arrest demanded when an enforcement ground as defined in section 4-1 of the EC Act exists. For example: When a claim secured by a mortgage is due and the mortgagee petitions for an arrest the special convention-based rules do not apply. Such a petition may be caused by fear that the ship will be taken abroad. Further, an arrest may be necessary to avoid prescription of a maritime lien (cf. MC section 55 on time limitation) but, as indicated, subject to what follows from the 1952 Convention, *see* MC Chapter 4. Finally, the rules of the 1952 convention do not, of course, restrict the rights of the authorities to detain vessels, e.g., when a vessel is considered to be unseaworthy (Article 2). It is not evident that detention related to payment of taxes and public dues is also outside the 1952 Convention, but this seems to be the generally accepted interpretation of Article 2 (implemented in MC section 91).

§3. The Ship

259. The preamble of the 1952 Convention limits its scope to 'seagoing ships', which probably should be understood as regularly ocean-going ships. The convention does not, however, prohibit the rules being given a wider application, and the Norwegian legislator has decided to use this opportunity. The convention-based rules in MC apply to any ship – seagoing or not – provided that there is an obligation to have the ship registered, which in practice means that arrest of vessels with a length of 15 m or more is subject to the 1952 Convention rules, while it is possible to arrest a pleasure craft of 45 foot for any type of claim. MC does not define the concept ship, but it indicates that ship should be construed as in other parts of MC. Drilling rigs and similar mobile constructions are, as per special stipulation in MC section 507, subject to Chapter 4 on arrest of ships, but as they cannot be considered as ships proper, the 1952 Convention-based rules are inapplicable.

For boats and floating units falling outside the 1952 Convention (and thus MC Chapter 4), the general enforcement rules will apply. This, *inter alia*, means that one can obtain arrest for any substantiated claim. This also would apply to wrecks. They are not 'seagoing ships'. MC section 91 also stipulates that to an arrest which is limited to cargo, freight, bunkers or parts of a ship, is outside the scope of MC Chapter 4.

260. There are also legal relationships which may limit the categories of ships which may be included. Norwegian arrest rules, in general, presuppose that the debtor is the owner of the asset. For example, if a bareboat chartered vessel causes damage, in most cases the bareboat charterer (not the owner of the vessel) will be liable. Accordingly, the arrest of the vessel is in this instance not permissible according to general Norwegian law. However, the 1952 Convention may be interpreted differently and was in fact understood in this way at an earlier stage. Later on, another view was advocated, i.e., that the main objective of the 1952 Convention was to reduce the number of claims which could lead to arrest. Consequently, it cannot be considered as contrary to the 1952 Convention if national law limits the number of claims even further by requiring personal liability on the part of the shipowner of an arrested vessel. Norway has adopted this view – *see* MC section 93 subsection 4: Arrest can be granted only if the vessel can 'serve as an object for the enforcement of a claim according to the general provisions of the Enforcement of Claims Act'. In other words, when the bareboat charterer or the time charterer is liable for damage to cargo carried on the vessel, the cargo owner cannot arrest the vessel.

There is, however, an important exception hereto. In spite of the principle indicated above and with no apparent justification in the text of the former or present enforcement legislation, it has been accepted that when a claim is secured by a *maritime lien*, then the vessel may be arrested even if the owner is not personally liable for the claim. For example, if a vessel on bareboat charter causes a collision, the bareboat charterer (not the owner) in most cases will be the responsible party, but the bareboat chartered vessel may be arrested because the claim for damage is secured by a maritime lien.

261. Not only the ship in relation to which the claim has arisen may be arrested. So-called sisterships may also be arrested, *see* MC section 93 subsection 1 letter b (corresponding to the 1952 Convention Article 3(1) and (4)).

Letter (b) deals with the situation where A is the owner of ship No. 1 and is personally liable for a claim connected with this ship. Here it is permissible to arrest other ships which A owned at the time the claim arose, but not ships acquired thereafter. It is irrelevant what kind of ship No. 2 is. The decisive factor is ownership. At the time of petitioning for arrest, it may happen that B has become the owner of No. 2. It follows from the reference in MC section 93 subsection 4 to the EC Act that No. 2 is now immune to an arrest request from A's creditors. The rules on maritime liens do not help as a maritime lien attaches to ship No. 1 only.

When both ships are owned by joint-stock company X, then they are, of course, in the same ownership, as is the situation where limited partnership Y owns both vessels, etc. However, the vessels may be considered to be under the same ownership in other instances as well (MC section 93 subsection 2 and the 1952 Convention Article 3(2)). This is so where ship No. 1 is owned by partnership or limited partnership Z, and ship No. 2 is owned by partnership or limited partnership W – provided that the partners (including the general partner of a limited partnership) are the same in both companies. However, the shares need not be equally distributed in both companies. The conditions for invoking this last rule on same ownership will rarely exist.

Letter (c) is applicable where the person (or company) personally liable for the maritime claim is not the owner of the vessel to which the claim is connected. The rule is aimed at chartering situations in particular. For example, the time charterer or the bareboat charterer is responsible in respect of delivery of bunkers to ship No. 1. Letter (c) permits arrest of ship No. 2 which the personally liable person or entity, in the example the time or bareboat charterer, owns. Whether he owned ship No. 2 at the time when the claim arose, is immaterial. The essential factor is that he is the owner of the ship at the time when arrest is asked for.

Finally, if the claim is secured by a maritime lien, arrest of the vessel to which the claim is linked may be allowed.

§4. Maritime Claims

262. The main purpose of the 1952 Convention is that arrest of a vessel should be allowed only in respect of certain claims called 'maritime claims'. These are defined in a long list containing seventeen partly overlapping items in the 1952 Convention Article 1 letters (a)–(q), and correspondingly in MC section 92. In the present context, a short overview has to suffice:

- Letter (a) covers damage caused by any ship in collision or otherwise, e.g., by collision with another object than a ship. A number of different types of damage may follow from a collision, e.g., environmental damage from leaking oil (carried as cargo or as fuel for the vessel's engines). It is submitted that even without a collision, such environmental damage, e.g., caused by tank washings being pumped over board, falls within letter (a).
- Claims for personal injury occasioned in connection with the operation of the vessel (passengers injured while boarding the vessel, longshoremen injured during loading operations, etc.) are maritime claims according to letter (b).
- Claims for salvage and removal of wrecks.

- Letters (d), (e) and (f) comprise claims deriving from contracts of affreightment, e.g., the charterer's claim when his cargo has been damaged or because the vessel arrived late at the port of loading.
- Letter (g) defines a claim for general average contribution as a maritime claim. The same is the position in respect of claims arising from towage and pilotage.
- Letters (k) and (l) concern deliveries to the vessel of commodities (stores, spare parts, bunkers, etc.) and services (building and repair costs, dock dues, etc.). It is immaterial whether delivery takes place abroad or in the home port, and, furthermore, it does not matter whether the deliveries are necessary for the maintenance of the ship and/or the continuation of the voyage.
- Closely related is letter (n): a claim for refund of disbursements made by the master, shipper, charterer or agent, on behalf of the ship or its owner, is a maritime claim.
- Wages and other forms of compensation to the master and others employed on board the vessel are, according to letter (m), of a maritime nature. Thus a longshoreman's claim is not maritime, in contrast to the claim of a waiter working on board a cruise ship, employed by the catering company which services the restaurants on board as an independent contractor. It may be argued that in this respect, the definition in MC is wider than in the 1952 Convention.

263. Finally, the last three letters (o), (p) and (q) stand in a class of their own. Disputes as to ownership of the vessel or, if the vessel is owned by two or more, disputes among the co-owners are of a maritime nature. The same applies to claims secured by a mortgage on the vessel. This group is exceptional in as much as the claims in this group are not necessarily monetary, and as a consequence, there are some special rules.

Article 3(1) states that for these three types of claims, arrest of a sister ship is not allowed. However, Article 10(b) permits a state to make a reservation in respect of letter (q), i.e., the mortgage provision. Norway has chosen to exercise this option – *see* MC section 93. Article 5(1) delimits the rule that an arrest shall be lifted on security being furnished: When arrest is granted for a maritime claim listed in Article 1(1) letter (o) or (p), i.e., disputes concerning ownership of the vessel or disputes between owners of the vessel, giving security is not sufficient ground for releasing the vessel. Putting up security is not, however, immaterial. The court may permit the person in possession of the ship to continue trading the ship when adequate security is arranged. The Norwegian legislator was in some doubt as to the implementation of this part of the 1952 Convention that in most instances amounts to a decree relating to letter (o) or letter (p) on a non-monetary claim; consequently ACL Chapter 34 gives the pertinent provisions, which means that one is outside the 1952 Convention unless the decree is one relating to detaining the vessel. Chapter 34 distinguishes between the decree and its implementation, as does Chapter 33. According to Chapter 16, giving security concerns the implementation. Subject to the discretion of the Court, security may lead to postponement of the implementation or to revocation of an actual implementation (sections 34-3 and 34-6). The Ministry of Justice considered that these rules were sufficient to meet the requirements of the 1952 Convention, pointing out that the primary objectives of the 1952 Convention were to protect the claimant against the arrest being lifted when security was not an adequate measure compared to arrest and to protect the claimant against the risk of having to start from scratch if the decision to allow trading against security appeared to have been unfortunate.

If the claim directly concerns money – see the alternative earnings' in letter (p) – then ACL Chapter 33 is applicable, with rules giving the defendant an absolute right to postponement or revocation of the implementation of the arrest by furnishing security. The Norwegian legislator has taken the view that Article 5 does not really intend to exclude the ordinary rules on security, in this instance concerning a regular monetary claim.

The outcome is that the Norwegian law does not contain special provisions reflecting Article 5(1). The rules of the ACL are considered compatible with the 1952 Convention when the presumed objectives of the 1952 Convention in this sector are taken into account.

Chapter 15. Carriage of Passengers

§1. Introduction

264. Questions relating to the carriage of passengers and luggage are regulated in MC Chapter 15 sections 401–432. The rules are based on the *Athens Convention* of 1974 with Protocol of 2002 on carriage of passengers and their luggage by sea, however, adjusted to EU No. 392/2009. In 2016 EC No. 2006/2004 as amended by EU No. 1177/2010 was implemented.

§2. Statutory Provisions

265. MC section 401 defines the parties to a contract of carriage of passengers by sea as *carrier* and *passenger*. The carrier promises to provide carriage, irrespective of whether he happens to own or control the tonnage necessary to perform the obligation. A travel agency can thus be considered the carrier, but will typically act as agent for the carrier/owner. A party will only be considered the carrier if the promise of carriage is made 'commercially or for remuneration'. Thus, a person onboard a pleasure craft will in most cases not be covered by the rules in the MC. In case of an agreement regarding the carriage of vehicles or live animals, the attending person (the driver of the lorry, the animal keeper) will be treated as passengers.

266. The contract for carriage of passengers is usually expressed in a *ticket*. This document may contain specific carriage conditions or may refer to the carrier's (shipowner/ferry company's) ordinary conditions. At first glance, there appears to be freedom of contract – *see* MC section 402. However, there are such extensive exceptions under sections 430–432, that this freedom is in fact strictly limited: The law protects the passengers and their luggage. Therefore, the ticket will often refer directly to the rules in the MC.

The mandatory rules place to some extent restrictions also on the passenger. The provisions of section 408, obliging the passenger to 'comply with regulations relating to good order and safety on board', cannot be avoided.

267. Accordingly, most of the rules in Chapter 15 cannot be departed from to the disadvantage of the passenger, viz. when (1) the place of departure or arrival is in Denmark, Finland, Norway or Sweden; or alternatively, (2) the carriage according to Norwegian law is subject to Norwegian jurisdiction.

In either case, the mandatory restrictions relate to agreements prior to the carriage. Thereafter there are no such restrictions relating to specific incidents. If for example, an incident involving personal injury has taken place, there is full freedom of contract with respect to establishing the basis of liability and the scope of damages.

The rules which cannot be set aside or varied to the detriment of the passenger are the following:

- Sections 411–429: The content of these rules is discussed below with exception of section 429, which regulates where a legal action can be commenced (although an alternative venue can be agreed once a dispute has arisen).
- Section 501 first paragraph Nos 4–6: covers time limitation.

268. When a carriage is performed wholly or in part by another than the carrier, the carrier remains liable according to Chapter 15 (section 426 subsection 1). However, if the contract specifies that the carrage shall take place on a named ship, the carrier cannot perform his obligation by using another ship, *see* section 406. Whether or not the ship used is named in the contract, section 405 applies: the carrier is obliged to ensure that the ship is seaworthy, both at the commencement of and during the voyage. The ship must, *inter alia*, be properly equipped, manned and provisioned. This requirement relates to the ship's general safety – it must be able to withstand the perils of the voyage and have a competent crew and the necessary safety equipment. It also concerns the fact that the individual passenger's health and welfare must not be threatened in any unreasonable manner: there must be railings for the passenger to hold on to, there must not be oil stains or loose items on deck which the passenger can slip on or trip over, when bad weather is approaching the necessary notices and warnings must be given, etc.

Section 418 a, implementing EU No. 1177/2010, gives the passengers a number of rights, e.g., concerning information, equal treatment and assistance to disabled persons.

§3. Liability and Limitation of Liability

269. The rules relating to liability for personal injury and for delay are a central feature of MC Chapter 15. MC section 428 determines who is entitled to bring a claim against the carrier. The passenger is entitled to sue, as can anyone who succeeds to his rights. In case of death, only the deceased's legal successors or dependants can claim damages.

Liability for *personal injury* is imposed where the injury is caused by the fault or neglect of the carrier or of persons for whom he is responsible (section 418). For example, the deck is slippery because of oil patches or the railings are weak and unreliable. The claimant must prove the extent of the damage and also that the injury arose as a result of an incident during the carriage. The claimant also has the burden of showing fault or neglect by the carrier, but his burden of proof is reversed where the damage arises from or in connection with shipwreck, collision, stranding, explosion or fire – *see* section 421.

The rules on liability for personal damage in section 418, implementing the Athens rules as adjusted by EU No. 392/2009, are complicated.

Subsection 1: For transport within the the area to which the EU regulation applies (inclusive carriage within Norway, *see* subsection 2) one has to distinguish between (i) damage due to a shipping incident – which is defined as 'shipwreck, capsizing, collision or stranding of the ship, explosion or fire in the ship, or defect in the ship', and (ii) damage due to other cause. In the first case, there is a strict liability up to 250,000 SDR – unless the carrier proves that the damage resulted from act of war or a natural phenomenon of an exceptional, inevitable and irresistible character, or was wholly caused by an act or omission done with intent to cause the incident by a third party. For loss exceeding this amount the carrier is liable unless he proves that there was 'no fault or neglect on the carrier'. In the second case (damage due to other causes) the carrier is liable if the claimant can prove that there was 'fault or neglect' on the carrier's side.

In all instance, there is a liability ceiling of 400,000 SDR.

Section 418 subsection 3 has special provisions where the Athens Convention applies but not the EU regulation No. 392/2009.

If the voyage is *delayed* or does not take place, the passenger may suffer loss. The carrier is liable for foreseeable losses caused by fault or neglect for which he was responsible (section 418 d). The passenger has the burden of proof 'regarding the scope of loss and whether the loss resulted from delay to the carriage' (section 421 subsection 1). For the carrier's liability for delay, the limit is 4,694 SDR, *see* section 422 subsection 1.

Section 431 permits the carrier to exempt himself from liability pursuant to Chapter 15 for delay arising in the period before the passenger embarks and for the period after the passenger disembarks. This exception also applies when the passenger goes ashore at an intermediate port. However, carriage by boat to and from the ship is subject to the mandatory rules if such carriage is included in the ticket price or is undertaken with a means of transport provided by the carrier (e.g., boat transport organized by a cruise vessel during a port call).

270. The extent of economic liability must be determined according to general tort rules on assessment of damages. In addition to the limits described above the carrier may have to cover interest and costs. MC section 423 establishes a deductible to avoid too many small claims being brought. The deductible is applied before liability is limited. No deductible applies to cases of personal injury, but in cases of delay, there is a deductible of 20 SDR per passenger. The right to limit liability can be lost in instances of wilful misconduct or qualified gross negligence. The rule corresponds to the equivalents in MC Chapters 9, 10 and 13, *see* section 424.

As is the case with carriage of goods, claims based on tort can be brought against the non-contractual party who actually caused the damage. MC sections 425 and 427 provide parallel solutions: a passenger cannot improve his position by pleading 'pure tort rules' against the contractual carrier, and if he sues a person not party to the contract, such person is entitled to the same protection as the contractual carrier.

271. The carrier is liable for lost, damaged or delayed luggage caused by his own or his servant's negligent actions. In the case of hand luggage, the rules relating to the burden of proof is on the passenger. For other luggage, the carrier always has the burden of showing that there has been no fault.

The carrier can limit his liability also in respect of luggage. For luggage which the passenger has in his custody (hand luggage), typically in his cabin, the maximum liability is 2,250 SDR. In the case of other luggage which is in the custody of the carrier, the limit is 3,375 SDR. These limits operate per passenger and not per item of luggage lost or damaged. A vehicle brought along by the passenger is deemed to be luggage, but a special limit of 12,700 SDR applies. *See* section 481, cf. Athens Convention Article 8.

Part III. Other Transport

Chapter 1. Road Transport

Hans Jacob Bull

§1. Introduction

I. The CMR Convention and Norwegian Internal Law

272. The Convention on the Contract for the International Carriage of Goods by Road of 19 May 1956 (the CMR) has been ratified by Norway. The CMR was made part of Norwegian internal law first by the act passed by the Parliament on 31 January 1969 No. 3 – the *Act on International Carriage of Goods by Road*. The 1969 Act transformed the provisions of the CMR to internal Norwegian law and dealt solely with international transport.

In 1974, a new act was passed by the Parliament – the *Act on Carriage of Goods by Road* of 20 December 1974 No. 68 (CGR). The CGR replaced the 1969 Act, and contains regulations which in the main apply for both international and domestic transport.

II. Compulsory Regulations

273. The provisions of the CGR are (with few exceptions) mandatory both for international and for domestic road transport. It means that the CMR provisions (as transformed to internal Norwegian law in the CGR) may not be deviated from by specific agreement either to the detriment of the carrier or to the cargo interests, *see* CGR section 5 subsection 1. For a domestic transport, the mandatory nature of CGR only serves to protect the cargo interests, *see* CGR section 5 subsection 2. Accordingly, the carrier is for domestic carriage at liberty to agree upon a heavier responsibility and to undertake a greater risk than that which follows from the provisions of the CGR.

§2. The Scope of the Act on Carriage of Goods by Road

274. The scope of the CGR is set out in section 1 subsection 1:

> The Statute applies to contracts for carriage of goods by road in vehicles provided the transport is carried out against remuneration and, according to the contract, takes place between locations in Norway (domestic transport) or to or from Norway or between foreign nations of which at least one has ratified the CMR (international transport). In the event the contract stipulates an international transport, the Statute will not apply to the extent it deviates from the law of another state that is a party to the CMR and it follows from general rules on choice of law that the law of the latter is to apply.

CGR section 1 makes it clear that only transport against a consideration is covered by the provisions of CGR. Hence, gratuitous transport falls outside the scope of the act. It would be inappropriate to apply the CGR provisions, in particular on carrier liability, on transports performed as a friendly service.

The cases in RG 1987 831 NCC and ND 1982 265 NCA indicate that road carriage usually will require a firm agreement on a remuneration for the transport in order for the transport to be subject to theCGR. However, the remuneration may be recognized as sufficient even if it is modest.

In order for a transport to be governed by the CGR, it is required that the means of carriage be a 'vehicle', *see* CGR section 3. Typically it would be a trailer, lorry or a van. The term 'goods' has not been defined in CGR, but will in principle cover all physical things and devices, whether they are carried in or on the vehicle or are being pulled by the vehicle. In ND 2005 295 NSC, the Supreme Court found that the CGR applied to a transport of money. However, furniture removal and funeral consignments fall outside CGR, as does carriage that is part of the mail delivery service, *see* CGR section 2 subsection 1. Finally, road transport which forms part of a contract for a railway carriage is not governed by CGR, but by terms governing railway carriage (the CIM), *see* CGR section 2 subsection 2. The term 'goods' obviously does not cover transport of people (passengers). For transport of passengers, *see* §6. below.

Vehicles are by their nature designed to travel on the road. The mentioning of 'road' in the CMR and the CGR indicates a specific type of contract different from, typically, transport at sea, in the air or by rail. Where the vehicle containing the goods is carried over part of the journey by sea, rail or air, CGR still applies in the main to the entire transport, provided the goods have not been unloaded from the vehicle (CGR section 4 subsection 1). An exception is made in CGR section 4 subsection 2 for loss, damage or delay resulting from an incident that may be allocated solely to the other means (mode) of transportation. If so, the law governing such means of transportation (e.g., a vessel) is to apply. The condition for allowing the law of another mode to govern is that the law then applicable offers mandatory protection to the cargo interests at least matching the protection of CGR. The burden of proving the applicability of the exception, foremost the allocation of the incident in question, e.g., a railway transport, rests with the claimant.

To determine whether or not a transport is a domestic or international transport is normally quite easy. Norwegian law has, however, not resolved yet whether a transport from Norway, intended for delivery abroad, is to be considered a domestic or international transport if the transport is aborted in Norway. Looking at the law of other CMR states, it is envisaged that the intended and not the actual place of delivery will be decisive in this respect. The transport would thus be considered an international transport. That will apparently be the case irrespective of whether the reason for the aborted transport was an unforeseen hindrance preventing the carriage, or a modification of the contract for carriage instructed by the sender.

A typical international transport is from a place of loading in Norway to a place of delivery abroad, or the other way around. It should be added that the criteria to determine the applicability of CGR are not dependant upon the nationality or domicile of the parties to the contract for carriage. The CGR provisions for international transport will apply even if the transport departs from and has an intended destination in two foreign countries. The condition is that the country of departure or the country of destination is a party to the CMR.

Recognizing that there are no fully consistent interpretations of the CMR as implemented within internal law in the various CMR states means that the CMR, and in Norway the CGR, to some extent invite 'shopping' of forum and governing law. Any 'shopping' will, however, be subject to the restrictions of the choice of law provision of CGR section 1.

§3. Rights and Obligations of the Carrier, the Sender and the Receiver

I. General

275. The typical contract for carriage of goods by road will be concluded by a sender of goods and a carrier, in which case the contracting carrier also performs the transport using his own vehicles.

Unless otherwise provided in the contract for carriage, the carrier will be at liberty to subcontract the performance of the transport to a sub-carrier, and the sub-carrier at liberty to subcontract the performance of the carriage to yet another carrier and so on. The liberty to sub-contract does not require any express consent from the cargo interests (i.e., a liberty clause). To the contrary, the cargo interests will in fact have to expressly prohibit transshipment in order to secure performance by the contracting road carrier, *see* CGR section 10 subsection 2 litra (a). Similarly, the sender will need an undertaking from the carrier not to sub-contract to another road carrier in order to claim that a performing sub-road carrier as such will represent a breach of contract.

The contracting carrier remains in any case liable for his employees, servants and for any sub-carrier towards the cargo interests as if their performance were his own, *see* CGR section 6.

276. A lot of contracts for carriage of goods by road are concluded through *freight forwarders* and freight forwarding companies. The freight forwarders may act on behalf of the carrier or on behalf of the cargo interests. Acting as an intermediary, the freight forwarder does not become a party to the contract for carriage.

The freight forwarder will under Norwegian law easily be considered as the contracting carrier if he does not clarify his role as an intermediary during the negotiations.

The CMR and the CGR do not contain regulations for the obligations and responsibility of the freight forwarder acting as such. The Nordic Association of Freight Forwarders has concluded an agreed document containing general conditions for freight forwarding (NSAB/85, revised as NSAB 2000 and NSAB 2015).

II. The Consignment Note

277. In order to determine whether a contract for carriage of goods by road has been concluded, general principles of Norwegian contract law relating to entering into and concluding contracts have to be applied (*inter alia*, the *Agreements Act* of 31 May 1918 No. 4). As regards international transports, CGR section 7 presupposes and specifies that the terms of the contract for a road carriage of goods that have been fixed are to be laid down in a separate document, the *CMR consignment note*. The consignment note shall be made out in three original counterparts, *see* CGR section 8 – one for the sender, one for the carrier and one for the receiver, all signed by the sender and the carrier. The counterpart of the carrier is supposed to accompany the goods through the transport.

Even though the wording of CGR section 7, when applicable to international transports, indicates a requirement under the law for the consignment note to contain certain information, it is not disputed that such a requirement is not a condition to the validity of the contract for carriage. Hence, an international transport may in principle be based on an oral agreement that will be governed by the CMR provisions as same are laid down in the CGR.

The parties to a domestic transport are not required under the CGR to issue a consignment note. CGR section 9 stipulates that in the event a consignment note in fact is issued, certain information shall be included. Such information will include the name and address of sender, carrier and receiver, place and time for receipt of the goods and the destination, together with information on the lot and nature of the goods. In addition, both the sender and the carrier may require that information on the particulars stated in CGR section 10 be included in the consignment note.

The CMR consignment note is not a negotiable document of title or otherwise a representative of the goods to be traded. The CMR and the CGR offer no legal framework to enable negotiable road transport documents for carriage of goods to be issued. Nevertheless, the provisions of the CMR and the CGR Act still make the consignment note a handy instrument for effecting international transport of goods, and to allow a proper transfer of title to the goods in exchange of payment under a purchase contract.

The terms and information (for instance, as to the condition of the goods) included in the consignment note will serve as strong evidence in a legal dispute related to same. It means, perhaps in particular, that the carrier ought to scrutinize the correctness of the terms and information actually entered on the consignment note. Additionally, the carrier ought to be conscientious about taking reservations that might be appropriate in the circumstances as allowed for in CGR section 10 subsection 3.

In practical terms, the information in the consignment note usually will be recognized as prima facie evidence, *see* CGR section 13. The consequence is that the information in the consignment note will be decisive unless rebutted by sufficient contrary evidence.

According to CGR section 10 subsection 1, the consignment note for an international transport shall contain the following particulars:

(a) place and date of issuance;
(b) name and address of sender;
(c) name and address of carrier;
(d) place and date for receipt of the goods and place designated for delivery;
(e) name and address of receiver;
(f) usual description of the nature of the goods and the way of packing; in the event of dangerous goods, a generally recognized description of them;
(g) number of units, their specific marking and counting number;
(h) gross weight of the goods, or its quantity otherwise stipulated;
(i) charges relating to the transport (freight, additional costs, custom duties, and other costs to be incurred from conclusion of contract to delivery);
(j) required instructions as to customs and other formalities;
(k) a statement to the effect that, irrespective of agreements to the contrary, the transport is subjèct to the CMR (cf. CGR section 1) or internal law conforming to the CMR.

CGR section 10 subsection 2 stipulates that further information shall be included when appropriate:

(a) a statement that transshipment is not allowed;
(b) costs undertaken to be paid by the sender;
(c) the amount for 'cash on delivery' charges;
(d) stipulated value of the goods, and the amount to constitute 'special interest' in the goods, compare CGR sections 33 and 35 subsection 2;
(e) the sender's instructions to the carrier on insurance requirements;
(f) agreed time limit for completion of the transport;
(g) list of documents at the disposal of the carrier.

In addition to inclusion of information as described above, the parties have the option to include all other information deemed to be necessary, compare CGR section 10 subsection 3.

III. The Carrier

278. The dominant obligations of the carrier under a road carriage are to take delivery of the goods at the place of loading, perform the transport (drive) to the place of delivery and to unload and present the goods to the disposal of the receiver within the agreed time.

As to sanctions for breach of contract by the carrier, the CMR and the CGR strongly focus on the liability to pay *damages*. The focus on damages is in line with the law of the other modes of transport regarding a specific transport distance. The damages offered are usually intended as a full settlement of the consequences of loss, damage or delay.

Contractual sanctions such as recision of contract or reduction of freight payable, are not specified in any detail in the CGR. Still, a claim for refund is envisaged as an additional remedy to the liability for damages in CGR section 32 subsection 5 (total or partial loss) and in section 35 subsection 1 (delay). Retention of lawfully unpaid freight and charges should be recognized to secure a set-off against the claim for damages due.

The carrier is expected to *examine the goods* upon receiving them for loading. CGR section 12 subsection 1 provides that the carrier shall compare the goods to the information in the consignment note on lot number, marking and counting numbers. In the event that the examination cannot reasonably be performed, or the information contained in the consignment note is doubtful, the carrier is to make a reasoned reservation in the consignment note. Similar reservations should be made on the apparent (visible) condition of the goods and their packing, *see* CGR section 12 subsection 2. Any reservation made by the carrier is not binding on the sender unless expressly accepted, *see* CGR section 12 subsection 3. The sender, in his capacity as seller, may have made different representations towards the purchaser as to the condition of the goods. However, the sender may in these circumstances have an incentive to secure evidence to the effect that the reservations made by the carrier are ill-founded.

Further, the carrier has obligations relating to lost or *misused documents* concerning the goods and the carriage those have been made available to the carrier by the sender, *see* CGR section 16 subsection 3. The basis for liability will be a presumption of fault on the part of the carrier (maximized to the limit operating for total loss). The burden of proof, other than for the costs and losses, rests with the carrier.

A transport of goods by road may for several reasons be impeded or *prevented from timely delivery* at the agreed destination. In the event that the transport is aborted or otherwise cannot be completed as intended (completion of carriage as agreed is impossible), the carrier is under an obligation to collect relevant instructions from the sender, *see* CGR section 23 subsection 1. Given that the right to modify the contract for carriage has passed on to the receiver, the same principle applies, *see* CGR section 23 subsection 3. All costs as a consequence of instructions given to the carrier in this respect are for the account of the sender or receiver, as appropriate. An exception applies provided the dominant cause of the costs is fault on the part of the carrier, *see* CGR section 24.

In the event that the carriage cannot be completed as intended, the carrier is entitled to unload the goods at the expense of the cargo interests. The transport is then to be deemed completed at the place of abortion. The carrier is still expected to *take care of the goods* on behalf of the cargo interests. The carrier is at liberty to appoint a third party to carry out the handling of the goods. In such a case, the carrier's liability is only to exercise due care in selecting such a third party. The *right of detention* of the goods to secure freight and other amounts due under the consignment note is maintained with the carrier towards the cargo interests even if a third party physically performs the keeping of the goods, *see* CGR section 25.

The unloading of the goods by the carrier, and possible storage, etc. undertaken by a third party, may not in all instances bring about a final solution as to the proper handling of goods carried in an aborted transport. Of course, the carrier should as a general rule *await appropriate instructions*. Such instructions may very well be to sell the goods at the place of abortion of the transport. However, such instructions may not be forthcoming. In any case, CGR section 26 provides that the carrier, under certain conditions, is *entitled to sell the goods*. First of all, a sale can take place if the goods are exposed to rapid deterioration or otherwise are in a condition that requires prompt action. Second, the carrier is at liberty to sell the goods in the event that the costs of storing or otherwise keeping the goods are not in proportion to the market value of the goods. The procedure of such a sale should be proper, and the carrier should endeavour to notify the cargo interests as to time and place of the sale. The carrier maintains his security interest in the proceeds of the sale. In the event of the costs of selling exceeding the sales revenue, the carrier has a valid claim for the unsettled amount. Reference is made to CGR section 26.

IV. The Sender

279. The dominant obligations of the sender under a road carriage are to pay the freight and related charges and to deliver the cargo at the place of loading. These obligations are not dealt with in any detail under the provisions of the CMR or otherwise the CGR.

The nature of the obligations of the sender, and any breach thereof, has to be determined in accordance with general Norwegian contract law. Under general Norwegian contract law, the sender, in the event of *default of payment of freight*, will face a strict liability to pay damages for all direct and consequential losses. The exceptions from liability will only be certain force majeure events relating to overall hindrances in carrying out banking transactions, etc.

Non-delivery of cargo at the place of loading– totally or in part – may be considered as a cancellation of the carriage by the sender. The sender will then be liable to pay damages in full.

Further, non-payment of freight and/or non-delivery of cargo may constitute a substantial breach of contract by the sender that entitles the carrier to rescind the contract. In this respect, the non-delivery is not only a cancellation by the cargo interests, but at the same time, also a breach of contract.

Insufficient or substandard *packing* of the goods will render the sender liable to pay damages for costs, personal injury, damage to other goods and material (typically the vehicle) as a result thereof. The liability is subject to the carrier's duty to ascertain apparent deficiencies or indicate that they otherwise were known to him, *see* CGR section 14.

As is the case with other modes of transport, the transport of *dangerous goods* also imposes certain obligations on road carriage. The sender is under an obligation to give specific information as to the nature of the danger, and, if appropriate, what precautions have to be taken. The sender has the burden of proving that sufficient information has been given, and a liability to pay damages for the consequences of not properly informing about dangerous goods. Under certain conditions, the carrier may instantly unload the dangerous goods and even destroy them as a protective measure, *see* CGR section 15.

The sender is to provide all *documents* needed to accompany the goods in order for the carrier to be able to deliver the goods at the agreed destination. The more practical alternative is to furnish the carrier with all relevant information in order for the carrier to obtain the documents. The carrier holds a claim for damages against the sender for incompleteness and inaccuracy of the information furnished or contained in documents made available, *see* CGR section 16.

The consignment note may expressly stipulate that the receiver (consignee) exercise the *right to modify the contract for carriage*. Unless such express transfer of authority has been granted to the receiver, the sender holds the right to modify the contract for carriage during the transport. The right to modify the contract for carriage includes the right to order stoppage while the goods are in transit, to alter the place of delivery, and to change the name of the receiver, *see* CGR section 17.

The carrier is obliged to adhere to instructions as long as they do not harm the normal activities of the carrier or represent a hindrance to the interests of other cargo. The carrier is liable to pay damages for the consequences of not complying with a valid instruction. The rather discretionary nature of the provisions stipulating the responsibility of the carrier in this respect indicates that the requirements for the standard of the conduct to be asked from the carrier should not be exaggerated. Reference is made to CGR sections 18 and 19.

V. The Receiver (Consignee)

280. The CMR and the CGR do not set out extensive provisions regarding the rights and obligations of the receiver (the consignee).

Often, but certainly not always, the receiver of the goods will be the purchaser under a sales contract with the sender. The receiver may, under certain conditions, *have the right to modify the contract for carriage* from the time of loading at the place of departure, *see* CGR section 17 subsection 3. First of all, the right to modify must have been expressly transferred by the sender to the receiver by signing the consignment note. Second, the receiver should hold the first counterpart of the consignment note for presentation. The receiver may also, like the sender, transfer the interest in delivery of the cargo (assign the consignment note). The next receiver so appointed does not possess the authority to appoint yet another receiver, *see* CGR section 17 subsection 4.

Upon arrival of the goods at the place of delivery, the receiver is *entitled to claim delivery* of the goods from the carrier against signing a receipt, *see* CGR section 20 subsection 1. Furthermore, the receiver is entitled to launch any claims against the carrier based on the contract for carriage (consignment note).

Upon claiming delivery, the receiver becomes *obliged to cover outstanding amounts* under the consignment note (or otherwise contract for carriage). Typically, the receiver will have to pay freight and charges relating to costs of the transport for the carrier. In addition, the receiver may have to pay 'cash on delivery' amounts to the carrier relating to any underlying purchase agreement. If a dispute on the amount payable arises, the carrier may detain the goods in his possession unless the receiver provides sufficient security, normally a bank guarantee, *see* CGR section 20 subsection 3.

§4. Liability and Limitation of Liability

I. The Basis for Liability

A. The Starting Point: The Carrier Is Strictly Liable

281. The starting point when deciding the carrier's liability is found in CGR section 27 subsection 1. The provision stipulates that the carrier is liable for losses and damage to the goods that occur from the time the carrier receives the goods for transport until delivery, and for delay. The way the provision is formulated implies that the carrier bears a strict liability.

However, the succeeding sections contain several exceptions from this starting point. CGR section 28 sets out some general exceptions, whereas CGR section 29 contains several specific exceptions. The central difference between the two categories of exceptions lies in the rules on burden of proof.

The most important exception in practice – and also the exception most difficult to apply – is found in CGR section 28 subsection 1 *in fine*: 'circumstances which the carrier could not avoid and the consequences of which he was unable to prevent.' This exception has formed the basis for the debate both in Norwegian and foreign law on whether the CMR liability is to be considered as a strict liability with force majeure exceptions or a liability based on a presumption of fault. It may be observed that the Supreme Court has referred to the CMR liability as 'strict' or 'basically strict' without deriving specific legal effects from the statements, *see* ND 1995 238 NSC and ND 1998 226 NSC.

282. The period of liability for loss of or damage to the goods is stipulated as 'the time when the carrier takes over the goods and the time of delivery', *see* CGR section 27 subsection 1. The decisive starting point for the period of liability will be when the carrier takes over the goods physically, and the termination when he physically delivers the goods to the receiver. How these principles are to be applied in the individual case, may depend on the agreements and the commercial practice established between the carrier and the sender and the receiver, respectively. Important factors will be the arrangements made between the parties regarding how the goods should be loaded on to and unloaded from the vehicle, and which one of the parties should be responsible for the actual loading or unloading. Where the sender, respectively the receiver, is in charge of loading or unloading, loss of or damage to the goods occurring during these periods will fall outside the period for carrier's liability. Are such tasks performed by a person other than the carrier, sender or receiver, it will have to be demonstrated whether that person acts on behalf of the carrier or the sender/receiver. If the loading/unloading is in fact a joint operation between the carrier and the sender/receiver, loss or damage occurring during this operation falls within the carrier's period of liability, but the carrier may be relieved for (part of) his liability due to a wrongful act or negligence on the part of the claimant, *see* CGR section 28 subsection 1.

283. CGR section 6 establishes that the carrier will be responsible for the acts and omissions of his agents and servants and of any other persons of whose services he makes use for the performance of the carriage as if such acts or omissions were his own. This rule conforms with ordinary Norwegian contract law. A carrier will be responsible for independent contractors performing all or part of the transport he has contracted for, but also for persons engaged to help him with loading or unloading operations, storage, etc. Persons helping out after the transport has been hit by an incident, will also be seen as the carrier's agents under the provision. The carrier's liability under CGR section 6 is not conditioned on the servants or agents having acted negligently, compare the expression 'as if such acts were his own' and ND 1985 212 NCA.

Whereas the CMR Article 3 expressly states that it is a condition for the carrier's liability for servants and independent contractors that they are 'acting within the scope of their employment', such a condition is not to be found in CGR section 6. However, such a condition would follow from general Norwegian contract law.

284. Usually, the determination of whether or not the goods have been *damaged* may be based on objective criteria. Additionally, the rules on prima facie *evidence* contribute to establishing workable rules in this regard.

As to *delay* in delivery, the carrier will be late in delivery if the specific time limit for delivery stipulated in the consignment note as allowed for in CGR section 10 subsection 2 litra (f) has not been met. Further, the absence of delivery of the goods (delay) of thirty days after a fixed time of delivery, or sixty days after receipt of the goods by the carrier, may be converted into a *total loss*, *see* CGR section 31 subsection 1. In the absence of a firm stipulation on time for delivery, the general rule as to delay is that the carrier is to be deemed late in delivery only if the time consumed by the transport exceeds what in the circumstances reasonably could be expected by a prudent carrier for the transport distance in question (*due dispatch*), *see* CGR section 27 subsection 2. Further, it should be emphasized that the carrier will be excused from meeting even a fixed time limit for delivery in the event that the transport is prevented or delivery of the goods is impossible as envisaged in CGR sections 22 and 23.

The fixing of an exact time of delivery may be reinforced in the consignment note by stipulating a '*special interest*' for the cargo interests in timely delivery, *see* CGR section 35 subsection 2, compared with section 10 subsection 2 litra (d). The general effect of a 'special interest' will be that the claimant may recover compensation in excess of the limited liability otherwise operating.

A domestic transport allows the carrier to undertake a heavier responsibility than set out by the CGR. The bare fixing of an exact time of delivery in a contract for domestic carriage normally will have to be construed to the effect that the carrier has a liability to pay damages in accordance with the liability scheme in the CGR, and not as a guarantee to pay full damages for all direct and consequential losses actually suffered by the claimant.

B. General Exceptions

285. The general exceptions from the liability of the carrier are set out in CGR section 28. Exoneration from liability will first and foremost be granted if the carrier can prove that the loss, damage or delay was caused by 'conditions that the carrier neither could avoid nor was able to prevent the consequences of', *see* CGR section 28 subsection 1 *in fine*. This exception covers several different situations, as may be seen from the short presentation below.

War, civil war, natural disasters, etc. are typical examples of force majeure events which the carrier could not avoid. However, the carrier will still have to prove that he was unable to prevent the consequences of the event, for example by choosing another route for the transport. These classical force majeure events have not created great problems in the Norwegian courts.

Another category that has come up in the Norwegian courts quite often, is (armed) *robbery*, *theft* and similar events. As regards theft, the typical situation seems to be that the goods are stolen, alone or together with the carrying vehicle while the vehicle is parked, normally during nighttimes, *see* ND 1982 186 NCA, where the carrier was held liable since he was not able to prove that the theft could have been avoided. As for armed robbery, the carrier was not held liable in ND 1998 226 NSC, where the driver was forced to hand over the control of the vehicle to two armed men at the place where he had chosen to park for the night. Fraud is a third example of third party intervention.

In contrast to international court practice, there are hardly examples in Norwegian court practice of cases where the vehicle has caught *fire*, with the effect that the goods have been damaged or completely destroyed.

Traffic accidents are often the reason why goods are destroyed or damaged during transport. In all the three central Norwegian cases, ND 1981 137 NSC, ND 1982 149 NCA and ND 1985 212 NCA, the carrier was found liable. In the Supreme Court case, the vehicle landed in a fjord after having been parked nearby. Neither the technical experts nor the court itself had been able to establish why the accident had happened.

286. As for the other general exceptions found in CGR section 28 subsection 1, exoneration from liability will be granted in the event that the carrier proves that the loss, damage or delay was caused by:

(1) negligent acts or omissions of the cargo interests (fault);
(2) instructions from the cargo interests that were not a consequence of fault on the part of the carrier;
(3) inherent vice of the goods.

In Norwegian court practice, these three general exceptions do not seem to have played any major role.

C. Defective Condition of the Vehicle

287. The carrier cannot be excused from liability if the cause of the default was deficiencies in the vehicle used for the carriage, *see* CGR section 28 subsection 2. The liability of the carrier for the condition of the vehicle has been structured as an exception from the general exceptions from liability. The effect of the exception to the exceptions is that one is back at the starting point in CGR section 27 subsection 1, i.e., a strict liability for the carrier without a possibility for him to call on the exceptions found in CGR section 28 first paragraph.

D. Special Exceptions

288. The *special exceptions* from the carrier's liability stipulated in CGR section 29 subsection 1 are:

(a) the use of an open vehicle without coverage according to express agreement entered in the consignment note (or, for domestic transport, acknowledged by the sender);
(b) deficient or substandard packing of the goods that cause the goods to be exposed to wastage or damage;
(c) handling, loading, stowing, unloading of the goods performed by the sender or the receiver, or somebody acting on their behalf;
(d) the nature of certain lots of the goods that makes them vulnerable to loss or damage;
(e) inadequate or incorrect marking or numbers on the goods;
(f) the carriage of livestock.

The central element in these special exceptions is that they give the carrier a better position regarding the burden of proof, *see* CGR section 29 subsection 2. If he is able to establish that in the circumstances of the case, the loss or damage could be attributed to one of the special exceptions, it shall be presumed that it was so caused. The claimant is, however, entitled to prove that the loss or damage was not, in fact, attributable to this exception.

There are certain alterations in the applicability of the special exceptions in CGR section 29 subsections 3 and 4 (i.e., exceptions from the special exceptions). The reason for the adjustments in subsection 3 is that the reason for the special exception found in CGR section 29 subsection 1 litra (d), based on the increased exposure of certain types of goods, is not present in the event of the vehicle being specially equipped to handle the particular exposure to damage. An example would be a trailer with a cooler or a heater handling goods otherwise subject to the special exception.

E. Concurrent Causes

289. In the event that the carrier is partly exempted from liability due to the general or special exceptions, the carrier may only be held liable to the extent the loss, damage or delay was caused by reasons for which the carrier is liable (concurrent causes), *see* CGR section 30.

II. The Limitations of Liability

A. General

290. The general rule under Norwegian contract law is that a liability to pay damages comprises *all adequate direct and indirect (consequential) losses actually suffered* by the claimant. The CMR liability scheme contains however provisions in order to *standardize* the amount of damages due (standardized valuation of the goods), *see* CGR sections 32 subsection 1 (loss) and 34 subsection 1 (damage). It follows that an assessment of the actual losses suffered by the particular cargo interest will not be pursued. The value stipulated through the standardized valuation of the goods is, in addition, subject to the *limitations* set out in CGR sections 32 subsections 2–5 (loss) and 34 subsection 2 (damage).

As for delay, CGR section 35 subsection 1 contains provisions both regarding the valuation of loss and the limitations.

Additionally, the CMR allows the sender to declare a special interest in the goods against a surcharge, *see* CGR sections 33 and 35 subsection 2. The interest declared may exceed the limitations of the CMR and the CGR, and it will operate as the upper limit of the carrier's liability. The bilateral compulsory nature of the CMR is not an obstacle to the declaration of a special interest.

B. Loss

291. For total or partial loss of the goods, the damages due (standardized) are equal to the value of the goods at the place and the time for receiving them for transport by the carrier. The value will primarily be stock exchange quotations. If quotations are not available, the market value will prevail. Lastly, the value will be fixed as for the common value for goods of a similar nature and quality, *see* CGR section 32 subsection 1.

Additionally, the damages due are *not to exceed* 8.33 SDR per kg of the gross weight of the lost goods for international (CMR) transport, *see* CGR section 32 subsection 3. The corresponding limit for domestic carriage is 17 SDR, *see* CGR section 32 subsection 2. As for domestic transport, the CMR limitation was considered low and therefore increased in favour of the cargo interests.

In addition to the damages, the claimant may demand a refund of freight and related charges paid – fully in the event of a total loss, and proportionately in case of a partial loss, *see* CGR section 32 subsection 5.

C. Damage

292. For damage to the goods, the valuation is as for total or partial loss (including special interest), *see* CGR section 34 subsection 1. The damages due are, in any case, *not to exceed* the limit recoverable if the goods had been totally or partially lost, *see* subsection 2.

D. Delay

293. Delay may have been declared converted into a total loss, *see* CGR section 31 subsection 1. For other delay than total loss, the actual economic loss suffered is to be compensated, *see* CGR section 35 subsection 1. The loss compensated will always be *limited* to the freight payable. Charges related to the freight are not to be added to the freight in fixing the limitation amount.

E. Domestic Transport: Special Relief

294. For domestic transport only, CGR section 39, in accordance with the *Act on Tort Claims* of 13 June 1969 No. 26 (the Tort Act) section 5-2, may allow an additional relief of the non-professional road carrier's liability. The assessment of relief is based on a discretionary evaluation of the specific circumstances of the case, including the financial ability of the carrier.

F. Interest

295. The claimant may claim interest on unpaid amounts. For international transport, the interest accrues from the time of sending a demand for payment to the carrier, or, alternatively, from filing of writ/points of claim with the courts. The claim earns interest at the rate of 5% per annum. For domestic transport, the claim earns interest in accordance with the *Act on Late Payment* of 17 December 1976 No. 100, basically entailing interest being triggered from one month after the claim for payment has been demanded. Interest will (January 2019) run at a rate of 8.75% per annum.

G. Extra-Contractual Claims

296. The claimant may in certain instances have an interest in directing his action or an additional action against persons or entities other than the contracting carrier, e.g., a hired driver or another servant at fault. The claimant may also construct the claim on rules outside contractual liability, for example, a tort action. A motive for the claimant to change the address of the claim from the contracting carrier may be an attempt to overcome the limitations.

In order to discourage actions for such extra-contractual claims, and to make the issues clear, CGR section 37 provides that claims based on other law than breach of contract for the carriage are still subject to the liability scheme in the CGR. The protection of CGR also operates to the benefit of the employees or servants, etc. for whom the carrier is liable according to CGR section 6.

The CGR implies that in the event that claims are made against both the carrier and the servant, the limitation amounts in CGR will serve as the *aggregate limit* for both or more claims. As is also the case with the CMR, the 'aggregate effect' has not been expressly spelt out in CGR.

III. Wilful Misconduct and Gross Negligence

297. The CMR Article 29 sets aside the otherwise offered exceptions from liability and the limitations of liability in the event that the default was caused by *wilful misconduct* by the carrier or by the agents or servants of the carrier or by any other persons of whose services he makes use for the performance of the carriage. The CMR Article 29 continues to provide that the default of the carrier, etc., 'considered as *equivalent to wilful misconduct*' under the law of the court or tribunal seized of the case, is to have the same effect.

CGR section 38 transforms the CMR Article 29 to Norwegian law and excludes the right to invoke exceptions or limitations if the default was caused by intent or '*gross negligence*'. 'Gross negligence' in the context of piercing limitations in liability is well known in other areas of Norwegian contract law.

In the case in ND 1995 238 NSC, the Supreme Court held that the concept of 'gross negligence' in CGR section 38 is the same as the commonly recognized concept for gross negligence under Norwegian contract and tort law. The case dealt with a road transport from Germany to Norway. The essential facts on the assessment of the carrier's (in fact a sub-carrier's) conduct as gross negligent appear to be that the trailer driver had over a long period of time driven too fast on bad roads in Norway combined with stiff suspension on a wagon which made it less than suitable for the carriage of a fairly light cargo. The burden of proving gross negligence or wilful misconduct rests on the claimant. A general observation on Norwegian – and indeed Scandinavian – case law over the last fifteen to twenty years is the sharp increase in the number of cases where the claimant is asking for the carrier's right to limit his liability to be set aside, and – similarly – a considerable increase in judgments where the claimant is granted such a right. Mention should be made of, on the one side, ND 1997 255 NCA, ND 2007 197 NCC and ND 2007 280 NCA (gross negligence) and on the other ND 2005 305 NCA (not gross negligence),

§5. Claims and Actions

I. General

298. The CMR contains regulations as to assertion of claims, and barring same, and on jurisdiction. The CMR regulations in this respect are a bit different from general Norwegian contract law. The CGR rules are therefore not the same for international and domestic carriage.

Generally, the regulations for both international and domestic transport encourage quick settlement of disputes. The regulations on international transport are in some respects not requirements for the claimant to swiftly assert the claim, but instead drafted as rules on shifting the burden of proof. The effect will be that the condition of the goods at the time of delivery is to be deemed contractual if apparent deficiencies were not pinpointed by the claimant upon delivery. It follows that the claimant then does not have a claim to assert at all.

II. Claim

299. For international transport, CGR section 40 subsections 2–4 stipulates that in the event that the receiver takes delivery of the goods without examining their condition, and without alleging loss or damage, the delivery is to be deemed contractual unless the claimant proves the opposite. Apparent (visible) defects are to be stated in writing by the receiver instantly upon delivery, and otherwise within seven days, Sundays and public holidays not included. When the receiver and the carrier have undertaken a mutual examination of the condition of the goods upon delivery, their findings are to be decisive as to the factual condition of the goods. Evidence to the contrary is then not admitted, except for hidden defects. In such a case, the claimant is expected to launch his claim within seven days, calculated likewise. For delay in delivery of an international transport, the receiver has to assert his claim in writing within twenty-one days after the goods have been made available to him.

For domestic transport, the claimant has to notify the carrier – not necessarily in writing – of the claim for loss, damage or delay 'without undue delay', *see* CGR section 40 subsection 1. The claimant is allowed slower action if the cause of the breach of contract was intent or gross negligence on the part of the carrier.

III. Time-Bar

300. Given that the claim has been duly asserted, the claim will be time-barred after one year, but after three years if based on intent or gross negligence, CGR section 41 subsection 1.

The time-bar period starts to run from the day of delivery of the goods in the event of partial loss, damage or delay, CGR section 41 subsection 2. For total loss, it runs from the thirtieth day after the expiry of the agreed delivery date or – if no delivery date has been agreed – from the sixtieth day from the date on which the goods were taken over by the carrier. For international transport, the time bar period may on certain conditions be suspended relating to written presentation of the claim on the carrier, CGR section 41 subsection 3.

To prevent the claim from being time-barred, it is usually required that the proper legal steps have been initiated. Generally, it means that the claimant will have to file the writ or points of claim with the courts. In the event of arbitration being the appropriate forum, the claimant will have to start the arbitration proceedings in accordance with the Arbitration Act of 14 May 2004 No. 25 section 23.

A claim that has been time-barred may not be utilized as a counterclaim or through set-off during court action even if the claims arise from the same contract for carriage, *see* CGR section 41 subsection 5.

In ND 2005 295 NSC, the Supreme Court found that the CGR was applicable to a transport of money. Consequently, the claim was time-barred after one year according to CGR section 41 subsection 1, and not subject to the time-bar rules with a three-year limit otherwise in general operative under Norwegian law.

IV. Jurisdiction and Venue

301. CGR sections 42–44 contain quite extensive regulations on jurisdiction and legal venue. One reason for the regulations is that other CMR states may under their internal law have jurisdiction to specific international road carriage.

In a CMR transport, the contracting parties may, within certain limits, *see* CGR section 42 subsections 1, second sentence and 2, agree upon the venue. With no agreement, a suit relating to such a transport may, according to CGR section 42 subsection 1, only be initiated in the state:

(1) where the defendant is domiciled;
(2) where the defendant has his principal place of business;
(3) where the representative through which the contract for carriage was concluded is situated; or
(4) where the carrier received the goods, or where it was destined to go.

In a domestic transport, the rules in CGR section 42 subsection 3 apply.

The parties are also at liberty to agree upon settlement of the dispute through arbitration proceedings. The agreement may be concluded already upon entering into a contract for carriage, or following an incident and after an actual dispute has arisen. This is expressly stated for international transport in CGR section 44.

V. Successive Carriage and Direct Action

A. *Successive Carriage*

302. CGR sections 45–49 contain regulations as to transport performed by successive road carriers, i.e., road carriers performing separate parts of the overall transport distance.

In the event of multiple successive carriers transporting goods for which there is one contract for carriage (as confirmed in a consignment note of which a counterpart is accompanying the goods), each carrier is responsible for the whole of the transport. Upon receipt of the goods and the consignment note, the 'second' and each subsequent carrier becomes a party to the contract for carriage in accordance with the terms of the consignment note. The consignment note serves as prima facie evidence also for the successive carriers, CGR section 46 subsection 1 third sentence. Each successive carrier is at liberty upon receipt of the goods to take reservations relating to the condition of and schedule for delivery of the goods in the consignment note, CGR section 46 subsection 1, second sentence. A reservation may be of importance in connection with recourse claims among the successive carriers.

The main effect of addressing a successive transport is that the claimant is at liberty to claim and sue the first and/or the last carrier of the transport distance and/or the carrier responsible for the part of the carriage under which the loss, damage or delay occurred, *see* CGR section 47. It follows that the carrier receiving a claim may not have caused the breach of contract himself and that he may be held liable for the performance of a carrier who is not a sub-carrier in relation to the carrier who is held responsible.

Unless otherwise agreed among the successive carriers, the division of responsibility among them basically conforms to the extent the carrier has contributed to causing the loss, damage or delay, *see* CGR section 48 subsection 1 litra (a) and (b). In the event of the causes of damage, etc., not being established, the responsibility is to be divided between all the carriers in accordance with the portion of the total freight due to them, *see* CGR section 48 subsection 1 litra (c) The same principle applies in the event that one of the liable carriers is unable to meet his payment obligations in this respect, *see* CGR section 48 subsection 2.

B. *Direct Action*

303. The CMR does not contemplate *direct action* against any sub-carrier of the contracting carrier. For successive carriage, a degree of direct action is nevertheless acknowledged, as described in A. above.

Under Norwegian law, it follows from the case in ND 1995 238 NSC that a direct action claim can be laid directly towards a performing and even a non-performing sub-carrier of the contracting carrier. The Supreme Court held that the sub-carrier was deemed 'the carrier' under CGR section 27 and liable according to the CMR liability scheme. In the opinion of the Supreme Court, the interpretation did not conflict with a prudent understanding of the wording of the CMR Article 17.

Further, the Supreme Court stated that the promise to perform road carriage by the sub-carrier also vests to the benefit of the owner of the goods (most likely referring to the sender or receiver as appropriate). The result is – at least for direct claims against defaulting performing sub-carriers – in line with statutory maritime and air transport law.

§6. Transport of Passengers

304. Transport of passengers on the road is not subject to the provisions of the CGR, not even for hand luggage or related items transported together with the person. Under Norwegian law, legislation relating to contracts for transport of passengers by road vehicles is nearly absent. It appears that passenger transport is not in any particular need of general international conventions. Under Norwegian law, the issue of passenger transport (apart from liability for delay) is basically a question of insurance cover.

The overall interest of losses suffered by passengers in car or bus transport, concentrates on *personal injury,* etc. Claims for personal injury relating to transport by road in a vehicle are governed by the *Act on Liability for Vehicles* of 3 February 1961. The 1961 Act sets up a mandatory insurance scheme. The scheme aims at full (*unlimited*) insurance compensation for losses suffered as a consequence of personal injury, including settlement of claims from relatives of a deceased passenger. The protection of the 1961 Act may not be contractually waived by the passenger prior to an incident.

The liability of the insurer is *strict* with *no exceptions* offered whatsoever (apart from contributory negligence). It is also necessary for the accident to have been caused by the vehicle (including, *inter alia*, the actions of the driver or the driver of another vehicle).

The liability of the insurers operates irrespective of whether the reason for the transport is a contract for carriage against a consideration (e.g., by taxi or bus), or a car owner allowing friends to join for a ride as a friendly service. Additionally, the insurer carries the same strict liability for pure tort claims, e.g., from a pedestrian who has been run down by the vehicle. The fact that the insurers carry a strict mandatory liability to cover the full losses suffered from personal injury, means that attempts to fix a liability as caused by breach of a contract is of less importance.

Calculation of the damages due from the insurance company for personal injury, etc., is governed by the Tort Act Chapter.

Under general Norwegian contract law, it is envisaged that the road carrier of passengers against a consideration has a liability to pay damages for *delay* with a presumption of fault. It will probably be appropriate to also apply the principle of the CMR Article 17 No. 3 as to the defective condition of the vehicle as an independent basis for liability. Moreover, economic loss relating to a delay in transport by taxi or bus will, under general Norwegian contract law as applied to road transport of passengers, in practice often be considered to be an unlikely consequence of the contract being breached.

Transport by bus of passengers may, in the circumstances, be subject to standard conditions for carriage. In such context, it is known that some bus operators undertake a limited guarantee for delay on prefixed inter-city route services. The guarantee usually covers the costs to the passenger of a substitute ride in a taxi to the intended destination, after an initial fixed period of delay. The guarantees that have been seen are not without exceptions from liability but do seem to offer a firmer basis for liability than the ordinary liability with a presumption of fault.

Chapter 2. Transportation by Rail

Thor Falkanger

§1. INTRODUCTION

305. Previously the railway system was – with a few exceptions – owned and operated by the state. Based upon an Act of 22 November 1996 No. 66 (now repealed) on the state's railway traffic company, the state-owned company Norges Statsbaner BA (NSB) was founded. The transportation activities were taken over by this company, subject to the rules of the act. By an Act of 21 June 2002 No. 43, the company was converted to a limited company (NSB AS). This company serves carriage of passengers, while carriage of goods is undertaken by the (since 2010) wholly-owned subsidiary CargoNet AS. However, both transportation of passengers and goods may be undertaken by others, using the railway infrastructure, subject to a license from the Ministry of Transport and Communications, *see* Act of 11 June 1993 No. 100 section 6.

Ownership and management of the infrastructure have been retained by the state, today in charge of the administrative body originally named Jernbaneverket (JBV), now Bane NOR.

There is a supervisory body: The Norwegian Railway Authority (SJT) with the practical control and supervisory authority for rail traffic, i.e., for anyone having the permission to undertake railway traffic (including tramways and metros).

I. The Legislation

306. Railway transportation is regulated in three acts:

- Act of 10 June 1977 No. 73 on railway liability, primarily in regard to damage to passengers and their luggage in national traffic (Chapter II). The act has also some provisions on liability for other personal injury and property damage which 'the driving causes' (Chapter III).
- Act of 11 June 1993 No. 100 on building and operation of railways, with provisions on competition in regard to agreements on transport of passengers by railway (Chapter IIA).
- Act of 10 December 2004 No. 82 on Convention concerning international carriage by rail (the COTIF Act), stating that the Convention of 9 May 1980 together with Protocol of 3 June 1999 has force as Norwegian law.

This means that the following instruments (listed in section 2 of the Act of 2004) are to be considered as enacted Norwegian law:

- CIV – Uniform Rules concerning the Contract of International Carriage of Passengers by Rail.

- CIM – Uniform Rules concerning the Contract of International Carriage of Goods by Rail.
- RID – Regulation concerning the International Carriage of Dangerous Goods by Rail.
- CUV – Uniform Rules concerning Contracts of Use of Vehicles in International Rail Traffic.
- CUI – Uniform Rules concerning the Contract of Use of Infrastructure in International Rail Traffic.
- APTU – Uniform Rules concerning the Validation of Technical Standards and the Adoption of Uniform Technical Prescriptions applicable to Railway Material intended to be used in International Traffic.
- ATMF – Uniform Rules concerning Technical Admission of Railway Material used in International Traffic.

307. In addition, the European Parliament and Council Regulation EF No. 1371/2007 of 23 October 2007 on rail passengers' rights and obligations have been implemented in Norway by Regulation of 3 September 2010 No. 1241.

Broadly speaking, this means that:

- *international railway transportation* – of passengers or goods – is subject to the international instruments listed above;
- *domestic passenger traffic* is regulated by the Act of 1977, supplemented by the mentioned Regulation No. 1241 of 2010;
- *domestic transportation of goods* is subject to the private contract.

II. Compulsory Regulations

308. In international transportation, the CIV rules on liability of the carrier in regard to passengers are mandatory, but the carrier may assume 'a liability greater and obligations more burdensome' (Article 5), and so are the rules in CIM on carriage of goods (Article 5). Other regulations may supplement, but not derogate from the rules In domestic passenger carriage, the rules in the Act 1977 cannot be derogated from to the detriment of the passenger (section 8). For goods transported domestically, there are no explicit mandatory rules, but it should be noted that the Contract Act 1918 section 36 empowers the court to set aside – wholly or partly – a contract where it would be 'unreasonable or against good business behavior' to apply the contract term(s).

III. Distinction Between International and National Railroad Transport

309. As stated above, different sets of regulations are applicable to international railroad transport and to domestic railroad transport. The scope of the provisions of CIV and CIM is set out in Article 1 of each document; the rules apply to every contract of carriage of passengers/carriage of goods by rail 'when the place of departure and the place of destination are situated in two different Member States'. This conforms to the COTIF Act of 2004 section 2 letter a which states that the CIV rules apply to 'all paid and free transport of passengers on rail when the place of departure is in Norway and the place of destination is in another Convention State or vice versa'. With respect to the CIM rules an equivalent definition is found in section 2 letter b.

The Act of 1977 on railway liability is in principle all-embracing, but its scope of application is delimited in section 2. Subsection 2 excludes traffic covered by the Act of 2004, i.e., when CIV applies. Furthermore, subsection 3 excludes transportation which comes under Regulation EF No. 1371/2007, i.e., rail carriage performed in accordance with license under Directive 95/18/EC on the national railway network.

§2. International Railroad Carriage of Passengers and Luggage

310. It will appear from the above that Norway has ratified and implemented the COTIF convention; consequently, there is no need for a detailed account of the rules. Only an outline will be given, with special comments where national law modifies or supplements what follows from the Convention with its Appendices.

I. The Obligation of the Railway to Carry

311. The dominant obligation of a railway undertaking is to transport the passenger, as well as his hand luggage and registered luggage, from the station of departure to the station of destination against the stipulated fare (tariff). The railway undertaking is under an obligation to enter into a contract for carriage, and it is expected to offer the same tariffs to all users on the same conditions (CIV Articles 6 and 7). The obligation to carry on equal terms should be seen in the light of railway services being means of transportation open to the public in general.

II. The CIV Ticket

312. For transport of passengers, one or more ticket shall be issued, each complying with CIV Article 7. The ticket, containing a reference to CIV, shall name the station of departure and destination, and what is 'necessary to enable the passenger to assert the rights resulting from this contract'.

Tickets not issued in the name of the passenger are transferable provided the journey has not started. The passenger is allowed to bring his hand luggage without extra charge, provided it can he handled easily by the railway (Article 12). The passenger shall at all times be in the possession of a valid ticket to be produced at the request of the railway staff (Article 9).

III. Liability of the Passenger

313. The liability of the passenger as against the carrier is stated in CIV Article 53. He is liable for loss or damage resulting from non-compliance with administrative formalities, or from non-compliance with proper marking of registered luggage. When damage occurs in connection with the carriage of vehicles, the Conditions of Carriage are decisive. In respect of damage from dangerous cargo, the rules in RID apply. Finally, for loss or damage caused by 'articles and animals' the passenger is liable unless he proves that he 'exercised the diligence required of a conscientious passenger'.

IV. Registered Luggage

314. The obligations of the parties with respect to registered luggage are established by a luggage registration voucher; such voucher has important evidentiary effects (Article 16). The voucher – with some minimum requirements on contents stated in Article 17 – is only issued on the presentation of a valid ticket, unless the General Conditions of Carriage otherwise provides (Article 18).

V. Liability for Personal Injury and Damage to Luggage

315. According to CIV Article 26 section 1, the railway is *in general liable* for loss resulting from the death of or personal injury to the passengers. The condition is that the damage iscaused by accident arising out of the operation of the railway and happening while the passenger is in, entering or alighting from railway vehicles (the liability period). Thus, the railway is not liable under CIV for injury or loss occurring on the platform or in the railway service area. Liability under Article 26 is generally strict, with some exceptions in Article 26 section 2 letters a, b and c (roughly: force majeure, fault on the side of the passenger, act by third person). According to the 1977 Act section 3 the liability for damage occurring in Norway is strict – with the same limitations regarding place of accident. Some modifications follow from section 12 – the liability may be reduced when the passenger has contributed to the damage or the damage is due to force majeure-like events.

If the railway is liable, the compensation to be paid is regulated in CIV Articles 27–30, leaving some questions to national law. In particular, it should be noted that 'the amount of damages ... shall be determined in accordance with national law' (*see* Act 13 June 1969 No. 26 on damages), but with 175,000 SDR as a limit for each passenger (Article 30). This limit may be considerably below the amounts awarded based upon general Norwegian principles. However, in the *travaux preparatoires* it is said that the limitation amount is not a maximum amount: If national law does not fix a limit for damages or the maximum limit in national law exceeds 175,000 SDR, Article 30 does not apply at all (Ot.prp. No. 93 (2003–2004) pp. 14–15). EF No. 1371/2007 Chapter III Article 11 allows national law to grant 'further compensation' than what follows from the Regulation.

CIV Articles 33–37 have rules on liability for damage to hand luggage, animals and registered luggage.

VI. Delayed Transportation

316. CIV Article 32 on liability in case of failure to keep to the timetables, leaves it to national law to 'determine whether and to what extent the carrier must pay damages'. There are no such provisions in Norwegian formal law, but Regulation No. 1241 of 2010 gives – as previously mentioned – EF No. 1371/2007 status as a regulation in respect of 'travels and railway services on the national railway net'. Chapter IV of this EU instrument has detailed rules on delays, missed connections and cancellations, which are reflected in NSB CC section 7. The main rule is that in case of 'significant delay'– defined as sixty minutes for the main lines and otherwise thirty minutes –'the passenger may submit a claim for coverage of documented foreseeable direct expenses, limited to a maximum of two-tenths of the Norwegian national insurance basis amount' (January 2019 NOK 96,883, approximately about 8075 SDR).

§3. International Railroad Carriage of Goods

317. For international carriage of goods CIM applies as Norwegian law for all contracts on carriage of goods by rail against compensation where the place of taking over the goods is in Norway and the place of delivery is in another Convention State, or vice versa (2004 COTIF Act sections 1 and 2). The Convention rules are supplemented by some procedural rules in the Act of 2004, *see* section 4 on acceptance and enforcement of foreign judgments, section 5 on procedure in recourse actions and section 6 concerning enforcements liens and arrest.

§4. Domestic Railroad Carriage of Passengers and Luggage

318. As stated above, the basic regulation is formally the Act of 1977 on railway liability. The substantial rules follow, however, from EU No. 1371/2007, *see* the Act section 2 subsection 3, stating that the rules in Chapters II and IV of the Act do not apply to carriage subject to EU No. 1371/2007. There are three exceptions to the application of the EU rules: First, as mentioned above, the strict liability is extended by the exclusion of CIV Article 26 section 2 letters a, b and c. Second, as also mentioned above, the limitation of liability amount of 175,000 SDR. in respect of personal injury is not considered as a maximum; the national rules on determining the compensation are decisive. Both these two sets of rules apply to international as well as domestic carriage. Third, the CIV and EU limitation when luggage is damaged is replaced by the Act section 5, which lifts the maximum to half the basis amount in the national insurance scheme (January 2019 – half of NOK

968,823) abt. NOK 47,000, approximately 4,100 SDR); this right to limit liability is lost if the damage is caused 'with intent or gross negligence by anyone on the side of the railway' (subsection 2).

§5. Domestic Railroad Carriage of Goods

319. For domestic rail carriage there is no specific mandatory legislation, but the Court may – as mentioned above – intervene on the basis of the Contract Act section 36.

The rules of CargoNet are of particular interest. The liability of CargoNet is defined in Terms and Conditions Article 9 (covering more than two printed pages!). The starting point is that CargoNet is liable for loss, damage or delay 'affecting load carriers and goods … during the period from takeover to delivery' (Article 8.2). There are a number of exceptions as well as limitation of extent of liability – basically to 17 SDR per kg (Article 8.8).

Chapter 3. Air Transport

Thor Falkanger

§1. Introduction

I. General

320. Like the shipping industry, an important feature of air transport is its international aspect. Transport by air has the additional advantage of being the swiftest way of providing transport for distances beyond a certain minimum. For that reason, transport by air is frequently chosen by many passengers and by many senders of goods suitable for air transport, even though the costs of air transport are often greater compared to alternative modes for the same distance. However, transport by air is particularly exposed to severe consequences if accidents do occur (e.g., due to inevitable technical or human failure).

In order to facilitate the smooth and safe operation of flights across national borders, a great number of states, including Norway, have entered into multinational conventions. One important aspect of such civil regulations is that they define the terms for foreign aircraft to use airspace above each state. In addition, the international regulations pertaining to qualifications for the captain, the manning of the aircraft and other elements of the airworthiness of the aircraft, reflect the public interest in the safety of civil aviation operations. Another public aspect is the necessity of aircraft marking and national registration of ownership. Such registration also enables recording of mortgages for financing of aircraft and jet engines. In this respect, air law offers a close parallel to ship mortgages and ship financing.

II. Air Transport Public Law: The Chicago Convention

321. The *Chicago Convention* on international civil aviation of 7 December 1944 establishes the International Civil Aviation Organization (ICAO). The convention which deals mainly with public air transport issues has been ratified by Norway and is implemented in Norwegian internal law. The closely connected agreements of the same date – the International Air Service Transit Agreement and the International Air Transport Agreement – have also been signed by Norway and transformed to Norwegian internal law.

III. Air Transport Private Law: The Warsaw Convention as Amended

322. Regarding private law, the most important international document is the *Warsaw Convention* on certain uniform rules relating to international air transport of 12 October 1929. The convention has been amended by the *Hague Protocol* of

28 September 1955, and supplemented by the *Guadalajara Convention* of 18 September 1961 as well as the *Guatemala Protocol* of 8 March 1971, and amended by the *Montreal Protocols* Nos 1–4 of 25 September 1975.

The most recent and important convention is the *Montreal Convention* for the Unification of Certain Rules for International Carriage by Air of 28 May 1999. These rules had to a great extent already been formulated in Regulation EU 2027/97.

Norwegian law, based upon the Warsaw Convention and the Hague Protocol, was amended when the Montreal Convention was ratified in 2004 (without formal denunciation of Warsaw/Hague; with the effect that some situations may be governed by a special Warsaw act of 1936 – *see* AAO Act of 11 June 1993 No. 101 section 19-3). In respect of passengers, the adoption of the Montreal rules was not as important because Norway had already implemented Regulation EU 2027/97.

IV. Internal Norwegian Law

323. The governing rules are today laid down in the AAO Act of 11 June 1993 No. 101 – repealing a previous act of 1960. The rules on transport of passengers as well as goods are primarily found in Chapter X, and are supplemented by Regulation EU 2027/97 (as amended by Regulation EU 889/2002) on liability for passengers and their luggage. On the relationship between the AAO Act and the rules from the EU regime that are binding according to the EEA Agreement (the agreement between EU and Norway), *see* the AAO Act section 1-1 subsection 2, stating that the rules flowing from this agreement have priority over the rules of the Act.

The AAO Act section 1-1 subsection 1 provides that air transport within Norway has to be performed in accordance with the provisions of the AAO Act and promulgated regulations, with reservations for what follows from the EEA Agreement. Furthermore, the Act is applicable to any Norwegian registered aircraft also when it is outside Norwegian territory, provided the opposite does not follow from the Act itself and the application is compatible with agreements with foreign states and 'general principles of law' (*see* section 1-2 subsection 2). It should also be noted that Chapter X applies to foreign aircraft outside Norway 'to the extent this follows from agreements with foreign states and general principles of law' (*see* section 1-2 subsection 3).

Section 19-3 has a reservation. The special Warsaw Act of 1936 is still applicable when we have an international transport from or to a state which is a party to the Warsaw Convention but has not ratified the Hague Protocol.

V. Compulsory Regulations

324. The transport rules in the AAO Act, first of all in Chapter X, are normally only operative for transport against remuneration (section 10-1). However, when they are operative they cannot be deviated from by contract to the detriment of the carrier's contractual counterparty (the passenger/the owner of the goods). This applies to the basis of liability as well as the calculation of damages (AAO Act section 10-23 subsection 2). The act does not prevent the carrier from accepting more onerous rules (subsection 1).

VI. International and Domestic Air Transport

325. In most instances Norwegian law, in particular Chapter X of the AAO Act, does not distinguish between international and domestic air transports.

For domestic flights, the requirements regarding transport documents may, however, be moderated (AAO Act section 10-39). And in domestic relations the *Act on Tort Claims* of 13 June 1969 No. 26 (the Tort Act) sections 5-1 and 5-2 are applicable (AAO Act section 10-21 subsection 3). These sections give the court a discretionary power to reduce the liability of the defendant in case of contributory negligence (section 5-1), and also in other situations when 'having regard to size of the damage, the defendant's ability to pay, existing insurances and the circumstances in general it is considered that the liability would be unreasonably burdensome for the defendant' (section 5-2). In international matters, it follows from AAO Act section 10-21 subsections 1-2 that contributory negligence shall have the effect of reducing the amount of damages. By how much is within the discretion of the court.

§2. Air Carriage of Passengers and Luggage

I. Transport Documents

326. The Warsaw Convention contains rather extensive regulations on information to be inserted in the transport documents. This is particularly true for the *air waybill* (Article 8), but it also applies to the *passenger ticket* and the *luggage check* (Articles 3 and 4).

According to AAO Act section 10-3, the passenger ticket is to contain information on place of departure, place of destination and, in addition, at least one intermediate landing place if places of departure and destination are in the same state and one or more intermediate landings are made in another state. Regarding luggage, section 10-4 says that a luggage check is to issued fo each item registered for transport.

Following the technological development as recognized in the Hague Protocol and perhaps especially in the Montreal protocols, the requirements on the contents of transport documents have been relaxed. In addition, the issuance of the prescribed document is not a condition for the validity of the contract for carriage – *see* AAO Act sections 10-3 subsection 4 (passenger ticket) and 10-4 subsection 2 (luggage check).

II. Liability for Death of and Injury to Passenger

A. *The Montreal Convention Liability*

327. AAO Act section 10-17 holds the carrier *strictly liable* for death or injury (bodily and mental) to passengers, provided the death or injury was caused by an accident on board the aircraft or in connection with the passenger embarking or disembarking the aircraft. There is no requirement that the cause of the injury be specifically related to air transport risks. For example, the carrier is liable for the consequence of bad food or beverages served during the flight, and even for an injury wilfully inflicted on a passenger by a co-passenger. The use of the word 'accident' implies that damage solely due to the health status of the passenger is outside the carrier's liability. 'Injury' covers, of course, bodily injury, and also mental damage (shock, etc.) in connection with a bodily injury. Whether mental damage unconnected with bodily injury is recoverable is, according to the *travaux preparatoires*, not tested before the Norwegian courts.

However, there is a ceiling for this strict liability (*see* paragraph No. 333 below on limitation amounts). For damage exceeding the limit the carrier may be liable, but now provided that the damage is caused negligently – *see* paragraph No. 334 below.

The question of liability for death or injury caused by occurrences outside the liability period described in section 10-17 – e.g., in the airport waiting hall – has to be answered on the basis of other rules. A border line situation is damage in connection with bus transport from the terminal building to the aircraft (or vice versa). It is, however, not likely that liability for such damage will be assessed on the basis of section 10-17.

B. *Regulation EU 2027/97*

328. As a consequence of the EEA Agreement, Norway has adopted parts of EU transport law. This is reflected in the AAO Act section 10-17a whereby Regulation EU 2027/97 (as amended by Regulation EU 889/2002) is incorporated.

The initial incorporation, which took place in 1998, was at that stage a significant change of the liability regime. Because this regulation 'implements the relevant provisions of the Montreal Convention' the subsequent implementation of the Montreal convention in 2004 is of limited importance for aviation companies with license from a state within EEA. The convention may be of importance for carriers that are not aviation companies.

C. *Liability for Fault*

329. AAO Act section 10-22 states that in case of liability exceeding an amount fixed by the Ministry, the carrier is not liable according to section 10-17 for the excess amount *provided* that the carrier shows (Norway: '*godtgjør*', which an Appeal Court has construed as proving 'something more than preponderance of probability', *see* ND 2003 374 NCA:

- either that the damage is not caused by fault on the part of the carrier, his employees or others for whom he is responsible;
- or that the damage exclusively is caused by a third party.

By Regulation 6 January 2011 No. 9 the amount is fixed to 113,100 SDR per passenger. In other words: up to 113,100 SDR the carrier's liability is strict, but the passenger (or the relatives of the deceased passenger) may be entitled to further (unlimited) compensation if a loss is proved and the carrier cannot meet the indicated burden of proof. In practice, this means that the carrier must show how the damage occurred and that neither he nor anyone for whom he is responsible has acted negligently.

These rules are in conformity with the Montreal Convention Article 21 (with amount revised as per Article 24).

III. Liability for Damage to or Loss of Luggage

330. Under AAO Act section 10-18 subsection 1 first sentence, the carrier is *strictly liable* for damage to and partial or total loss of checked luggage. This rule applies where the damage occurred in the aircraft or while the luggage was in the custody of the carrier.

The second sentence exempts the carrier to the extent that the loss or damage was caused by inherent vice of or otherwise defects in the luggage. The carrier has the burden of proof; i.e., he must show that he is entitled to benefit from the exception.

Subsection 2 concerns unchecked baggage including personal items, for which the carrier is liable only if the damage resulted from fault of the carrier or anyone for whom he is responsible. It seems that the burden of proof for fault will rest on the claimant.

IV. Liability for Delay in Transport of Passengers and Luggage

331. Under the AAO Act section 10-20, the carrier is liable for delay in transporting passengers or luggage unless the carrier proves that he and those for whom he is responsible have taken all necessary measures to avoid the loss or that such measures were impossible. As a consequence, hindrances to transport due to force majeure events will relieve the carrier of liability. Traffic congestion on take-off, landing or otherwise access to airport facilities are likely to be accepted as relief either as force majeure or a not relevant fault on the part of the carrier. The exception may be practical e.g., in terms of certain weather conditions.

V. Advance Payment. Insurance

332. Important elements in the protection of the interests of the passenger or his successors are the rules on advance payment of liability amounts and the obligation of the carrier to have adequate insurance covering his liability.

AAO Act section 10-22a has rules on advanced payment. The rules following from Regulation EU 2027/97 are made applicable also outside the scope of this Regulation. The basic rule is that at the latest fifteen days after an *aircraft accident* resulting in death or personal injury the carrier shall pay an advance amount to 'physical persons' entitled to compensation to cover their immediate needs. Such payment is not considered as an acknowledgement of liability. There is, however, no absolute obligation to repay the advance: if the carrier eventually is held not liable, repayment is subject to the carrier proving that the injured or killed person by negligence has caused or contributed to the damage.

The insurance obligation is stated in section 10-38a. For Norwegian carriers, the obligation is to have 'sufficient insurance to cover the liability according to Chapter 10' (subsection 1), and non-Norwegian carriers shall be in a position to 'document' that they have such insurance (subsection 2).

VI. The Extent of Liability: Limitation of Liability

333. In case of *death of or injury to passengers*, including mental harm and disfigurement, the starting point under Norwegian internal law is that the passenger shall receive damages for the *full economic loss actually suffered* by the claimant in accordance with the Tort Act sections 3-1 through 3-10 – provided that the damage is not too remote (the requirement of adequate causation). The liability will also comprise compensation to cover inability to enjoy a normal life – section 3-2. A practical loss component is loss of income from work.

The claimant carries the burden of proving the economic loss suffered.

The carrier may *limit* his strict liability for the proven loss of each dead or injured passenger to 113,100 SDR (AAO Act section 10-22 subsection 1 first sentence, compare Regulation 6 January 2011 No. 9). However, if the damage is due to fault on the part of the carrier (*see* above in paragraph No. 334), there is no right of limitation.

For *delay in transport of passengers*, the passenger must likewise prove the actual economic loss suffered, while the carrier may *limit* his liability to 4,694 SDR for each passenger – the AAO Act section 10-22 subsection 2, compare Regulation 6 January 2011 No. 9.

In case of delay, damage, or partial or total loss of *luggage*, the actual loss must be proven by the passenger in the same manner. The carrier may *limit* his liability to 1,131 SDR – AAO Act section 10-22 subsection 3, compare Regulation 6 January 2011 No. 9. The limit operates per passenger irrespective of the number of items delayed, damaged or lost.

Legal fees and costs relating to filing and pleading the claims may be recovered in addition to the limitation amounts.

If a claim is pursued against the carrier and also (or instead) against the servant at fault, the limitation serves as the *aggregate amount* recoverable – AAO Act section 10-25. There is an exception in subsection 2 in case of serious negligence.

VII. Wilful Misconduct and Gross Negligence

334. AAO Act section 10-22 subsection 5 takes away the right to limit liability regarding personal injury and delay in carriage of passengers if it is proved that the damage resulted from an act or omission of the carrier, his servants or agents (within the scope of their service), done with intent to cause damage or grossly negligent with the understanding that damage would probably result.

VIII. Fault by the Passenger

335. AAO Act section 10-21 distinguishes between international and national flights. Subsection 1 relating to contributory negligence during *international flights* entails that in the event that the passenger by own acts or omissions negligently contributes to the damage, the liability of the carrier shall be reduced; he may also be wholly exonerated. The same applies to claims from relatives of an injured or deceased passenger. The burden of proving contributory negligence rests on the carrier. Reduction of a claim or total exoneration will depend upon what is considered reasonable with a view to the seriousness of the contributory conduct, *see* subsection 2.

For *domestic flights*, AAO Act section 10-21 subsection 3 refers to the general rules under Norwegian law on contributory negligence according to the Tort Act sections 5-1 and 5-2.

§3. Air Carriage of Goods

I. The Air Waybill and Cargo Receipt

336. In conformity with the Montreal Convention, AAO Act section 10-5 requires that transport of goods by air is evidenced either by an air waybill or a cargo receipt, but the carriage agreement is not invalidated if such a document does not exist or, if it exists, does not conform with the requirements dealt with below (section 10-9).

We shall first discuss the air waybill.

The air waybill shall, according to section 10-8, contain this basic information:

(1) place of departure and place of destination;
(2) the place of at least one intermediate landing place when place of departure and destination is in the same country and one or more intermediate landing places are in another country;
(3) weight of the goods.

In practice, the waybill will give additional information, *see* below.

The waybill is issued in three originals by the sender (the consignor) (section 10-6 subsection 1). No. 1 is marked 'for the carrier' and is signed by the sender. No. 2 is marked 'for the receiver' (consignee) and is signed by both the sender and the carrier. Original No. 3 is signed by the carrier and given back to the sender when the goods have been received for transport. A common practical approach may be that the air carrier, at the request of the sender, issues the air waybill, in which case the carrier will be deemed to have done so on behalf of the sender if not otherwise proven (section 10-6 subsection 2).

The issuance of a waybill has several important consequences as given below.

The waybill is, according to section 10-11 subsection 1, a refutable evidence of the conclusion of a contract of carriage of the receipt of cargo and the terms of carriage mentioned in the waybill. And the same applies to information included in the waybill regarding the weight of the goods, its dimensions, packing and number of pieces (subsection 2 first sentence). Description of the visible condition of the goods is in the same category, while other information regarding quantity, volume, contents or condition has not this evidentiary effect, unless the carrier has inspected the correctness in the presence of the sender and has confirmed this by a statement in the waybill (second sentence). The importance of the information in the waybill is, first of all, demonstrated where a claim for loss or damage is set forth. Usually, the condition of the cargo at the place of destination is not disputed. Any difference from the description in the waybill is assumed to represent transport damage – unless the carrier succeeds in establishing that the goods received at the place of departure were not as described.

Another effect of the air waybill is that it is, as mentioned, evidence of the carriage agreement. The carrier's obligation to deliver the goods at the place of destination depends on the payment of outstanding amounts and otherwise fulfilment of the terms mentioned in the carriage agreement (section 10-13). This is of particular relevance for the buyer of the goods.

A third effect to be mentioned here, is connected with the sender's far-reaching right to dispose of the goods, also when it is in transit: he may stop the carriage, require that the goods are returned or that the goods are delivered to another than the one named as receiver in the air waybill. However, the carrier will insist upon being shown the original air waybill No. 3 – otherwise he may be held liable for the damage caused to any person who is lawfully in possession of the air waybill (section 10-12 subsection 2).

The air carrier may require that the sender issues separate air waybills where the goods consist of more than one lot – one waybill for each lot (section 10-7).

The air waybill and, of course, the cargo receipt are non-negotiable documents. The international obligations do not prevent making the air waybill a negotiable document, but such a step has not been taken under Norwegian law.

337. There is, as indicated, an alternative to the air waybill: It is not necessary to issue an air waybill if information regarding the goods is 'registered in another manner' (section 10-5 subsection 2). In such a case, the carrier shall, on the sender's demand, give the sender a cargo receipt containing sufficient information for the identification of the goods, and the sender shall have access to the information recorded. In addition, section 10-8 says that the cargo receipt shall contain the same information as the air waybill. And furthermore, the evidentiary effects of the cargo receipt are the same as for the air waybill (sections 10-11 and 10-12 as well as 10-13).

338. The sender is the issuer of the air waybill and he is also the one who in most instances will supply the information included in the cargo receipt. Incorrect information may cause difficulties for the carrier: his operations are made more difficult, the goods may be damaged or delayed, there may be difficulties in respect of goods belonging to others. Section 10-10 holds the sender responsible for the information supplied. If the information is 'incorrect or insufficient the sender is obliged to pay the damage suffered by the carrier or anyone for whom the carrier is responsible'.

II. Rights and Obligations of the Carrier, the Sender (Consignor) and the Receiver (Consignee)

339. The *air carrier* is under an obligation to receive and transport the goods from the place of departure to the place of destination according to the flight schedules operating or as specifically agreed, against payment of the applicable charges. The carrier enjoys the right to *detain the goods* until all amounts due under the contract of carriage have been settled.

The *sender of the cargo* is under an obligation to furnish documents or information, *see* paragraph No. 336 above concerning the air waybill, or alternative registration of information otherwise included in the waybill. The sender has also an obligation to present information or documents required by the customs authorities or other public bodies, necessary for the delivery of the cargo to the receiver (consignee), *see* section 10-16. If the sender does not comply with this obligation the goods may be delayed and delay may cause physical damage to the goods (the flowers wither, the fruit rots). Should the carrier be held liable towards the cargo owner for delay or cargo damage, the carrier has a recourse claim against the sender.

Carriage of dangerous goods is dealt with in Regulation 11 January 2003 No. 41.

Provided the sender fulfils his obligations under the contract for carriage, the sender has a *right to modify the contract of carriage*, *see* section 10-12 subsection 1. The option to modify comprises a right to withdraw from delivery at place of departure or place of destination, to instruct stoppage in transit, to instruct delivery to a receiver other than the one named in the air waybill, and to have the goods returned to the place of departure. Other instructions are not binding on the air carrier except for minor adjustments. This right to modify the contract of carriage is, however, subject to an important qualification. The air waybill No. 3 or the cargo receipt should be presented to the carrier at the time when the sender chooses to modify the contract. The background for this rule is, of course, that if the sender sells the goods, the buyer needs to know that he eventually will get the goods. With possession of the air waybill or the cargo receipt the buyer is reasonably sure that the contract of carriage will not be altered to the detriment of his interests. Should a modification nevertheless take place, the carrier is liable for the damage caused to the true holder of the bill or the receipt (with recourse to the sender) – *see* section 10-12 subsection 2.

Agreements deviating from section 10-12 or section 10-13 are not valid unless inserted in the air waybill or the cargo receipt (section 10-15).

III. Liability for Loss, Damage and Delay

A. *Loss and Damage*

340. If the goods are damaged or totally lost the air carrier is liable for the economic loss of the cargo owner. According to the AAO Act section 10-19 subsection 1 this is a *strict liability* with a *few exceptions*. The air carrier is exonerated to the extent he proves (Norway: 'godtgjør'– *see* above paragraph No. 151) that the damage, etc. was caused by:

(1) inherent defect, quality or vice of the goods;
(2) substandard packing of the goods not performed by the carrier;
(3) act of war or similar hostile armed action;
(4) an act of public authority relating to import, export or reloading of the goods.

The liability period of the air carrier for cargo transport runs from taking custody of the goods at the airport to the time of delivery at the destination. The period may also comprise complementary transport to the airport, e.g., by a lorry (AAO Act section 10-19 subsection 2).

Delay is to some extent treated as total loss of the cargo. Section 10-14 states that delayed goods are considered totally lost if the carrier admits that they are indeed lost, or the goods have not arrived at the latest seven days after they should have.

B. *Delay*

341. The liability of the air carrier when loss is caused by late delivery of the cargo is not strict; liability is based upon a presumption of fault. The carrier is held liable unless he succeeds in proving that the delay was not caused by his fault or a fault of those for whom he is responsible (section 10-20).

IV. Limitations of Liability

342. The liability of the air carrier in respect of loss of or damage to the goods or delay is, according to the AAO Act section 10-22 subsection 4 limited to 19 SDR per kg (Regulation 6 January 201w1 No. 9, reflecting the Montreal Convention Article 24). This limitation is applicable in international as well as domestic traffic.

Legal fees and costs relating to filing and pleading claims with the courts may be recovered in addition to the limitation amount, provided the air carrier has not within six months from the incident or six months after the filing of an action with the court offered in writing an amount at least matching the awarded sum.

The sender may have declared a *special interest* in the goods. The amount declared will then serve as the upper limit for the liability of the air carrier (section 10-22 subsection 4 second sentence). Usually, the amount declared will have to be compensated unless the carrier proves that the value of the goods is actually lower (third sentence).

V. Wilful Misconduct and Gross Negligence

343. The limitations operate no matter on what legal and factual basis the claim is brought. However, section 10-22 subsection 5 declares that the right of limitation is lost if it is proved that the damage resulted from an act of the carrier himself or anyone for whom he is responsible (within the scope of their service), provided that the damage was caused intentionally or grossly negligent with the understanding that damage would probably result.

VI. Fault by the Sender

344. According to the AAO Act section 10-21, the liability of the carrier shall be reduced and he may even be completely exonerated, if it is proved that the cargo owner or anyone for whom he is responsible, negligently contributed to the damage – having due regard to what is considered reasonable in view of the degree of contribution. This is the same principle that applies for a passenger's contributory negligence, *see* § 2.VII. above.

§4. Claims and Actions

I. Assertion of Claim

345. Transport law for most modes of transport requires prompt assertion and prosecution of claims by the claimant in order to avoid the claim being extinguished. Air transport is no exception in this respect.

According to AAO Act section 10-26, checked luggage and goods received without complaint from the owner are deemed to have been delivered in sound condition and in conformity with the information in the transport document or what has been registered. The owner has, however, the possibility of proving the opposite.

If the goods are damaged or partly lost a complaint must be presented immediately after the damage or loss was discovered, and at the latest within seven days after receipt of checked luggage and fourteen days after receipt of goods.

For delay, a complaint must be made within twenty-one days from the date when the goods were placed at the disposal of the receiver.

Complaints should be in writing, presented or mailed to the carrier before the period allowed for assertion of a claim expires. If these requirements on assertion of claims are not complied with, the claim is extinguished unless the air carrier has acted in bad faith (section 10-27).

The AAO Act does not contain provisions on assertion of claims relating to injury, etc. to passengers or for total loss of checked luggage or goods. This means that the claim may be brought until it is time-barred – *see* section 10-29 and II. below. In the event that a claim is not promptly asserted it may be more difficult for the claimant to verify his claim (when and how the damage occurred, the extent of the damage, etc.).

II. Time-Bar

346. According to section 10-29 – based upon the Warsaw Convention Article 29 – all liability claims under AAO Act Chapter X are subject to a two-year time-bar (extinction) running from the arrival of aircraft at the destination or from the scheduled arrival or from the time carriage stopped.

The convention rules have to be supplemented by internal law in respect of the precise calculation of the time-bar period and how to breach the time-bar. Such rules are found in the Act on Time-Barring of Claims of 18 May 1979 No. 18. There are a number of ways for breaching the time limit. Acceptance of the claim – explicitly or by action (e.g., payment of interest, advance payment) – is a practical and important one (section 14). The fallback position is taking legal steps, i.e., commencing a suit. For example, if goods arrived on 1 June 2018 the petition (points of claim) should be submitted to the court at the latest 1 June 2020 (section 15); delivery to the authorized post distributor on this date is sufficient (section 29 No. 3, compare the Act on the Courts of 13 August 1915 No. 5 section 146). The Convention rule is very strict: the claim is extinguished in two years, regardless of whether the cargo owner at that time was aware of the damage. Furthermore, an agreement to extend the period is not valid. In other words: if the parties are negotiating towards the end of the two years period and an amicable solution appears to be near, the claimant should nevertheless for the sake of security commence legal proceedings. The Norwegian enactment has to be understood in the same way.

III. Law and Venue

347. AAO Act section 10-28 is based upon the Montreal Convention Article 33. It limits peremptorily the possible venues for a claim for damages based upon Chapter X of the AAO Act. The possibilities are, however, numerous. Regarding a suit in Norway the position is: A suit can be commenced if the carrier has his domicile or his principal place of business in Norway, or has a place of business in Norway through which the contract has been made. So is also the situation when the place of destination is in Norway. In case of passenger's death or personal injury, there is an additional venue, viz. where the passenger had his permanent residence at the time of the accident in Norway – provided that the carrier operates airborne passenger service in Norway from premises in Norway (owned or rented).

IV. Successive Carriage and Direct Action

348. Special liability questions arise when a carriage is performed by successive carriers. AAO Act section 10-30 has rules on division of liability in such cases where successive air carriers are performing different parts of the total transport distance.

The main rule in subsection 1 is that each successive carrier is liable for the part of the transport distance performed by him.

For checked luggage and for goods, the sender (consignor) may in addition to suing the contracting carrier sue the first performing air carrier. The receiver (consignee) may in addition to the contracting carrier claim the last performing air carrier. In both cases, such claims may be pursued even though the loss, damage or delay occurred while the luggage or goods was in the custody of an other carrier. If two carriers are liable, the liability is jointly.

Section 10-30 has to be read together with section 10-32 which defines the concept of 'carrier' (in conformity with the Guadalajara Convention). Both the carrier concluding the contract and the carrier actually performing (the total or a part of the carriage) are deemed to be 'carriers' in respect of Chapter X. For instance: If damage occurs while the goods are in the custody of the performing carrier he is liable according to the rules in Chapter X, and so is the contracting carrier. While the contracting carrier is liable for what happens during the total transport period, the performing carrier is liable only for what happens during his period of custody of the goods.

In case both carriers are sued, the claimant cannot recover an aggregate amount in excess of the highest applicable limitation for one carrier.

The option for the claimant to direct actions against more than one carrier requires special rules on venue. A claim for damages against both carriers or one of them may be pursued where the contracting carrier has venue according to section 10-28 (*see* paragraph No. 347 above) or where the performing carrier has his domicile or principal place of business (section 10-36 subsection 1). The claimant's choice of defendant may give rise to recourse actions; section 10-36 subsection 2 has special rules on venue in such a suit.

Chapter 4. Multimodal Transports

Thor Falkanger

§1. Introduction

I. General

A. Definitions

349. The international conventions established in order, *inter alia*, to facilitate transport in trade that often requires the use of different modes of transport have almost exclusively aimed at regulating one mode of transport.

If the mode of transport is the same – liner shipment from Oslo to Gothenburg, with a new line taking the goods to US – we usually talk of a *successive transport* arrangement. What we will discuss in the following is the combination of different modes of transport – typically truck transport from the inland factory to the port where the goods are taken on board the liner vessel to the port of destination. Then we have a *multimodal transport*. The transport may be arranged in a manner whereby the sender of the goods becomes the contracting party in relation to several carriers performing parts of the total transport distance: There is one contract with X for the sea voyage, another with Y for the rail transport etc. The delivery of the goods from one carrier to the next one – in our example from the ship to the railway – may raise some problems, which we shall not deal with here. What we will discuss is the situation where one carrier undertakes to have the cargo transported from A to B, using two or more different modes of transport. The person giving such a promise is often called a *multimodal transport operator* (MTO).

Clearly, in some instances it may be doubtful whether a person has given a multimodal promise or whether he, e.g., has undertaken the carrier's role for the sea-voyage and in addition agreed to act as an intermediary for the railway part. Here we assume the former is accepted. The issue is what rules are applicable when the cargo is damaged or do not arrive on time.

B. The Use of Multimodal Transport Arrangements

350. The background for the multimodal transport agreement has been the growing demand for door-to-door delivery services. In this development, the freight forwarders have played an important role; they have gradually increased their activities as contracting carriers, which means that the actual carriers to a great extent are subcontractors of the freight forwarders.

Theoretically, a number of different modes of transport may be combined. In practice, there are, of course, important restrictions, depending upon factors such as available infra structure, type of cargo (volume, weight, value, etc.), time element, etc.

C. Multimodal Transport of Passengers

351. Also, transport of passengers may be arranged as a multimodal undertaking, either by a travel agent or by the passenger himself. The following presentation will concentrate on multimodal transport of goods.

II. The Multimodal Transport Problem

A. Common Legal Issues in Transport Law

352. From a legal perspective, multimodal transport poses several questions to which there are no clear answers. There are no binding international conventions on the subject of multimodal transports; neither has Norwegian internal law (as already indicated) a general legislation hereof.

The four major modes of transport (by sea, road, rail and air) are individually governed by quite detailed legal regimes founded on international conventions reflecting certain factual dissimilarities. Still, a number of legal issues are common to the regimes governing each mode of transport. Common issues that are usually addressed may be transport documents/negotiability, modifications of contract of carriage, basis of liability, limitation of liability, exclusion of limitations, assertion of claim, time-bar, governing law and venue, and direct action. The legal solutions for each mode do, however, vary. An example of a difference is the limitation amounts for damage, loss and delay applicable for each mode.

B. Compulsory Regulations

353. Freedom of contract may, to some extent, allow an MTO and a sender of goods to agree on an overall distribution of risk and liability for the entire multimodal transport. However, the legal regimes for each of the four major modes of transport are to a great extent compulsory for the subject mode. An international road transport of goods is, for example, subject to mandatory regulations to the protection of both the carrier and the sender (the CMR Article 41). The compulsory nature of the applicable rules constitutes a challenge for the MTO undertaking an overall liability towards the sender and simultaneously ensuring a feasible contractual back-to-back position towards the sub-carriers.

C. Three Main Problems

354. Among the problems related to multimodal transport we shall mention three. First, we have the gap-problem: there may be gaps between the liability periods for the various regimes for each mode of transport. Second, the MTO may be hold liable for damage, loss and delay, but it may be difficult or impossible to establish exactly when the liability arose ('unlocalized damage'). What kind of limitation rules are, e.g., applicable in such a situation? A third issue of a general nature is designing an adequate and cost-effective insurance cover for the entire multimodal transport.

D. Sources of Law

355. The following presentation will focus on some of the sources of law available from a Norwegian law perspective. The aforementioned absence of international law and conventions (on the Geneva convention, *see* below in §3.), and the lack of specific Norwegian internal law regulation of multimodal transport make it necessary to examine the fragments of multimodal transport rules (statutory) that exist in some of the regimes governing the four major modes of transport (§2. below). Further, some of the multimodal transport standard rules and formulas may be of greater interest in this context than any mandatory or supplementary legislation (statutory) that may be at hand (§4. below).

§2. Statutory Provisions and Treaty Law

I. Sea Carriage

356. Sea transport of cargo by a vessel is, under Norwegian internal law, governed by the MC; this Code has no regulations for multimodal transport, but there are some regulations of importance for multimodal transport.

The adaptation to the Hamburg Rules means i.a. that the carrier no longer may exonerate himself from liability by inserting 'tackle-to-tackle' clauses in, e.g., the bill of lading. Accordingly, the gap between sea carriage and a subsequent transport is reduced.

Where the total transport is performed by two or more vessels – successive carriage – the MC has to limited extent rules on the problems that may arise, *see i.a. above* paragraph No. 162.

II. Road Carriage

357. The CMR and the Act on Carriage of Goods by Road of 20 December 1974 No. 68 (the CGR Act) address to some extent international transport by road combined with other modes of transport – *see* the CMR Article 2 and the CGR Act section 4, which are discussed above in paragraph No. 274.

On successive carriage and direct action, *see* paragraph Nos 302 and303 above.

III. Railway Carriage

358. CIM Article 38 has provisions on liability when a railway vehicle is to be carried on board a vessel. If the sea passage is considered as a part of the regular railway route it is allowed to widen the scope of exceptions from liability.

On successive carriage, *see* CIM Articles 26 and 27.

IV. Air Carriage

359. In the event of a multimodal transport, the Warsaw Convention Article 31 provides that the rules of the convention (*inter alia*, on liability) are applicable to the air carriage only. This is reflected in the AAO Act of 11 June 1993 No. 11 §§ 10-37.

§3. International Regulation: UNCTAD 1980

360. Under the auspices of the UNCTAD the 1980 Geneva convention on *International Multimodal Transport Of Goods* was agreed.

The rules of UNCTAD 1980 are drafted to accommodate any combination of two or more modes of transport not necessarily involving a vessel. The UNCTAD 1980 requires thirty states to sign and ratify before the convention becomes effective twelve months thereafter (Article 36). Only a few states have signed the convention. Norway is not one of them. Nevertheless, if faced with a specific multimodal transport issue, the principles of the UNCTAD 1980 may be considered as valid arguments also under Norwegian law.

The scope of the UNCTAD 1980 is international multimodal transport (Article 2) and the rules are mandatory (Article 3), except that the MTO may contract a greater risk or a heavier responsibility than that which follows from the rules of the convention (Article 28). The liability of the MTO is based on the principle of presumption of fault or neglect and covers liability also for servants, agents and other persons for whom the MTO is responsible (Articles 14, 15 and 16). The liability period runs from taking the goods in charge, as further defined, until delivery. The liability is as a main rule limited to the higher of 920 SDR per package or 2.75 SDR per kg of gross mass. Provided the multimodal transport does not comprise of a sea or inland waterways transport, the limit is 8.33 SDR per kg of gross mass, which is in line with the CMR. Where it can be ascertained that the damage or delay occurred during an identified transport mode (localized damage) governed by mandatory convention or national law rules offering a higher limit than UNCTAD 1980, such rules take priority. The MTO loses the right to limit his liability if the damage or delay was caused intentionally or recklessly.

A multimodal transport document shall be issued, in a negotiable or non-negotiable form, with the contents and reservations as described in Articles 5 through 9. The multimodal transport document serves as prima facie *evidence* of receipt of the goods by the MTO as described in the document. To rebut evidence is not admitted if a negotiable document has been acquired in good faith by a consignee.

§4. STANDARD RULES AND FORMULAS

361. The fact that the UNCTAD 1980 so far has not become effective has encouraged the preparation of standard formulas for multimodal transport. A few of them will be mentioned.

362. A joint UNCTAD/ICC work group has prepared the UNCTAD/ICC *Rules on Multimodal Transport Documents*, effective from 1 January 1992 – the UNCTAD/ICC Rules. The UNCTAD/ICC Rules are drafted to apply to multimodal transport documents and have to a great extent absorbed the UNCTAD 1980 regime.

363. The Baltic and International Maritime Conference (BIMCO) has issued a Negotiable Combined Transport Bill of Lading 1971 with the code name Combiconbill. The document was drafted to serve unimodal or mulitimodal transports that do not necessarily involve transport by a vessel. Still the document reflects its origin in the shipping community, and that sea carriage often will be a part of a Combiconbill multimodal transport. The Combiconbill contains liberty clauses for the performance of the transport (clauses 6 and 7). The liability regime regarding liability and the exceptions is similar to that in the CMR.

Later, BIMCO has prepared the *Negotiable Multimodal Transport Bill of Lading* which is subject to the UNCTAD/ICC Rules – with code name Multidoc 95. There is also a *Non-Negotiable Multimodal Transport Waybill* of 1995, subject to the UNCTAD/ICC Rules, and the CMI *Uniform Rules for Sea Waybills*, with the code name Multiway 2016.

From the Norwegian – or rather Scandinavian – point of view NSAB 2015 (General Conditions of the Nordic Association of Freight Forwarders) is of particular importance. The document may be used for single mode transports as well as for multimodal transports. Where the freight forwarder is acting as contractual carrier, the formal main rule is that he is liable for loss or delay (clause 16), but there are important exceptions, notably for 'circumstances which the freight forwarder could not avoid and the consequences of which he was unable to prevent' (letter h). The liability for damage is limited to 8.33 SDR per kg gross of the part of the goods which has been lost, depreciated or damaged (clause 22). If it is proved, however that 'loss, depreciation, damage or delay has occurred whilst the goods were being carried by a particular means of transport, the freight forwarder shall instead be liable in accordance with the law applicable to such mode of transport' (clause 2).

Selected Bibliography

Maritime Law

Brækhus, Sjur, Alex Rein, and Jeremy Kingsley. *Handbook of P&I Insurance*. 3rd ed. Arendal: Assuranceforeningen Gard-Gjensidig, 1988.

Bull, Hans Jacob, and Terje Hernes Pettersen. *Skipssikkerhetsloven: Med kommentarer*. Oslo: Fagbokforlaget, 2010.

Bull, Hans Jacob. 'Insurance Law and Marine Insurance Law: The Unequal Twins.' *Scandinavian Studies in Law* 46 (July 2004): 11–33. http://www.scandinavianlaw.se/pdf/46-1.pdf.

Bull, Hans Jacob. 'Identification in Cargo Insurance.' *Scandinavian Institute of Maritime Law Yearbook, MarIus*, no. 295 (2002): 173–196.

Denisova, Ekaterina. 'The Role of Environmental Civil Liability in Regulation of Marine Oil Pollution in Norway.' *MarIus*, no. 383 (2009).

De Vibe, Kaja. 'Reinsurance Contracts. Application of the Law, the Reinsured's Duty of Disclosure and the Reinsurer's Obligation to Indemnify the Reinsured.' *Scandinavian Institute of Maritime Law Yearbook, MarIus*, no. 346 (2006): 265–306.

Eftestøl-Wilhelmsson, Ellen. 'Regulating European Multimodal Transport.' *Scandinavian Institute of Maritime Law Yearbook, MarIus*, no. 400 (2010): 27–46.

Eftestøl-Wilhelmsson, Ellen. 'EU Intermodal Transport and Carrier Liability – Content and Context.' *Scandinavian Institute of Maritime Law Yearbook, MarIus*, no. 360 (2007): 133–166.

Eftestøl-Wilhelmsson, Ellen. 'EC Agency Law and Intermediaries in Shipping.' *Scandinavian Institute of Maritime Law Yearbook, MarIus*, no. 346 (2006): 141–178.

Erdal, Leiv Mikael. 'Legal Implications of Security Assignment: Comparing the Norwegian and English Law of Security Assignments in the Context of Building Finance for High-Value Movable Property.' *MarIus*, no. 365 (2008).

Falkanger, Thor, Hans Jacob Bull, and Lasse Brautaset. *Scandinavian Maritime Law: The Norwegian Perspective*. 4rd ed. Oslo: Universitetsforlaget, 2017.

Falkanger, Thor. 'Cargo Damage – Who is Entitled to Sue the Maritime Carrier?' *Scandinavian Institute of Maritime Law Yearbook, MarIus*, no. 400 (2010): 47–64.

Falkanger, Thor. 'The Freight Forwarder's Security for Earnings and Outlays – with Particular View to NSAB 2000 and Norwegian Domestic Law.' *Scandinavian Institute of Maritime Law Yearbook, MarIus*, no. 394 (2009): 139–165.

Selected Bibliography

Falkanger, Thor. 'Credit Based upon Security in Ships.' *Scandinavian Studies in Law* 46 (July 2004): 35–59. http://www.scandinavianlaw.se/pdf/46-2.pdf.

Falkanger, Thor. 'Time Limitation of Cargo Claims Against the Sea Carrier.' *Scandinavian Institute of Maritime Law Yearbook, MarIus*, no. 309 (2003): 17–60.

Falkanger, Thor. 'Maritime Liens on Cargo: A Survey of the Provisions in the Norwegian Maritime Code.' *Scandinavian Institute of Maritime Law Yearbook, MarIus*, no. 295 (2002): 83–113.

Falkanger, Thor. 'Mortgages on Ships According to Norwegian Law.' *Scandinavian Institute of Maritime Law Yearbook, MarIus*, no. 281 (2001): 3–39.

Falkanger, Thor. 'Arrest of Ships under Norwegian Law.' *Scandinavian Institute of Maritime Law Yearbook, MarIus*, no. 258 (2000): 3–34.

Falkanger, Thor. 'Forced Sale of Vessels – According to Norwegian Law.' *Scandinavian Institute of Maritime Law Yearbook, MarIus*, no. 247 (1999): 3–27.

Falkanger, Thor. *Leie av skip*. Oslo: Universitetsforlaget, 1969.

Falkanger, Thor. *Konsekutive reiser*. Oslo: Universitetsforlaget, 1965.

Hempel, Maria. 'The End of the Shipping Pool as We Know It? EC Competition Law and the Legality of Shipping Pools.' *Scandinavian Institute of Maritime Law Yearbook, MarIus*, no. 360 (2007): 189–213.

Holme Støylen, Joar. 'The End of Liner Conferences? The New Competition Regime for Liner Shipping: Legal and Practical Consequences for European Maritime Transport.' *Scandinavian Institute of Maritime Law Yearbook, MarIus*, no. 394 (2009): 269–331.

Kang, Byoungil. 'Shipbuilding Contracts between Norwegian Buyers and Korean Builders.' *Scandinavian Institute of Maritime Law Yearbook, MarIus*, no. 360 (2007): 57–103.

Karsten, Jens. 'The Athens Regulation Is Heading into Harbour – the EU on the Point of Regulating Liability for Maritime Passengers.' *Scandinavian Institute of Maritime Law Yearbook, MarIus*, no. 376 (2008): 161–195.

Kristiansen, Camilla Nyhus. 'The Forwarding Agent's Storage Service Agreements: The Expansion of the Forwarding Agent's Traditional Role'. *Scandinavian Institute of Maritime Law Yearbook, MarIus*, no. 295 (2002): 197–274.

Kvaløy, Siri. '"Conditions of Use" at Gas Terminals: Risk Allocation and Insurance Coverage.' *Scandinavian Institute of Maritime Law Yearbook, MarIus*, no. 376 (2008): 57–131.

Michelet, Hans Peter. *Håndbok i tidsbefraktning*. Oslo: Sjørettsfondet, 1997.

Pozdnakova, Alla. 'Anonymity of Shipowners as a Maritime Security Problem – EU Law Implications.' *Scandinavian Institute of Maritime Law Yearbook, MarIus*, no. 360 (2007): 105–132.

Ringås, Cassia. 'The Bunker Convention: International Convention on Civil Liability for Bunker Oil Pollution Damage.' *Scandinavian Institute of Maritime Law Yearbook, MarIus*, no. 376 (2008): 277–344.

Røsæg, Erik. 'New Laws on Passenger Rights.' *Scandinavian Institute of Maritime Law Yearbook, MarIus*, no. 400 (2010): 325–344.

Røsæg, Erik. 'The Rotterdam Rules as a Model for Multimodal Transport Law.' *European Journal of Commercial Contract Law* 2, no. 1/2 (2010): 94–97.

Røsæg, Erik. 'The Athens Convention on Passenger Liability and the EU'. In *The Hamburg Lectures on Maritime Affairs 2007 & 2008*, edited by Jürgen Basedow, Ulrich Magnus, and Rüdiger Wolfrum. Berlin: Springer, 2010, 55–75.

Røsæg, Erik. 'Multinational Transport Company Groups above and beyond Nation States'. In *General Trends in Maritime and Transport Law 1929-2009: XI Hässelby Colloquium 2009*, edited by Johan Schelin, . Stockholm: 2009, 15–27.

Røsæg, Erik. 'Implementing Conventions – Scandinavian Style.' *Scandinavian Institute of Maritime Law Yearbook, MarIus*, no. 394 (2009): 167–199.

Røsæg, Erik. 'A System for Queuing in Ports.' *Scandinavian Institute of Maritime Law Yearbook, MarIus*, no. 376 (2008): 133–160.

Røsæg, Erik. 'Passenger Liabilities and Insurance: Terrorism and War Risks'. In *Liability Regimes in Contemporary Maritime Law*, edited by D. Rhidian Thomas. London: Informa, 2007, 207–230.

Røsæg, Erik. 'Too Many Claimants, Too Little Insurance.' *Scandinavian Institute of Maritime Law Yearbook, MarIus*, no. 346 (2006): 123–140.

Røsæg, Erik. 'Misapprehension of Peril in Salvage.' *Scandinavian Institute of Maritime Law Yearbook, MarIus*, no. 321 (2004): 1–43.

Røsæg, Erik. 'News under the Athens Sun: New Principles and Lost Opportunities of the Athens Convention 2002.' *Scandinavian Studies in Law* 46 (July 2004): 153–173. http://www.scandinavianlaw.se/pdf/46-7.pdf.

Røsæg, Erik. 'The Applicability of Conventions for the Carriage of Goods and for Multimodal Transport.' *Lloyd's Maritime and Commercial Law Quarterly* (August 2002): 316–335.

Røsæg, Erik. 'Refugees as Rescuees: The Tampa Problem.' *Scandinavian Institute of Maritime Law Yearbook, MarIus*, no. 295 (2002): 43–82.

Røsæg, Erik. 'Compulsory Maritime Insurance.' *Scandinavian Institute of Maritime Law Yearbook, Marius*, no. 258 (2000): 179–205.

Røsæg, Erik. 'On Electronic Bills of Lading – in Particular on BOLERO Bills of Lading.' *Scandinavian Institute of Maritime Law Yearbook, MarIus*, no. 247 (1999): 129–154.

Selmer, Knut. *The Survival of General Average: A Necessity or an Anachronism?* Oslo: Oslo University Press, 1961.

Selvig, Erling. 'Limitation of Shipowners' Liability and Forum Shopping in EU/EEA States.' *Scandinavian Institute of Maritime Law Yearbook, MarIus*, no. 400 (2010): 359–390.

Ward, Ezekiel. 'Collaboration in Liner Shipping under Article 81 EC: Agreements Between Liner Shipping Undertakings Following the Repeal of Regulation 4056/86'. *MarIus*, no. 364 (2008).

Wilhelmsen, Trine-Lise. 'When Pirates Capture the Cargo.' *Scandinavian Institute of Maritime Law Yearbook, MarIus*, no. 400 (2010): 443–464.

Wilhelmsen, Trine-Lise. 'Transport Liability Regimes and Economic Efficiency'. In *Law and Economics: Essays in Honour of Erling Eide*, edited by Erik Røsæg, Hans-Bernd Schäfer, and Endre Stavang. Oslo: Cappelen akademisk forlag, 2010, 257–275.

Wilhelmsen, Trine-Lise. 'Marine Insurance Regimes and Their Impact on Shipping Competition.' *Scandinavian Institute of Maritime Law Yearbook, MarIus*, no. 394 (2009): 1–38.

Wilhelmsen, Trine-Lise, and Hans Jacob Bull. *Handbook in Hull Insurance*. Oslo: Gyldendal akademisk, 2007.

Wilhelmsen, Trine-Lise. 'Developments in Norwegian and Scandinavian Maritime Law.' *Scandinavian Institute of Maritime Law Yearbook, MarIus*, no. 360 (2007): 1–5.

Wilhelmsen, Trine-Lise. 'The Charterer's ("Befrakters") Right to Limit his Liability in Respect of a Claim from the Shipowner for Damage to the Vessel: Scandinavian and English Law'. In *Festskrift till Lars Gorton*, edited by Eva Lindell-Frantz, Björn Lindquist, Per Jonas Nordell, Christina Ramberg, and Jan Ramberg. Lund: Juristförlaget, 2007, 655–667.

Wilhelmsen, Trine-Lise. *Rett i havn: Risikofordelingen mellom transportøren og vareeieren ved transport gjennom havn*. Oslo: Gyldendal akademisk, 2006.

Wilhelmsen, Trine-Lise. 'Cargo Insurance for International Sales of Goods.' *Scandinavian Institute of Maritime Law Yearbook, MarIus*, no. 321 (2004): 87–135.

Wilhelmsen, Trine-Lise. 'Hull Insurance of "Latent Defects"- i.e., Errors in Design, Material or Workmanship.' *Scandinavian Studies in Law* 46 (July 2004): 257–285. http://www.scandinavianlaw.se/pdf/46-13.pdf.

Wilhelmsen, Trine-Lise. 'The Distinction Between One and More Than One Insured Event.' *Scandinavian Institute of Maritime Law Yearbook, MarIus*, no. 309 (2003): 105–186.

Wilhelmsen, Trine-Lise. 'Issues of Marine Insurance: Misconduct of the Assured and Identification.' *Scandinavian Institute of Maritime Law Yearbook, MarIus*, no. 295 (2002): 115–172.

Wilhelmsen, Trine-Lise. 'Issues of Marine Insurance: Duty of Disclosure, Duty of Good Faith, Alteration of Risk and Warranties.' *Scandinavian Institute of Maritime Law Yearbook, MarIus*, no. 281 (2001): 41–169.

Wilhelmsen, Trine-Lise. 'The Norwegian Marine Insurance Plan and Substandard Ships.' *Scandinavian Institute of Maritime Law Yearbook, MarIus*, no. 258 (2000): 209–238.

Wilhelmsen, Trine-Lise. 'The Provisions for Time Limit and Limitation in the Norwegian Marine Insurance Plan of 1996: Legal Framework and Some Problems.' *Scandinavian Institute of Maritime Law Yearbook, MarIus*, no. 247 (1999): 195–212.

Østreng, Iris. 'Vessel-Source Pollution in the Disputed Area of the Barents Sea – Norway's Access to Administrate Prevention Initiatives.' *Scandinavian Institute of Maritime Law Yearbook, MarIus*, no. 394 (2009): 201–267.

Road Transport Law

Bull, Hans Jacob. *Innføring i veifraktrett*. 2nd ed. Oslo: Tano Aschehoug, 2000.

Jahr, Anette. 'Direct Action Against Subcarriers under the CMR Convention.' *Scandinavian Institute of Maritime Law Yearbook, MarIus*, no. 247 (1999): 109–127.

Railroad Transport Law

Meidell, Andreas. 'Togpassasjerers rettigheter i Norden.' *TemaNord*, no. 544 (2004).

Air Transport Law

Andersen, Rolf Chr. Trolle. 'The Rights of Air Passengers in the Event of Delays and Cancellations.' *TemaNord*, no. 541 (2002).
Falkanger, Falkanger, Thor. *Lufttransport av gods*. Oslo: Universitetsforlaget, 2016.
Lødrup, Peter. *Luftretten anno 1975*. Oslo: P. Lødrup, 1997.
Lødrup, Peter. *Luftfart og ansvar: En undersøkelse av tredjemannsansvaret i norsk og fremmed luftrett.* Oslo: Tanum, 1966.

Selected Bibliography

Index

The numbers here refer to paragraph numbers.

Made in the USA
Monee, IL
13 September 2026

62974255R00125